COLLINS COMPLETE
GUIDE TO
BRITISH
BIRDS

PAUL STERRY
PAUL STANCLIFFE

BTO
British Trust for
Ornithology
Looking out for birds

Maps and
Calendars
by Simon
Gillings

This edition published in 2015 by William Collins,
an imprint of HarperCollins Publishers

1 London Bridge Street
London SE1 9GF

WilliamCollinsBooks.com

First published in 2015

ISBN 978-0-00-755151-4 (hardback)
ISBN 978-0-00-755152-1 (paperback)

William Collins uses papers that are natural, renewable and recyclable products made
from wood grown in sustainable forests. The manufacturing processes conform to the
environmental regulations of the country of origin.

Acknowledgements

Paul Sterry would like to thank in particular Andrew Cleave, Rob Read, David and Namrita Price-
Goodfellow, Shane O'Dwyer, Susi Bailey and his publisher Myles Archibald for their encouragement and
help with the creation of this book. In addition, the following people, in alphabetical order, helped with
photography: Ashley Barnes; Dominic Berridge of Wexford Wildfowl Reserve; Sheldon Cary of Calleva
Falconry School; Steve Castle; Mark and Susie Groves of Island Sea Safaris; Karl Hughes; Chris Keep of
Bentley Wildfowl Collection; Joe Pender of Sapphire Pelagics; James Sutherland; and Graham Vick.
Paul Stancliffe would like to thank Jeff Baker and Mike Toms for their help and support; Ieuan Evans for
his interest and wise words when needed; Andy Mason for the many shared birds; his girls, Abigail, Lily
and Hazel for their beauty, inspiration and endless patience; and of course the BTO for allowing him to
indulge in his passion.

Edited and designed by D & N Publishing, Baydon, Wiltshire
Colour reproduction by Paul Sterry, Nature Photographers Ltd
Printed and bound in Hong Kong by Printing Express

CONTENTS

AIM AND SCOPE OF THE BOOK

Collins BTO Guide to British Birds covers all species that breed regularly in the region, plus those that winter here or occur as common passage migrants. It is one of two books, the other being *Collins BTO Guide to Rare British Birds*, that provide an identification reference to all wild bird species that have occurred in Britain and Ireland, as of September 2014. The term 'wild' relates to birds that are naturally occurring or have self-sustaining populations.

Collins BTO Guide to British Birds has been written and illustrated as much with the beginner in mind as the experienced birdwatcher. Designed to be used in the field, the text and photographs describe and illustrate the key features needed to identify a species with confidence, and to separate it from similar, or 'confusion', species. In general, the species accounts follow the taxonomic running order provided by the British Ornithologist's Union (BOU) in its 8th edition of the British List. But for the benefit of the reader, in some instances the running order has been juggled subtly so that potentially confusing species are placed side by side. Throughout the book there are special pages that describe the key features needed for separating different families, and groups of birds that share the same habitat.

Over 1,200 photographs have been used in this book and many are seen here for the first time. They have been chosen carefully to show not only important identification features but also to give clues to a bird's usual habitat, and its typical posture. Annotations highlight key identification features that are discussed in the text.

Song and call are useful aids to identification, and reference is made to vocalisation for each species. Bear in mind that it is always difficult to describe the song and call of a bird phonetically; and, of course, some birds are essentially silent.

The taxonomy and names of all the birds illustrated in this book follow the recommendations of the BOU list. At the start of each species account the English name, scientific name and the British Trust for Ornithology (BTO) two-letter code are included. For example, with Dunlin is its scientific name, *Calidris alpina*, and its two-letter BTO code, DN. In the case of relevant races or subspecies, a third name follows the first two scientific names, so the British breeding race of Dunlin is written as *Calidris alpina schinzii*. The average size of each bird is included; in most species this is the length, measured from the tip of the bill to the tip of the tail, but in birds that are seen most frequently in flight (such as raptors), the given measurement is wingspan.

In the species description section of the book, labels are used to locate key features and traits for identification. Most birds depicted are adults and these are not labelled as such if the plumage does not vary seasonally. Where a photograph shows a seasonal variation of a bird's plumage, a plumage other than adult, or where differences exist between the sexes, this fact is labelled. For each species a UK population estimate is given in the species accounts. This figure does not include the Republic of Ireland as sufficient data are not available for all species.

For an explanation of how to interpret the maps and calendar wheels, see p.9.

DUNLIN

Calidris alpina | DN | LENGTH 17–21cm

scientific name | BTO code | average size (tip of bill to tip of tail)

What's in a name?

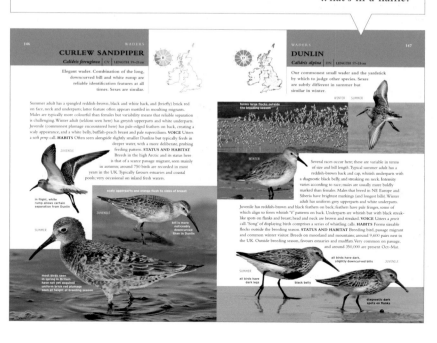

146   WADERS

CURLEW SANDPIPER
Calidris ferruginea | CV | LENGTH 19–21cm

Elegant wader. Combination of the long, downcurved bill and white rump are reliable identification features at all times. Sexes are similar.

Summer adult has a spangled reddish-brown, black and white back, and (briefly) brick red on face, neck and underparts; latter feature often appears mottled in moulting migrants. Males are typically more colourful than females but variability means that reliable separation is challenging. Winter adult (seldom seen here) has greyish upperparts and white underparts. Juvenile (commonest plumage encountered here) has pale-edged feathers on back, creating a scaly appearance, and a white belly, buffish-peach breast and pale supercilium. **VOICE** Utters a soft *prrrp* call. **HABITS** Often seen alongside slightly smaller Dunlins but typically feeds in deeper water, with a more deliberate, probing feeding pattern. **STATUS AND HABITAT** Breeds in the high Arctic and its status here is that of a scarce passage migrant, seen mainly in autumn; around 750 birds are recorded in most years in the UK. Typically favours estuaries and coastal pools; very occasional on inland fresh waters.

JUVENILE

in flight, white rump allows certain separation from Dunlin

scaly upperparts and orange flush to sides of breast

JUVENILE

bill is more noticeably downcurved than in Dunlin

SUMMER

most birds seen in spring in Britain have not yet acquired uniform brick red plumage seen at height of breeding season

WADERS   **147**

DUNLIN
Calidris alpina | DN | LENGTH 17–21cm

Our commonest small wader and the yardstick by which to judge other species. Sexes are subtly different in summer but similar in winter.

WINTER   SUMMER

forms large flocks outside the breeding season

WINTER

Several races occur here; these are variable in terms of size and bill length. Typical summer adult has a reddish-brown back and cap, whitish underparts with a diagnostic black belly, and streaking on neck. Intensity varies according to race; males are usually more boldly marked than females. Males that breed in NE Europe and Siberia have brightest markings (and longest bills). Winter adult has uniform grey upperparts and white underparts. Juvenile has reddish-brown and black feathers on back, some of which align to form whitish 'V' patterns on back. Underparts are whitish but with black streak-like spots on flanks and breast; head and neck are brown and streaked. **VOICE** Utters a *preeit* call. 'Song' of displaying birds comprises a series of whistling calls. **HABITS** Forms sizeable flocks outside the breeding season. **STATUS AND HABITAT** Breeding bird, passage migrant and common winter visitor. Breeds on moorland and mountains; around 9,600 pairs nest in the UK. Outside breeding season, favours estuaries and mudflats. Very common on passage, around 350,000 are present Oct–Mar.

all birds have dark, slightly downcurved bills

JUVENILE

SUMMER

all birds have dark legs

black belly

diagnostic dark spots on flanks

BIRDS AND THE BTO

Formed in 1933, the British Trust for Ornithology is a leading independent science research organisation, dedicated to studying UK birds; it is based in Thetford, Norfolk. It specialises in hands-on surveys and regards both its members and the volunteers who take part in these surveys as its greatest assets. As part of its work, the BTO organises and coordinates bird-ringing. This branch of research has been going on for more than 100 years and during that time it has informed bird conservation continuously.

Because it has been monitoring birds for more than eight decades, the BTO has some of the longest-running wildlife datasets in the world. Such data are essential to our understanding of changes in bird populations: increases and declines in numbers, and shifts in their ranges.

The lifeblood of the BTO is the 40,000 or so volunteers who regularly take part in its various surveys. In the early days, the data were recorded almost exclusively in hand-written notebooks; they would then be submitted to the BTO on paper recording forms, to be scanned and logged by staff at its headquarters. These days, although some records are still collected in traditional notebooks, data can now be submitted electronically, allowing analysis to be done much more quickly.

BTO volunteers undertaking work for the Breeding Bird Survey.

BIRD OBSERVATORIES

There are 19 bird observatories around the coasts of Britain and Ireland, all involved in monitoring bird movements. Ringing and catching birds is an integral part of their work and this is undertaken as part of the national ringing scheme run by the BTO. All the ringing data collected by the observatories is sent to the BTO and forms a significant contribution to the annual datasets that help the BTO in its fundamental role of monitoring bird populations.

ABOVE: Portland Bird Observatory.
RIGHT: Female Blackcap being ringed.

Until 1971, the BTO coordinated and monitored the work carried out at bird observatories. Since then, this role has been carried out by the Bird Observatories Council, on which BTO staff members still sit. Anyone can visit a bird observatory and assist the daily work of the observatory wardens. This might involve counting seabirds on nesting cliffs on Fair Isle, monitoring visible migration at Portland, or even helping with the ringing at any of them.

Coal Tit being ringed.

Nowadays, birdwatchers can use the *BirdTrack* app on their smartphones to record observations whilst out birdwatching; they can submit them on the spot, as well as directly to the relevant local recorder. This allows scientists at the BTO to track arrival and departure dates for both our summer and winter visitors in real time. And they can follow influxes of irruptive species like the Crossbill and Waxwing as they progress through the country. For observers, this free recording software allows them to look back through all their submitted records. And they can make comparisons between years, and with other observers in the area. All in all, *BirdTrack* is a great aid to conservation.

Advancements in technology have opened up new areas of scientific research for the BTO, particularly in the area of bird migration. For example, it has helped the organisation uncover the journeys that birds such as Swift, Nightingale and Nightjar undertake each year and has contributed to an understanding of the pressures they

Record your findings in the field, in real time, using the *BirdTrack* app on your smartphone.

face. And thanks to the work of BTO scientists, we are now able to follow Cuckoos as they migrate to and from their wintering grounds in the Congo rainforest.

To some, the BTO's name may sound a bit grand, but nothing could be further from the truth. It is a down-to-earth organisation that welcomes help from all birdwatchers and it conducts surveys that anyone can be involved with, regardless of their level of experience. The role of the Garden BirdWatch survey is self-evident: people monitor the birds they see in their gardens on a weekly basis and submit their data to the BTO for analysis. It was BTO Garden BirdWatchers who first highlighted the decline in our House Sparrows. The Breeding Bird Survey, whose data are used by the government and a variety of organisations, and Wetland Bird Survey require a little more experience; the Nest Record Scheme and the Ringing Scheme are for those who like to be a little more hands-on; and, of course, *BirdTrack* is a tool for those who just want to make their sightings and records count for something. For information on these and other surveys, visit www.bto.org.

MAPS AND CALENDAR WHEELS

The **maps** represent a new way to show how likely one is to see species throughout Britain and Ireland during summer and winter. They combine *where* species occur with *how common* they are into a single map, and are based on data collected for *Bird Atlas 2007–11* (2013). Purple areas on a map indicate a species is resident all year round and is equally abundant in summer and winter (e.g. Meadow Pipit, see map), but as the colour tends towards blue it means a species is more common in winter than summer; clean blues indicate a species is only present in

Meadow Pipit map.

winter (e.g. Fieldfare). The opposite trend, from purple to red, indicates a tendency towards summer dominance, with pure reds for summer visitors (e.g. Swallow). More intense colours indicate greater abundance and thus a higher chance of seeing a species in an area. White areas denote absence or an extremely low likelihood of seeing the species in summer or winter. Distribution maps do not show occurrence during migration. All maps cover only summer and winter periods; you may encounter some species in other areas during spring or autumn migration. To protect sensitive sites for rare breeding birds (e.g. Honey-buzzard), their maps are shown at a coarser scale.

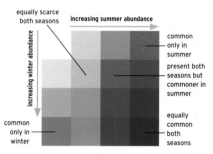

The colours used in the maps. Each colour relates to a particular combination of summer and winter abundance.

The **calendar wheels** show the best time of year to see each species in Britain and Ireland and are derived from data from the online bird recording software *BirdTrack*. The amount of orange in a segment shows the likelihood of seeing a species in that month in the parts of Britain and Ireland shown as occupied on the map. An empty (grey) segment shows a species is absent during that month, thus distinguishing summer and winter visitors. The highest likelihood of seeing a species in a month (a completely orange segment) is given by the number in the wheel's centre, and conveys how likely you are, on average, to encounter the species in occupied areas of Britain and Ireland. For a scarce species (e.g. Nightingale), the 16 indicates that people encounter Nightingales on up to 16% of birding trips where it is found in south-east England. Meadow Pipits can be encountered on up to 32% of visits, peaking in spring and autumn. Fieldfares are generally only seen in autumn and winter, peaking at 31% of visits in early winter.

All maps and data were supplied by the BTO (www.bto.org).

TOP TO BOTTOM:
Nightingale,
Meadow Pipit,
Fieldfare.

IDENTIFICATION AIDS
Bird Topography

In general terms, the features of a bird can be divided neatly into two sections: the bare parts (legs and bill); and the feathered parts (wings, body and tail). These elements can be subdivided even further to help describe individual parts of a bird, and it is useful to have a basic understanding of these subdivisions. It helps the reader make easier reference to the species description text in the book and is useful in the process of identification in the field. The following annotated photographs show the important anatomical and topographical features for a range of common bird species.

Mallard

speculum
underwing coverts
primaries
upperwing coverts
secondaries
nostril
axillaries
bill
collar
breast · belly · undertail coverts · bill

Teal

scapulars · mantle
tail
breast
undertail coverts

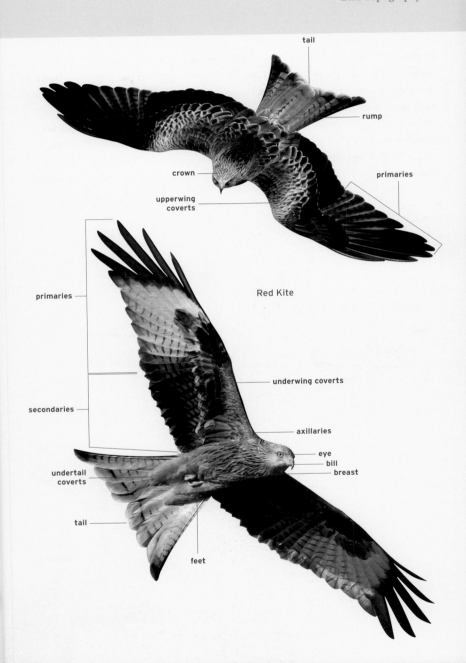

tail

rump

crown

upperwing coverts

primaries

primaries

Red Kite

secondaries

underwing coverts

axillaries

eye
bill
breast

undertail coverts

tail

feet

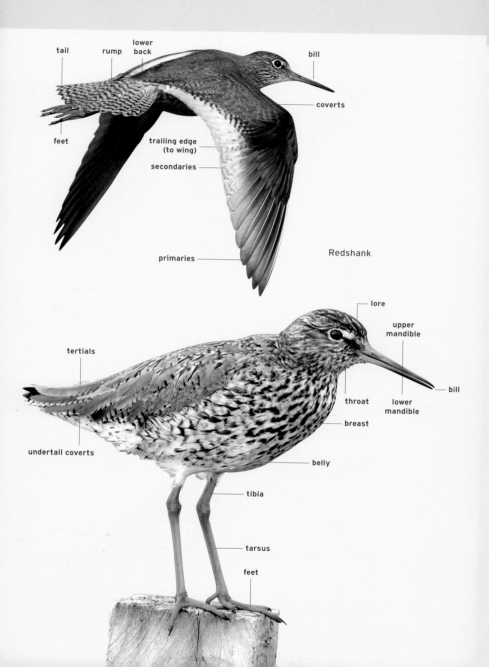

tail

rump

lower back

bill

feet

trailing edge (to wing)

secondaries

coverts

primaries

Redshank

tertials

undertail coverts

lore

upper mandible

throat

lower mandible

bill

breast

belly

tibia

tarsus

feet

Common Gull

crown

lore

upper mandible

supercilium

ear coverts

nape

lower mandible

mantle

throat

breast

Siskin

greater coverts
(forming a wingbar)

belly

tertials

secondaries

tarsus   feet

uppertail
coverts

primaries

tail

crown   supercilium

eye-ring

eye-stripe

lore

sub-moustachial
stripe

moustachial stripe

throat

malar stripe

Reed
Bunting

Acquiring bird identification skills can take a lifetime, and no matter how experienced you are there are always things to learn. But there are some shortcuts that make life a little easier for the beginner as well as the expert. One of the best tips is to familiarise yourself thoroughly with a selection of common birds – the most regularly encountered representatives from a wide range of bird families. Get to know their size (for relative comparison) as well as their plumage. These will be default birds that can be referred to when confronted with a tricky identification.

The better you know your default birds, the easier the identification of new species becomes. This applies to species included in this book, and a knowledge of common default birds will prove invaluable when your birdwatching skills progress and you start using the companion volume, *Collins BTO Guide to Rare British Birds*. Of course, not all bird groups require default species: some birds are unmistakable and members of some groups are all uniquely different. However, for those groups where it is useful, the following section describes the relevant default birds and provides the reader with some identification pointers.

WILDFOWL This group can be divided roughly into three sub-groups: swans, geese and ducks. Of the three swan species to occur here, Mute Swan (p. 44) is the one to get to know. Greylag Goose (p. 48) is the default 'grey' goose (*Anser* spp.), and Canada (p. 49) is the default 'black' goose (*Branta* spp.). When it comes to ducks, Mallard (p. 57) and Tufted Duck (p. 66) are the default dabbling and diving ducks, respectively, and are worth getting to know in terms of size as well as plumage details.

Mute Swan

Mallard

Tufted Duck

Greylag Goose

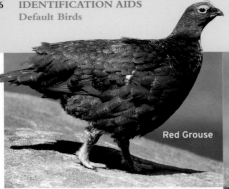

Red-legged Partridge

Red Grouse

Pheasant

Red-throated Diver

GAMEBIRDS These ground-dwelling birds are just as inclined to run from danger as they are to fly. Red Grouse (p. 76) is the default upland gamebird and Pheasant (p. 81) is the default lowland gamebird; adult males of the latter species are unmistakable, but young and female birds can cause confusion and are worth getting to know well. Red-legged Partridge (p. 82) is the default partridge.

DIVERS Of the three divers, Red-throated (p. 84) is the one to get to know well – in winter plumage in particular, a time when diver identification is most tricky.

TUBENOSES Storm-petrels, Shearwaters and Fulmar are consummate seabirds with specially adapted, large nostrils; collectively they are known as 'tubenoses'. European Storm-petrel (p. 88), Manx Shearwater (p. 90) and Fulmar (p. 91) are the default species, each with distinctive plumage and flight pattern.

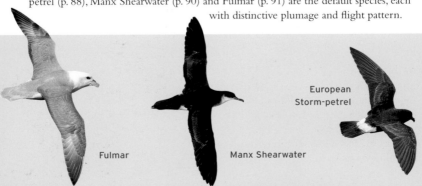

European Storm-petrel

Fulmar

Manx Shearwater

HERONS AND ALLIES Members of this group are long-necked and long-legged wetland birds. The pure white Little Egret (p. 97) is unmistakable, so Grey Heron (p. 96) is the default species to get to know in its various postures.

GREBES Identification of summer-plumaged grebes is straightforward but in winter it can be trickier. Little (p. 99) and Great Crested (p. 100) grebes are the default species here.

Little Egret

Grey Heron

Little Grebe

Great Crested Grebe

Sparrowhawk

Buzzard

Kestrel

Hen Harrier

BIRDS OF PREY When it comes to default raptors, become familiar with Common Buzzard (p. 112) and Hen Harrier (p. 108) among the larger species. Kestrel (p. 118) and Sparrowhawk (p. 117) are useful representatives of the smaller species; pay attention not just to their plumage but also to their habits and flight pattern. As a tip, raptors are often seen in flight, when size can be hard to judge. However, they are frequently mobbed by other birds; this can be a useful way of gauging size if you know what species is doing the mobbing.

Ringed Plover

Dunlin

WADERS Plovers are a distinctive group of short-billed waders and of these Ringed Plover (p. 139) is a good default bird. Most other waders are longer-billed and can be divided into small, medium and large species. If you get to know the default species for each group, then identification of something different becomes more straightforward. Default species are as follows: small waders – Dunlin (p. 147); medium-sized waders – Redshank (p. 163); large waders – Curlew (p. 157).

Redshank

Curlew

SKUAS These seabirds can be difficult to identify as they fly by offshore. Arctic Skua (p. 167) is the default bird here. Take particular note of its size and structure, and try to compare it to other birds seen in the vicinity.

Arctic Skua

GULLS For convenience, this group can be divided into two sub-groups: small and large gulls. Black-headed Gull (p. 174) is the default small gull and Herring Gull (p. 180) is the default large species. Both have a range of plumages as they age and throughout the year. Also, pay attention to leg and bill colours.

TERNS Invariably associated with water, tern species can look confusingly similar to one another. Common Tern (p. 188) is the default species in both adult and juvenile plumages.

Black-headed Gull

Herring Gull

Common Tern

Woodpigeon

Collared Dove

Tawny Owl

Great Spotted Woodpecker

PIGEONS AND DOVES

These are plump-bodied birds with relatively small heads, longish wings and a long tail. Woodpigeon (p. 197), with its striking neck and wing markings, is the default pigeon, while Collared Dove (p. 198) is the representative dove you should become familiar with.

OWLS

Most members of this group are nocturnal predators, although some species are often active in the daytime as well. All have relatively large heads and forward-facing eyes. Tawny Owl (p. 203), which is exclusively nocturnal, is the default species to get to know.

WOODPECKERS

These mainly woodland birds are adept at climbing trees and their outline is distinctive. Get to know Great Spotted Woodpecker (p. 212) as the default representative of the group and become familiar not only with its markings but also its relative size.

Carrion Crow

CROWS Of the black corvids, Carrion Crow (p. 226) is the archetypal crow. When comparing it with other black corvids, tail shape in flight is important; the presence or absence of bare skin around the face, and extent of feathered 'trousers' are other features on which to concentrate.

TITS When identifying the tits, Blue Tit (p. 229) is the default bird. When comparing this species with other tits, concentrate on face and crown patterns, colour, and the presence or absence of wingbars.

SWALLOWS, MARTINS AND SWIFT Swallows and martins are passerines (perching birds) that catch insects on the wing, and they have relatively long, narrow wings; in the default species, Swallow (p. 242), the tail is deeply forked with long streamers. The Swift (p. 208) is superficially similar but unrelated; it also feeds in flight and its wings are long and narrow, creating a horseshoe-like outline.

Blue Tit

Swallow   Swift

WARBLERS The best approach with this diverse group is to separate them into their most representative genera:

- *Sylvia* warblers have relatively long tails, grey in their plumage and short undertail coverts that just reach the wingtips; Whitethroat (p. 255) is the default species.

- *Acrocephalus* warblers have rich brown plumage with plain undertail coverts that are medium length and extend just beyond the wingtips; default species are the Reed Warbler (p. 259), which has unmarked plumage, and Sedge Warbler (p. 258), with streaked plumage.
- Grasshopper Warbler (p. 257) is the only common *Locustella* warbler; it has very long, spotted undertail coverts that almost reach the tip of the tail.
- *Phylloscopus* warblers are small, compact birds that are olive brown above with a yellow wash below; Chiffchaff (p. 251) is the default species.
- The genus *Cettia* has one representative in Britain: Cetti's Warbler (p. 248).

Whitethroat

Sedge Warbler

Grasshopper Warbler

Reed Warbler

Chiffchaff

Cetti's Warbler

THRUSHES All thrush species share the same rather plump-bodied appearance. The most widespread and familiar species is the Blackbird (p. 265) but get to know it in all its plumages. Among our remaining resident species, Song Thrush (p. 266) is a good default species.

Blackbird

Song Thrush

CHATS AND RELATIVES These compact birds include species that are present here year-round as well as seasonal migrants. To give you a head start with identification, get to know Robin (p. 274) and Stonechat (p. 279). Songs and calls are also important indicators of identity.

Robin

Stonechat

PIPITS AND WAGTAILS These perching birds share the same long-tailed appearance. Meadow Pipit (p. 287) and Pied Wagtail (p. 283) are the default representatives of the group. Get to know their appearance, but become familiar with their habits and calls as well.

Meadow Pipit

Pied Wagtail

FINCHES Several members of this variable group are commonly encountered in the region, but probably the best ones to concentrate on are Chaffinch (p. 290) and Siskin (p. 296). Both have striking plumage features, some of which are diagnostic and others of which are shared with related species.

Chaffinch

Siskin

Reed Bunting

BUNTINGS Some bunting species are almost unmistakable, particularly adult males. However, in other plumages identification (especially with poor or partial views) can be challenging. Reed Bunting (p. 303) is the default species, and head pattern, rump colour and leg colour are key features to concentrate on.

BEHAVIOUR

The behaviour of a bird can provide useful clues to identification; feeding behaviour and flight patterns are particularly important. For example, a small bird that creeps up tree bark, spiralling up a tree trunk, is likely to be a Treecreeper; a compact woodland bird that perches head down is sure to be a Nuthatch; a woodland bird whose flight is direct but undulating is going to be a species of woodpecker. Where behaviour is useful in identification, it is mentioned in the species text.

BELOW: Woodpecker flight is characteristically undulating – the result of alternative bouts of rapid wingbeats and gliding with folded wings.

ABOVE: Bouts of frantic feeding activity, with very rapid bill action, provide a clue to the identity of Little Stint and allow separation from other superficially similar waders, notably Dunlin.

JIZZ

Spend some time with experienced birdwatchers and sooner or later you will hear somebody use the word 'jizz', for example in the context of 'the bird had the jizz of a *Sylvia* warbler' or some similar phrase. It refers to an observer's overall impression of a bird: a distillation of characters such as size, proportions, shape, bill and leg length, combined with colour, posture, behaviour, voice and habitat preferences, all made with reference to other known species.

Although it is necessarily personal and subjective, the jizz of a bird can be a useful aid for any birdwatcher when it comes to sorting out the identification of a mystery species. The key is to be aware of your own skill level and experience, and to trust your instincts accordingly.

OPPOSITE PAGE: Both Dartford Warbler (*left*) and Long-tailed Tit (*right*) are similar in both their size and proportions. Apart from plumage differences, their behaviour and habits allow distinction of the two. Overall, these features create a different jizz for each species.

TRICK OF THE LIGHT

Plumage colours are obviously key features when it comes to identification. But limitations to our perception of colour need to be considered too. Some people see (and, more importantly, describe) the same colour in different ways. And more significantly, the ambient light plays a crucial role. For example, shades of red and yellow that appear intense when seen with sunlight behind the observer can look distinctly 'washed out' in the dappled shade of foliage, or if the bird is viewed into the light.

What a difference a bit of sunlight makes. In dappled shade, this Redstart looks to have rather sombre plumage, but when lit properly it is one of our most colourful birds.

IDENTIFICATION AIDS
Voice and Song

The importance of songs and calls in bird identification cannot be overemphasised, but learning bird vocalisation has to be one of the greatest challenges that any birdwatcher faces. The following pages contain tips to help the process.

All birds have a song and call that is unique to the species; this allows both the birds themselves, and us as observers, to be certain of identity. To appreciate the significance of vocalisation, consider the identification of two closely related and superficially similar birds: Chiffchaff and Willow Warbler. Silent individuals of these species, seen briefly, can be hard to distinguish, but their songs, when heard, identify them with certainty. The onomatopoeic song of the Chiffchaff is easily recognised and can be phonetically described as a repeated *chiff-chaff-chiff-chaff-chiff-chaff*. It is very different from that of the Willow Warbler, which can be described as a sweet, cascading *tswee-tswee-tswee-tswee-tswee-tswee*. The calls are more of a challenge, but with experience they can also be used to distinguish the pair: a Chiffchaff's call is a rather monosyllabic, whistled *hweet*, while that of a Willow Warbler is a plaintive, disyllabic *hoo-eet*.

There are few shortcuts when it comes to learning bird songs and calls. And there is no substitute for spending time in the field, preferably with someone who has knowledge of bird vocalisations. However, there are various ways to speed up the learning process. Listening to recordings of bird songs and calls is good 'homework', although recordings can sound very different from birds in the wild. There are also bird song apps for smartphones that allow the observer to compare instantly a song heard in the field with one played through the device.

Learning songs and calls can be a daunting prospect but the key is to start small. Begin by learning the vocalisations of four or five bird species that sing and call in your garden. Try

Song is the most straightforward way to distinguish Chiffchaff (*right*) from Willow Warbler (*far right*).

MNEMONICS

Using a mnemonic can help you to remember bird songs and calls. A classic example is the phrase 'wet-my-lips' that birdwatchers use to describe the song of the Quail; and the song of the Yellowhammer is traditionally transcribed as 'a little bit of bread and no cheese'. But why not try making up your own mnemonics? In any case, we all hear things in subtly different ways. So be creative and remember that the funniest mnemonics are often the easiest to remember.

'a little bit of bread and no cheese'

Listen to the dawn chorus in your garden and you will soon learn the rather plaintive song of the Robin.

to watch the birds in the act of singing or calling – that will help cement the association between the bird and its song.

Once these songs are learned, add a couple more species to your repertoire, and keep doing this until there are no more to learn in the garden. Then it is time to move beyond the boundaries of your garden. Choose a habitat, study what birds might be found there, observe them singing and add them to your growing list of recognised bird songs. You will find that the more species you know, the easier it gets to add new ones. But remember that while the calls and songs of some species do not vary much, others have large repertoires and may vary regionally.

BIRDS AND WEATHER

The weather can have a profound effect on the survival and success of birds, as with all wildlife. The seasonal nature of our climate is something that our birds have evolved to cope with, and respond to; they can deal with most of the vagaries of the weather and overcome most setbacks. However, the British weather is notoriously fickle and unpredictable, and birds do get caught out.

Cold springs can mean poor breeding success, either directly through the chilling of eggs and chicks, or as a result of lack of food for the developing brood if insects are part of the diet. While hot, dry summers may be good for holidaymakers, insect life can suffer, along with the birds that depend on them for food. On many people's minds at the moment is the issue of flooding – a consequence of unprecedented rainfall; in winter this can mean that feeding grounds become unavailable, while spring floods can result in the loss of vital nesting sites during the breeding season. In winter, excessive snowfall compounds the problems of cold weather by blanketing feeding sites for some species, just at a time when they need to build up their reserves more than ever.

Severe gales and winds can also be a problem for birds. To a degree they can affect breeding birds and the ability of all birds to feed. But since the worst weather often occurs in autumn, inevitably it coincides with periods of migration.

Autumn gales can have a profound effect on migrating birds, notably seabirds. But it is not just movements that are affected: prolonged strong winds can also make feeding difficult, or impossible.

Each spring around 15 million birds arrive in Britain and Ireland to breed, most of them having spent the winter months in sub-Saharan Africa. As they arrive, millions more winter visitors to Britain are leaving, heading north to their breeding grounds in northern Europe. This phenomenon is known as migration and is one of the greatest wonders of the natural world.

Many birds migrate at night under the cover of darkness. Nocturnal migration is, by its very nature, hard for us to observe. Sometimes the only evidence that migration is taking place comes in the form of new arrivals at a given location seen first thing in the morning, or the disappearance of flocks that were present the previous evening. However, with a few species migration can be discerned after dark. A classic example is the thin *tseep* call of the Redwing heard as birds fly overhead at night in late September or early October.

With the weather set fair, migrant Swallows begin to arrive on the south coast of England in good numbers in April. They will have travelled from wintering grounds in South Africa, an amazing journey for such small birds.

Birds that migrate in the daytime are, of course, more easily observed, particularly at coastal sites. However, the conditions have to be right for good observation. Clear blue skies and little wind are excellent for the migrating birds themselves but not promising for observation: the birds migrate high in the sky, out of sight and sound of observers on the ground. Spells of low cloud and drizzle are what get the pulses of 'visible migration' enthusiasts racing. During these conditions, migrating birds are forced closer to the ground and their calls are more easily heard.

HABITATS FOR BIRDS

A combination of geology, geography and historical land use has created a wealth of different habitats in Britain and Ireland. By and large, these are fragmented but the mosaic effect means that an amazing diversity of birdlife can sometimes be found in a comparatively small land area.

The character of any given habitat is influenced by factors such as its geology and botany, and Man also has a profound effect in most places. Only some of our coastal habitats and a few remote mountain tops have escaped human interference over the last few centuries.

Man's influence has not always been to the detriment of wildlife diversity. For example, some habitats owe their very existence to clearance of trees from the land. And appropriate woodland management can exert a positive influence on plant and animal diversity. Indeed, land management is undertaken on almost all nature reserves.

Most birds have rather specific habitat requirements. Their behaviour, feeding and nesting requirements, and indeed structure, have evolved to suit special niches in particular habitats.

For some birdwatchers, studying the distinctions between our different habitats may seem rather esoteric. However, an appreciation of habitat helps us understand more fully the lives of birds. And being able to recognise a habitat means you will save yourself time and effort when it comes to pinning down habitat-specific species. The following pages detail all of our most characteristic and distinctive habitats, their character and vegetation, and key bird species.

THE COAST

For many people, the British and Irish coastline is its crowning glory. Although development has marred stretches of the coast, those parts that remain unspoilt are truly wonderful and harbour some of our most charismatic birds. The rich intertidal zone, bathed twice daily by an advancing and retreating tide, and the offshore waters are fundamental to the diversity and abundance of birdlife around our coasts.

CLIFFS For breathtaking scenery and a sense of untamed nature, coastal cliffs offer unrivalled opportunities for the birdwatcher. In spring and summer, a few select locations are thronged with breeding seabirds. Indeed, we have some of the finest seabird cliffs in Europe, with populations of some species that are globally important. The best time to visit a colony is between April and July, when the sight, sound and smell of the birds will be at its height. Because each species has unique nesting requirements, not every seabird species will be found on every cliff. And a fundamental requirement for any seabird colony is the close proximity of good feeding grounds.

MUDFLATS AND ESTUARIES To the unenlightened eye, an estuary may seem like a vast expanse of mudflats, studded with a mosaic of bedraggled-looking vegetation and very

ABOVE: Although the scene may appear tranquil and harmonious, predation is an ever-present threat for nesting seabirds: these Guillemots are justifiably nervous about the scrutiny of the Herring Gull because a momentary lapse in attention could mean the loss of an egg or chick.
ABOVE RIGHT: Mudflat with lugworm casts.
RIGHT: A Dunlin feeding on mudflats.

little else. For the birdwatcher, however, this is one of the most exhilarating of all habitats to visit. Incredible numbers of marine invertebrates thrive in the oozing mud; benefiting from this biological richness are the waders and wildfowl that feed on our estuaries in huge numbers from autumn to spring. Our estuaries are globally important refuges for many bird species.

Waders are perhaps the most characteristic group to exploit this resource, each species having a bill length and feeding strategy adapted to suit a particular food source. Wildfowl, too, occur in huge numbers on many estuaries. Some feed on minute animals filtered from the mud with their bills, while others favour plant material; a few catch fish and crustaceans.

SANDY SHORES Beloved of holidaymakers, sandy shores are also of interest to the birdwatcher. Outside the breeding season, look for Sanderlings and other waders as they follow the line of breaking waves in search of small invertebrates. Offshore, fish and crustaceans provide a rich supply of food for those bird species that are adapted to catch them. In summer, terns plunge-dive for fish and crustaceans, and in the winter months grebes, Red-throated Divers and sea ducks exploit this resource. On the landward side of the beach, colonising plants establish stable dune systems where birds such as Ringed Plovers and

terns can nest. But human disturbance effectively excludes these species from almost all suitable areas in southern England.

FRESH WATERS

For the birdwatcher, freshwater habitats have the same magnetic appeal as do coastal sites. Habitat types range from small ponds and streams to large lakes and river systems, and few people have to travel far to visit one or more of these habitats. The abundance of freshwater life supports a splendid array of birds, some species of which are found nowhere else.

RIVERS AND STREAMS Birdlife abounds on many rivers and streams, larger ones supporting populations of Mute Swans, Mallards and Grey Herons. Small lowland streams are favoured by Kingfishers and Little Grebes, while, in the north and west of the region in particular, Dipper and Grey Wagtail are characteristic species. In a few parts of southern England, chalk streams have a long history of being managed as Watercress beds. These come into their own during the winter months, when Green Sandpipers, Water Rails and the occasional Water Pipit join forces with the resident Grey Wagtails.

TOP: A Sanderling feeding at the edge of the breaking waves on a sandy beach.
ABOVE: Wetland with extensive reedbeds.
BOTTOM: Bearded Tit, a reedbed specialist.

LEFT: The River Kennet, with flowering Stream Water-crowfoot *Ranunculus penicillatus*.
ABOVE: Little Grebes are often associated with streams during the breeding season.

LAKES AND PONDS Bodies of standing water usually support different plants and animals from those found in flowing water. Many seemingly natural lakes are man-made – flooded gravel pits, reservoirs and canals, for example. But with maturity they usually harbour an abundance of plant and invertebrate life, food for birds above and below the water.

Coots and Moorhens are almost ubiquitous, and larger lakes with good fish populations may harbour nesting grebe and diver species. Sedge Warblers and Reed Buntings nest in emergent vegetation of all types. Restricted to a few extensive reedbeds are unique

LEFT: A reed-fringed lake in winter.
BELOW: Pochard and other diving ducks congregate on lakes and flooded gravel pits outside the breeding season.

bird communities comprising Bittern, Marsh Harrier and Bearded Tit, along with more widespread species such as Reed Warbler.

In autumn and winter, areas of open water become refuges for flocks of diving ducks and Coots. For many species, reservoirs and flooded gravel pits fulfil the same role as natural and semi-natural lakes, with the added advantage to the birdwatcher that they are often within striking distance of urban areas.

MARSHES The encroachment of vegetation into areas of open water leads to the creation of habitats know as mires, often referred to in general terms as marshes. The underlying soil has a profound influence on the appearance of the marsh or mire in question, its invertebrate community, and hence the birdlife its supports.

Birds such as Snipe, Redshank, Sedge Warbler and Reed Bunting make use of these wetlands for nesting. When insect life is at its most abundant in spring and summer, Hobbies are sometimes attracted to feed on the dragonflies that are associated with these habitats. And numbers of ducks and waders (notably Snipe) build up outside the breeding season.

WOODLAND AND FOREST

The vast tracts of forest that once cloaked much of Britain and Ireland have long since gone, felled and cleared by Man over the centuries. Fortunately, pockets of woodland still remain, some of which are large enough to retain a wilderness feel and harbour a characteristic array of forest plants and animals.

DECIDUOUS WOODLAND Woodlands of deciduous trees are found throughout most of Britain and Ireland and are the dominant natural forest type in most areas. Deciduous trees shed their leaves in autumn and grow a new set the following spring. The seasonality seen in deciduous woodland is striking and is reflected in the seasonal occurrence and abundance in the birdlife.

Most deciduous woodlands are home to thriving populations of birds, with both residents and summer visitors breeding there. The tit family is well represented, and species such as Chaffinch and Robin are widespread and common. Nuthatch, Treecreeper and three species of woodpecker add to the variety of our resident woodland birds, with Sparrowhawk and Tawny Owl the most typical predators across the region.

Spring sees the arrival of migrant warblers, whose songs boost the dawn chorus across much of the region. Redstart, Pied Flycatcher and Nightingale are also welcome arrivals, albeit with local and patchy distributions. Outside the breeding season, migrants from northern mainland Europe arrive and boost resident numbers; species such as Brambling are almost exclusively winter visitors.

CONIFEROUS WOODLAND Unlike our deciduous trees, conifers are, with a few exceptions, evergreen and keep their leaves throughout the year. Areas of native conifer

LEFT: Deciduous woodland
in spring.
ABOVE: Nuthatch, a classic
woodland bird.

LEFT: A larch plantation
in winter.
ABOVE: The bill of a Crossbill is
uniquely adapted to extract
seeds from the cones of
coniferous trees.

woodland are restricted to a few relict pockets of Caledonian pine forest in the Highlands
of Scotland. Conifers seen elsewhere in Britain and Ireland either have been planted or
have seeded themselves from mature plantations. While our native conifer forests harbour an
intriguing selection of birds, some of which are unique or nearly so to this habitat, plantation
conifers are usually species-poor.

Caledonian pine forests harbour the only bird species unique to these islands, the
Scottish Crossbill. In addition, although widespread in Europe generally, the Crested Tit and
Capercaillie are also restricted to this habitat in Britain. Clearings and widely spaced trees
also encourage birds such as Tree Pipit and Redstart, making a trip to central Scotland an
extremely rewarding one for any birdwatcher.

Plantation forests elsewhere in the region still merit some attention. In particular, mature
plantations of larches and spruces are prime locations for Crossbills.

HEDGEROWS AND SCRUB

Although much reduced in extent, hedgerows are still a feature of the countryside, fringing roadside verges and marking boundaries between fields. Most will have been planted in the past, using local native woody shrubs and trees; they acquire additional species as they age. Scrub is a general term applied to the loose assemblage of tangled, medium-sized shrubs, bushes and Bramble patches that colonises open ground. Although despised by some, its value to wildlife is considerable. Hedgerows usually comprise the species, and acquire the character of, any woodland edge in the vicinity. Scrub, too, reflects the botanical composition of the surrounding area.

Most areas of hedgerow and scrub are good for nesting songbirds, both native species and summer migrants. All find the tangled undergrowth ideal for nesting, and the foliage and flowers of the component plants are a rich source of insects and other invertebrate food. When managed sympathetically, hedgerows and areas of scrub abound in fruits, berries and nuts in autumn. Several thrush species take full advantage of this food bonanza.

GRASSLAND AND FARMLAND

Full of wildflowers and native grass species, a good meadow is a delight to anyone with an eye for colour and an interest in natural history. Prime sites are comparatively few and far between these days, either lost to the plough or degraded for native wildlife by modern intensive farming practices. But if you do find an area of sensitively managed grassland, Skylarks may still be present.

Although arable fields may fall loosely under the category of grasslands – crop species such as wheat, barley and oats are grasses, after all – their interest to the birdwatcher tends to be minimal in many areas. Formerly, populations of insects and other invertebrates would have fed hungry broods in spring and summer, while weed seeds and spilt grain would have supported huge flocks of buntings and finches in autumn and winter.

In areas where farming is not too intensive, Lapwings and a few other species may still manage to breed. But on the whole, modern intensive farming is incompatible with native wildlife. Little wonder then that previously common and widespread birds such as Corn Bunting and Tree Sparrow have declined catastrophically in many areas.

HEATHLAND

Home to a number of specialised birds, heathlands are under considerable threat today and are the subject of much attention from conservation bodies. The habitat owes its existence to Man and came about following forest clearance on acid, sandy soils. Regimes of grazing, cutting and periodic burning helped maintain the habitat in the past, and continued management is needed to ensure an appropriate balance between scrub encroachment and the maintenance of an open habitat.

TOP: Skylark, the quintessential grassland bird.
ABOVE: Flower-rich grassland in early summer.

The habitat's name is clearly derived from dominance of members of the heath family of plants, all of which flourish on acid soils. For the best floral display, visit an area of heathland in July, August and September. But for birds, April and May are probably the best months. Specialities such as Dartford Warbler and Hobby can be seen then, and Nightjar and Woodlark are often also present in good numbers. Resident Stonechats and Linnets are

ABOVE: Dartford Warbler, emblematic of lowland heaths.
LEFT: Lowland heathland in Dorset.

other typical heathland species, and in winter look for Great Grey Shrike, Hen Harrier and Short-eared Owl.

UPLANDS

Upland areas retain a sense of isolation for the visitor and the appearance at least of being wild and untamed. Clearance of trees and animal grazing, along with the influences of soil type and climate, have ensured that moorland is the dominant upland habitat, with grassland or heathers the main vegetation. In a few areas, mountains dominate the landscape, sometimes rising to altitudes above the level at which trees cannot grow; these areas harbour unique communities of plants and animals.

During the breeding season, uplands are the domain of waders, the most evocative being the Golden Plover. Songbirds are comparatively thin on the ground, but Twite breed in northern Britain, alongside the ubiquitous Meadow Pipit. This latter species is essential to the diet of many avian predators, notably the Merlin.

Heather moors are perfect for Red Grouse; moors are encouraged by those with shooting interests in many parts of northern Britain. Its cousin, the Black Grouse, also favours moorland habitat but usually occurs where grassland and small conifer plantations are sited side by side.

Keen birdwatchers make regular pilgrimages to our higher mountains in search of more specialised birds. Many Scottish mountains still have good populations of Golden Eagles and Peregrines. Ptarmigan live unobtrusive lives on the higher peaks, and the confiding Dotterel still breeds there.

THE URBAN ENVIRONMENT

For the majority of people in Great Britain, the urban environment is the one with which they are most familiar. Although seemingly unpromising, it still has bird interest, in part because many features associated with our buildings and gardens mimic niches in natural

ABOVE: Dotterel - nests only on remote mountain plateaux.
LEFT: Cairngorm mountains, Scotland.

habitats. Mature gardens with hedgerows and shrubs recall woodland margins, while buildings resemble man-made cliffs with their roof spaces doubling as artificial caves.

Visit any mature urban park and you will find an array of birds more usually associated with woodland or farmland. These include Woodpigeon, Jay, Great Spotted Woodpecker, Blue Tit, Great Tit, Blackbird and Robin. A number of these also find town gardens much to their liking, although the more informal the garden, the more species it is likely to attract.

A few bird species seem inextricably linked to the urban environment, in our region at least. House Sparrows, Collared Doves and Feral Pigeons, for example, are seldom found far from human habitation, and Swifts rarely nest anywhere other than in the roofs of buildings. Starlings often feed in gardens and roost during the winter months in towns, sometimes in phenomenal numbers. In winter, Redwings and Fieldfares move into suburban areas when driven by severe weather and depletion of natural berry supplies in the countryside. And the Waxwing is more associated with urban settings than any other winter visitor.

ABOVE: **Waxwing - a regular urban visitor.**
BELOW: **Modern housing estate.**

RECOGNISING WILDFOWL

Wildfowl is the collective name given to birds belonging to the family Anseridae, familiar members of which are swans, geese and ducks. Most are associated with wetlands to a greater or lesser degree, and all have webbed feet designed for propulsion in water. Most wildfowl have bills with serrated margins designed for grazing on vegetation; a few species are carnivorous.

SWANS

ABOVE: **Mute Swan.** ABOVE RIGHT: **Whooper Swan.**

Swans are the largest members of the wildfowl family. They have a proportionately long neck that allows them to feed on submerged vegetation, and that is held outstretched in flight. Adult swan plumage is pure white, while immature birds are grey–brown.

GEESE

Amongst wildfowl, geese are second only to swans in terms of size. There are two major goose genera: *Anser* and *Branta*. *Anser* geese are often referred to collectively as 'grey geese'; subtle differences in plumage and more obvious differences in bill structure and colour allow separation of the four species that occur here regularly. *Branta* geese are smaller overall, with plumages that comprise black, white and grey elements.

TOP: White-fronted Geese (genus *Anser*).
LEFT: Brent Goose (genus *Branta*).

LEFT: Mallard, the archetypal dabbling duck.
RIGHT: Pochard, a typical diving duck, in the act of diving.

Ducks are the smallest members of the wildfowl family, with relatively compact bodies and proportionately shorter necks than swans and geese. Dabbling ducks belong to the genus *Anas*. Although they occasionally upend in shallow water to feed or make half-hearted attempts to submerge, their buoyancy means that much of their diet is necessarily consumed while dabbling in the shallows, or indeed by grazing on land.

Members of the genus *Aythya* are all ducks that dive routinely in order to feed. They are found on freshwater lakes and sheltered coasts, depending on the species and time of year. Most form sizeable flocks outside the breeding season.

While many ducks have a vegetarian diet, several diving species are carnivorous. Coastal species such as Eiders feed primarily on molluscs, while so-called 'sawbills' (members of the genus *Mergus*) specialise in catching fish. With a few exceptions, most of the species described are gregarious to a greater or lesser degree outside the breeding season.

FLOCKS AND FLIGHT

Outside the breeding season, geese and swans, and many duck species, form flocks. They feed and roost together, so there are always plenty of eyes on the lookout for danger. Migratory swan and goose species even migrate to and from their Arctic breeding grounds in flocks.

If you live in Scotland, then one of the most evocative sounds of autumn is the call of grey geese, flying high overhead as they migrate south from their Arctic breeding grounds. Typically, long-distance flights of geese take on a 'V' formation; these are known as 'skeins'. Such formations are not just the consequence of following the leader but are also thought to improve aerodynamic efficiency. When flying to and from roosts and feeding grounds, geese tend to fly in looser flocks, although 'V' formations are still sometimes in evidence.

Bean Goose flock in 'V' formation.

WHOOPER SWAN

Cygnus cygnus | WS | LENGTH 150–160cm

A large all-white waterbird. Similar in size to Mute
Swan but separable using bill colour. Typically holds
its neck straight, not curved. Sexes are similar.

Adult has essentially pure white
plumage, although in spring and
summer, head and upper neck can
become stained orange. Bill is
triangular and rather long, with a
triangular yellow patch that extends
beyond the nostril. Juvenile has
grubby buffish-grey plumage and
a dark-tipped, pale pink bill. In
flight, head and neck are held
outstretched in the manner of other
swans, but wedge-shaped head aids
identification. **VOICE** Utters loud,
bugling *ung-uk* calls. **HABITS**

in flight, neck looks
incredibly long

JUVENILE

Usually seen in flocks, within which family groups are readily discernible. Sometimes mixes
with other swan species. Feeds by grazing grasses. **STATUS AND HABITAT** A handful of
pairs breed in the region each year but best known as a winter visitor (Oct–Mar). Most
winter visitors (around 11,000 birds in the UK) come from breeding grounds in Iceland, and
favour open habitats ranging from arable farmland to wet meadows and lakeside marshes.
Many return to traditional sites each autumn, although
some dispersal does occur in severe weather.

extent of colour on bill is variable but
often looks more yellow than black

BEWICK'S SWAN

Cygnus columbianus │ BS │ LENGTH 115–125cm

Our smallest swan species. Compared to the larger Whooper Swan, the shorter neck, small round head and bill pattern are useful in identification, especially in flight. Sexes are similar.

FAMILY GROUP

typically seen in family groups

JUVENILE

Adult has essentially pure white plumage. Compared to Whooper Swan, wedge-shaped bill is proportionately shorter and yellow colour is less extensive (usually does not extend beyond start of nostrils). Size of rounded (not triangular) yellow bill patch is variable. Juvenile has grubby buffish-grey plumage and a pinkish bill that is pale-based with a dark tip. All birds hold neck straighter than Mute Swan. **VOICE** Utters various honking, bugling, yelping calls. More musical than Whooper. **HABITS** Usually seen in flocks, within which family groups can be discerned. Sometimes mixes with other swan species. Feeds by grazing grasses. **STATUS AND HABITAT** Winter visitor, mostly to traditional sites and involving around 7,000 birds. Flocks favour seasonally flooded grassland, marshy meadows and, occasionally, arable farmland. In severe winters, there is some dispersal southwards and weather-related influxes occur from mainland Europe.

compared to Whooper, bill is smaller and adult's yellow patch is less extensive

MUTE SWAN

Cygnus olor | MS | LENGTH 150–160cm

Large all-white waterbird and our only regularly
resident swan species. Bill knob is larger in males than
females and gives the impression of a steep forehead
(cf. Whooper and Bewick's). Sexes are otherwise similar.

Adult is white overall although crown
can be suffused orange-buff. Bill
is orange-red (brighter in male
than female) with a black base.
Juvenile has grubby grey-brown
plumage and a pinkish-grey bill.
All birds hold neck in an elegant curve
when swimming. **VOICE** Generally
silent but utters grunting calls on
occasions, and loud hissing when
alarmed near the nest. Wingbeats produce a throbbing whine. **HABITS** Family parties
(parents and young cygnets) are a familiar sight on lowland lakes and rivers in spring. Feeds
by upending while swimming and using neck to reach submerged plants; also grazes
grassland. **STATUS AND HABITAT** Our commonest and most widespread swan, with up to
7,000 nesting pairs in the UK. More than 70,000 individuals spend the winter in the UK. In
the breeding season, favours freshwater wetlands, besides which it nests; in winter, also occurs
on estuaries and sheltered coasts, and farmland adjacent to wetlands.

throbbing sound produced
by wingbeats is diagnostic

MALE

juveniles invariably
associate with adult birds

JUVENILE

study the size of the bill
knob to help determine sex

MALE

FEMALE

head and neck are sometimes stained grubby due to feeding

BEAN GOOSE

Anser fabilis | BE | LENGTH 65–85cm

Robust, heavy-looking 'grey' goose with a bulky bill and orange legs. Sexes are similar but adults and juveniles are separable. Two distinct subspecies occur in our region.

TAIGA, ADULTS

TAIGA, ADULT

TUNDRA, ADULT

the size and stoutness of the bill helps with subspecies identification, as does the extent of orange coloration

overall, body plumage is browner than superficially similar Pink-footed Goose

Adult has chocolate-brown head and neck, grading to paler brown on breast and belly. Neck appears long when compared to similar Pink-footed Goose. Undertail is white and back is dark brown, with pale feather margins. In flight, wings look rather uniformly dark, but at close range note the pale bars on upper surface. Dark rump and tail contrast with narrow white band that defines tail-base. Ssp. *fabilis* (breeds in the taiga of N Europe) is large and long-necked, with a large bill usually well marked with orange. Ssp. *rossicus* (breeds in the tundra of N Siberia) is smaller and shorter-necked, with a smaller bill showing a reduced amount of orange. Both subspecies sometimes show a hint of white at base of bill. Juveniles are similar to respective subspecies adults but bill and leg colours are subdued. **VOICE** A nasal, trumpeting cackle. **HABITS** Typically forms single-species flocks. Feeds by grazing grassland. **STATUS AND HABITAT** A winter visitor with fewer than 1,000 occurring in most years. Severe winter weather sometimes produces a small additional influx of birds from mainland Europe. Small numbers of ssp. *fabilis* are regular in Norfolk, otherwise its occurrence is unpredictable. Favours wet grassland, marshes and arable fields.

PINK-FOOTED GOOSE

Anser brachyrhynchus | PG | LENGTH 60–75cm

Similar to Bean Goose, but smaller and more compact; smaller bill is marked with pink, not orange. Pink legs are diagnostic. Sexes are similar but adults and juveniles are separable.

greyish back and flanks contrast with browner neck and head

combination of pink feet and bill is diagnostic among grey geese

Adult has a dark chocolate-brown head and upper neck, grading to buffish brown on breast and belly. Back is blue-grey, the feathers having pale margins. In flight, note the pale blue-grey back, rump and upperwing coverts; tail shows a considerable amount of white.

in flight, upperwings appear rather uniform except for subtly darker flight feathers

Juvenile is similar to adult but back is buffish (not grey) and feathers have less well defined pale margins; bill and leg colours are subdued compared to those of adult. **VOICE** Nasal, trumpeting cackles, interspersed with diagnostic *wink-wink* calls. **HABITS** Typically forms single-species flocks. Favours arable and stubble fields and permanent grassland, generally roosting on estuaries or large bodies of fresh water. Feeds by grazing grassland and stubble. **STATUS AND HABITAT** Locally common winter visitor, mainly from breeding grounds in Iceland, with smaller numbers from Greenland. The majority are found from East Anglia and Lancashire, northwards to E Scotland. Around 350,000 birds visit the region each winter, representing some three-quarters of the world population.

WHITE-FRONTED GOOSE

Anser albifrons | WG | LENGTH 65–75cm

Distinctive 'grey' goose, the adults with a striking white forehead patch. Sexes are similar but adults and juveniles can be separated.

EUROPEAN, ADULT

Occurs here as 2 subspecies: Greenland White-front, ssp. *flavirostris*; and European White-front, ssp. *albifrons*. Adults of both subspecies have a brown head grading to slightly paler brown on neck and underparts, with bold black patches on belly and a large white forehead blaze. Back is dark grey-brown and undertail is white. European is appreciably shorter-necked than Greenland, and slightly smaller and paler overall. Pale-tipped bill is orange in Greenland but pink in European (however, note that the colour can be difficult to ascribe in the field). Legs are orange in all birds. In flight, all birds have rather dark wings with faint, pale wingbars. Juveniles are similar to respective adults but lack the white forehead blaze initially and black belly markings; tip of bill is dark. **VOICE** In flight, utters barking, rather musical 'yodelling' calls. **HABITS** Forms sizeable flocks and feeds by grazing grassland. **STATUS AND HABITAT** Winter visitor with traditional haunts. In severe winters, occasionally turns up away from known sites. Greenland White-fronts (entire world population winters here) are found mainly in Ireland and N and W Scotland. European White-fronts favour S England and S Wales. In good years, the combined wintering population of both subspecies is around 16,000 in the UK.

EUROPEAN, FLOCK

EUROPEAN, 1ST-WINTER

juveniles acquire white on forehead after a few months; black markings on underparts do not begin to appear until following year

GREENLAND, ADULT

extent of black on underparts varies between adults

GREYLAG GOOSE

Anser anser | GJ | LENGTH 75–90cm

The largest 'grey' goose and the only one that breeds here. Ancestor of domesticated 'farmyard' geese. Sexes are similar.

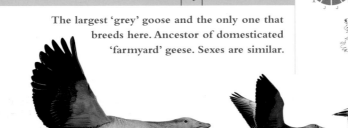

upperwing pattern shows more contrast than in other 'grey' geese

Adult has grey-brown plumage (more uniform than in other 'grey' geese) with dark lines on side of neck, barring on flanks and pale margins to back feathers. Large triangular bill is pinkish orange and pale-tipped; legs are pink. Juvenile is similar to adult but even more uniformly grey-brown; bill lacks adult's pale tip. In flight, all birds show pale forewings, rump and tail that contrast with darker flight feathers. **VOICE** Loud, honking calls, exactly like the familiar calls of farmyard geese. **HABITS** Forms small flocks. Feeding habitats include damp grassland, marshy lake margins and farmland. Birds seldom stray far from water, especially while moulting in summer. Typically, birds nest on islands in lakes and flooded gravel pits. **STATUS AND HABITAT** Natural range is confused by the presence of numerous feral populations. Patchily distributed in lowland England; more widespread and common in N England and S Scotland. More than 40,000 pairs probably breed in the UK. Resident numbers are boosted between Oct and Mar by migrants from Iceland; the winter population in the UK exceeds 200,000 birds.

proportions are more robust than other 'grey' geese: neck is thicker and bill is larger and stouter

legs are stout and pink

CANADA GOOSE

Branta canadensis | CG | LENGTH 95–105cm

Large wetland bird with a swan-like silhouette. An introduced species but now our most widespread and familiar goose. Sexes are similar.

Adult is mainly grey-brown, darkest on back (pale feather margins create barring) and palest on breast. Has white cheeks and chin on an otherwise black head and neck, blackish bill and dark legs. In flight, wings appear uniformly grey-brown and contrast with striking white undertail and dark tail. Juvenile is similar to adult but barring on back is less distinct. **VOICE** Loud, disyllabic trumpeting calls in flight. **HABITS** Usually found near water but typically feeds on adjacent grassland, or even on arable fields. In addition to natural habitats such as lakes and rivers, also favours flooded man-made gravel pits and reservoirs, and even urban parks with ornamental lakes; can become remarkably tame. **STATUS AND HABITAT** Introduced here from North America in the mid-17th century and now well established. More than 60,000 pairs breed in the UK and the winter population is nearer 200,000 birds. Most are concentrated in lowland England; it is scarce in Wales and absent from much of Scotland and Ireland.

neck is relatively thin and long; note the clear divide and contrast between neck and breast

black neck and white cheeks are striking at all times, even in flight

underparts grade from whitish on breast to grey-buff on belly

BARNACLE GOOSE

Branta leucopsis | BY | LENGTH 58–69cm

Small, well-marked goose, usually seen in large, noisy flocks. In flight, looks strikingly black and white. Sexes are similar.

combination of black head and white face allow easy separation from similar size Brent Goose

back is strongly barred

Adult has a mainly white face, with a black line from bill to eye, and a black crown and nape that merge with black neck and breast. Belly is whitish grey with faint dark barring on flanks; back is grey with well-defined black and white barring. Undertail is white, tail is black, and legs and bill are black. Juvenile is similar to adult but white elements of plumage are often tinged yellow and barring on back is typically less well defined. **VOICE** Flocks utter loud, barking calls. **HABITS** Forms sizeable flocks favouring a range of grassy habitats, from grazing pastures and arable fields to saltmarshes; often roosts on tidal mudflats or freshwater lakes. **STATUS AND HABITAT** A winter visitor to traditional, mainly coastal, sites. Birds from Greenland winter mainly on islands off NW Scotland (notably Islay) and also islands off NW Ireland. Birds from Svalbard visit the Solway Firth. Sometimes turns up elsewhere in severe winters; these records probably relate to birds displaced from mainland Europe, but escapees from captivity are a possibility too.

BRENT GOOSE

Branta bernicla | BG | LENGTH 56–61cm

Our smallest goose, roughly the size of a Shelduck. Sexes are similar but adults and juveniles are separable. Two subspecies occur: Pale-bellied Brent, ssp. *hrota***; and Dark-bellied Brent, ssp.** *bernicla***.**

Adult Pale-bellied has a blackish head, neck and breast, the neck with narrow white markings on side. Note neat division between dark breast and pale grey-buff belly. Back is uniform dark brownish grey. Adult Dark-bellied is similar but belly is darker and pale flank area smaller. All birds have a black bill and legs. Juveniles are similar to respective subspecies adults but note the pale barring (feather margins) on back and absence of white markings on neck. In 1st-winter birds, white on sides of neck is acquired in New Year. **VOICE** Extremely vocal, uttering a nasal *krrrut*. **HABITS** Seen in sizeable, noisy flocks. Birds favour estuarine habitats, feeding on eelgrasses and saltmarsh plants, plus seaweeds, after their arrival in autumn. The importance of grassland increases during their stay. **STATUS AND HABITAT** A mainly coastal winter visitor, favouring estuaries in S and E England, and much of the Irish coast. Pale-bellied Brents from Greenland winter mainly in Ireland, while birds from Svalbard winter around Lindisfarne in Northumberland. Elsewhere in S Britain, the visitors are Dark-bellied Brents from Russia, found mainly between N Norfolk and the Solent. In most years, the total UK population exceeds 90,000 birds.

DARK- and PALE-BELLIED

Pale-bellied birds look 'cleaner' and brighter than Dark-bellied, especially in flight

DARK-BELLIED ADULT

DARK-BELLIED 1ST-WINTER

PALE-BELLIED ADULT

1st-winter birds usually associate with their parents, forming loose family associations within larger flocks

EGYPTIAN GOOSE

Alopochen aegyptiaca | EG | LENGTH 65–72cm

Distinctive Shelduck-sized bird. In flight, the bold
white patch on innerwing assists identification.
Bill and legs are pink. Sexes are similar.

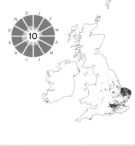

**white panels on wings are
obvious and striking in flight**

Adult has a grubby white
head and neck, its pale eye
surrounded by a dark patch.
Note the clear division
between pale neck and
orange-buff breast. Belly is
grey-buff with a small, dark
central patch. Back is dark
grey-brown, and white and
chestnut colours on wing
can be seen in resting birds.
Juvenile is similar to adult
but colours are duller; dark
breast spot and patch
around eye are absent.
VOICE Likened to a
braying donkey. **HABITS**
Usually seen in small

**legs are
stout and pink**

**white on wings is
obvious even in
standing birds**

groups, seldom far from water. Needs grassland for feeding and trees for breeding (typically
nests in tree-holes). **STATUS AND HABITAT** Has African origins; now established as a
breeding bird following a series of introductions dating back to late 18th century. Today,
more than 1,000 pairs breed in the UK. The population is scattered across lowland England,
with the bulk ranging from the Thames Valley corridor to East Anglia.

SHELDUCK

Tadorna tadorna | SU | LENGTH 55–65cm

A goose-sized duck with distinctive bold markings. Looks rather black and white in poor light. The shape of the colourful bill allows sexes to be separated.

looks strikingly black and white in flight

FEMALE

alert birds often stand upright, adopting a rather goose-like posture

JUVENILE

feeds by sifting invertebrates from the shallows

MALE

Adult male is mostly white but with a dark green head and upper neck (looks black in poor light), chestnut breast band, black belly stripe and orange-buff undertail. Legs are pink and bill is bright red with a conspicuous knob at base. In flight, wings show contrasting white coverts and black flight feathers. Adult female is similar but bill's basal knob is much smaller. Juvenile has mainly buffish-grey upperparts and white underparts. **VOICE** Courting male utters a whistling call, while female's call is a cackling *gagaga…* **HABITS** Coastal birds sift estuarine mud for small invertebrates. Nests in holes such as abandoned Rabbit (*Oryctolagus cuniculus*) burrows and tree-holes. **STATUS AND HABITAT** A familiar sight on estuaries and mudflats; also occurs in smaller numbers at inland freshwater sites. Around 15,000 pairs breed in the UK. In summer, many adults migrate to the Wadden Sea, Holland, and Bridgwater Bay, Somerset, to moult. Birds return to British estuaries in autumn and the UK population numbers around 60,000 birds in winter.

MANDARIN DUCK

Aix galericulata | MN | LENGTH 41–49cm

A striking duck species, males of which have elaborate and colourful plumage. The relatively dowdy female is still well marked and distinctive.

male's colourful plumage and sail-like feathers on back make identification straightforward

MALE

white markings on female's face show up at a distance

bold, pale spots on flanks are distinctive

MALE

FEMALE

surprisingly manoeuvrable in flight

Adult male head has a mane of orange, white, greenish and brown feathers, with white above eye and elongated orange facial plumes. Note the orange sail-like feathers on back, dark breast with vertical white stripes, brown flanks and white undertail. Bill is bright red with a pale tip. Adult female is grey-brown overall, darkest on back and with pale buffish spots on flanks. Belly, 'spectacles' surrounding eyes and throat are white. Bill is dull pink with a pale tip. Juvenile resembles adult female but colours are duller and patterns less striking. **VOICE** Mainly silent. **HABITS** Often seen in pairs, feeding unobtrusively around water margins. Nests in tree-holes. **STATUS AND HABITAT** Originates in E Asia, and popular in captivity. The British feral population comprises escapees and deliberate releases. Favours large, well-vegetated lakes with wooded margins.

WIGEON

Anas penelope | WN | LENGTH 45–47cm

Distinctive dabbling duck. Sexes differ, males being colourful and attractive. Forms flocks outside the breeding season and is a classic duck of winter estuaries.

white patches on male's wings are striking in flight

FEMALE

white belly contrasts markedly with otherwise reddish-brown plumage

Adult male has an orange-red head with a yellow forehead. Breast is pinkish. Plumage is otherwise mainly grey and finely marked except for white belly and characteristic black and white rear end. In flight, note the striking white patch on wing. Bill is pale grey and dark-tipped. In eclipse plumage, male resembles adult female, although white wing patch is still evident. Adult female is reddish brown, darkest on head and back; note the white belly. In flight, lacks male's white wing patch. Bill is grey and dark-tipped. Juvenile resembles adult female. **VOICE** Male utters a distinctive *wheeeoo* whistling call, an evocative sound of estuaries and wetlands in winter. **HABITS** Gregarious outside the breeding season and forms sizeable flocks. **STATUS AND HABITAT** A few hundred pairs breed here, but best known as a winter visitor: around 440,000 birds are present in the UK Nov–Mar in most years. Favours mudflats, estuaries and coastal grassland, but also occurs locally in significant numbers on inland wetlands and adjacent agricultural land.

MALE

pale forehead and forecrown are distinctive

male has very clean-looking plumage with striking black and white at rear end

GADWALL

Anas strepera | GA | LENGTH 46–55cm

An unassuming dabbling duck. Sexes differ. A close
view is needed to appreciate the beautifully intricate
vermiculate patterns on the
male's feathers.

black and white
patterning on
male's wings
is striking
in flight

often seen in pairs

MALE

FEMALE

Adult male has a buffish head and neck, with clear separation from the finely patterned grey
breast and flanks. Centre of belly is white and rear is black. Note the dark bill and yellow
legs. In eclipse plumage, male resembles an adult female. Adult female has mottled brown
plumage with a greyish head, and an orange-sided bill. White speculum can sometimes be
glimpsed in feeding birds. Juvenile resembles adult female. In flight, all birds show white in
speculum; extent of this is greatest in adult male, which also shows chestnut on innerwing.
VOICE Male utters a croaking call and female utters a nasal Mallard-like *quack*. **HABITS**
Dabbles in shallow water and sometimes upends to feed on water plants. Forms flocks
outside the breeding season. **STATUS AND HABITAT** Associated with freshwater habitats
with shallow margins, including lowland flooded gravel pits and reservoirs. Around 1,200
pairs breed in the UK, while up to 25,000 birds can be
present in
winter.

compared to a female Mallard, note female's
relatively smaller bill and more uniformly
brown head

FEMALE

MALE

male's black
rear end shows up
at quite a distance

MALLARD

Anas platyrhynchos │ MA │ LENGTH 50–65cm

Our most widespread and familiar duck. In flight,
all birds show a white-bordered blue speculum.
Sexes differ: males are more colourful
than females.

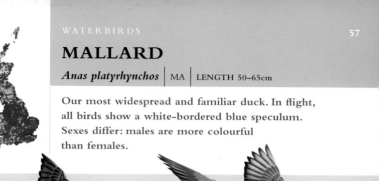

male's blue
speculum can
look dark in poor
light

FEMALE

MALE

Adult male has a yellow bill and shiny green head and upper neck, separated from chestnut
breast by white collar. Underparts are grey-brown except for black rear and white tail.
Back is grey-brown grading to reddish brown, and has diagnostic curled black central tail
feathers. Legs and feet are orange. In eclipse plumage, male resembles adult female but note
the yellow bill colour and reddish-brown breast. Adult female has an orange-brown bill
and mottled brown plumage. Legs and feet are dull orange-yellow. Juvenile is similar to
adult female. **VOICE** Male utters a range of whistles and nasal calls. Female utters familiar
quacking calls. **HABITS** Feeds by dabbling in shallow water. Accepts a wide range of other
food when fed by people and often becomes tame. **STATUS AND HABITAT** Found on a
wide range of freshwater habitats. Commonest on lowland lakes, rivers and flooded gravel
pits, but also on ornamental urban lakes. Around 100,000 pairs breed in the UK. An influx
of birds from N Europe boosts winter
numbers to around 680,000 birds.

FEMALE

colour of female's bill varies in
intensity between individuals

green gloss on male's
head is not always easy
to discern in poor light

curled tail feathers are
unique to this species

MALE

TEAL

Anas crecca | T. | LENGTH 34–38cm

27

Our smallest duck and one of the most widespread.
Flocks are a familiar sight in winter on estuaries,
mudflats and inland wetlands. Sexes differ.

flight is very rapid but white-bordered green
speculum often catches the eye

MALES and FEMALE

FEMALE

small size and uniform plumage
are good features for female Teal;
females invariably associate with
males, which aids identification

MALE

green colour on
male's head is
not always easy
to discern

black and white
lines on flanks and
black-framed yellow
patch at rear end both
show up at a distance

Adult male has a chestnut-orange head with a yellow-bordered green patch through eye.
Plumage is otherwise grey and finely marked, except for black-bordered yellow undertail
and distinctive horizontal white line along flanks. Bill is dark grey. In eclipse plumage, male
resembles an adult female. Adult female has uniform mottled grey-brown plumage; green
speculum can sometimes be glimpsed in feeding birds. Bill is mainly grey with a hint of
yellow at the base. Juvenile is similar to adult female but plumage is warmer buff; base of bill
is yellowish. In flight, all birds show a green speculum, defined by white borders. **VOICE**
Male utters a ringing whistle while female utters a soft quack. **HABITS** Usually nervous and
flighty, taking to the wing – and rising almost vertically – at the slightest sign of danger. Forms
flocks outside the breeding season. **STATUS AND HABITAT** Around 2,000 pairs nest in the
UK, favouring dense waterside vegetation beside upland and northern moorland pools and
bogs. Outside the breeding season, favours more open lowland and coastal habitats such as
freshwater marshes and mudflats. More than 200,000 UK birds are present in most winters.

GARGANEY

Anas querquedula | GY | LENGTH 37–41cm

**Slightly larger than a Teal, and well marked.
Generally unobtrusive; the male's call
is often the best clue to the species'
presence. Sexes differ.**

FEMALE

colours and
pattern on male's
innerwing are
diagnostic

MALE

Adult male has a reddish-brown head and broad
white stripe above and behind eye that almost
meets on nape. Breast is brown but plumage is
otherwise greyish, except for mottled buffish-
brown rear. In flight, male has a distinctive pale
blue-grey forewing and white-bordered
greenish speculum. In eclipse, male resembles
adult female but retains wing colours and
patterns. Adult female has mottled brown
plumage, similar to female Teal. Note uniform
grey bill and obvious pale facial spot at base of
bill. In flight, lacks male's pale forewing panel
and speculum is brown. Juvenile resembles adult
female. **VOICE** Male utters a diagnostic rattling
call, while female occasionally utters a very soft
quack. **HABITS** Unobtrusive on migration but
extremely secretive during the breeding season;
Apr and May are prime months. **STATUS AND
HABITAT** Migrant summer visitor to Britain
that winters in Africa.
Around 100 pairs probably
nest in the UK each year,
favouring well-vegetated
marshes and lake margins.
Seen regularly, and in
better numbers, on
migration.

compared to similar
size female Teal,
female Garganey has
more striking head markings and
more obviously pale-edged
feathers on back

FEMALE

markings on male's head
are unique and diagnostic

MALE

finely patterned greyish flanks
show up at a distance

PINTAIL

Anas acuta | PT | LENGTH 51–66cm

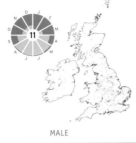

An elegant dabbling duck. Elongated appearance with a pointed rear end is a good clue to the identification of all birds. Sexes are dissimilar in terms of plumage: males are more colourful than females.

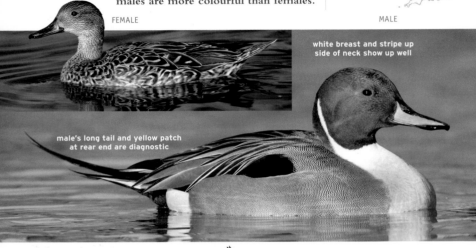

FEMALE

MALE

white breast and stripe up side of neck show up well

male's long tail and yellow patch at rear end are diagnostic

Adult male has a chocolate-brown head and nape, with a white breast extending as a stripe up side of head. Plumage is otherwise grey and finely marked, but note the cream and black rear, and long, pointed tail, often held at an angle. In flight, note the grey wings and green speculum (with white trailing edge). In eclipse plumage, male resembles adult female but retains pattern and colours on wings. Adult female has mottled buffish-brown plumage. In flight, white trailing edge on innerwing is an obvious feature. Juvenile is similar to adult female but the complex feather markings are less well developed. **VOICE** Male utters a whistling call, while female's call is grating and harsh. **HABITS** Unobtrusive during the breeding season but at other times feeds in the open in flocks. **STATUS AND HABITAT** Favours marshy waterside ground in the breeding season, but in winter is usually associated with estuaries. Perhaps as few as 20 pairs breed in the UK, but visitors from N Europe swell the winter UK population to around 30,000 birds.

looks long-necked and narrow-winged in flight

SHOVELER

Anas clypeata | SV | LENGTH 44–52cm

The distinctive long, flattened, spatulate bill makes identification easy. Sexes differ: male is more colourful than female. Often forms small single-species groups.

FEMALE

male shows a lot of white in flight; in both sexes leading half of innerwing shows blue

MALES

Adult male has a shiny green head (looks dark in poor light), white breast, and chestnut patch on flanks and belly. Rear is black and white, and back is mainly dark. Has a yellow eye and dark bill. In flight, shows a blue forewing panel and white-bordered green speculum. In eclipse plumage, male resembles adult female although body is more rufous and head is greyer. Adult female has mottled buffish-brown plumage and yellowish bill. In flight, wing pattern is similar to male's but blue is replaced by blue-grey. Juvenile is similar to adult female. **VOICE** Male utters a sharp *tuk-tuk*, while female utters a soft quack. **HABITS** Unobtrusive, favouring well-vegetated water margins and marshes. Filters food with its bill. **STATUS AND HABITAT** Associated with shallow water, sometimes on estuaries and mudflats in the winter but more usually on freshwater lakes and marshes. Nests in marginal vegetation. Around 700 pairs breed in the UK, but best known as a winter visitor. Population peaks in midwinter (around 18,000 birds may be present then); by late winter, numbers begin to fall.

FEMALE

the large bill is a feature shared by both sexes; with female birds, its colour varies in intensity

MALE

white elements of male's plumage show up well even on distant, sleeping and partly hidden birds

WILDFOWL IN FLIGHT – WINTER ESTUARY

Winter is the best time of year to watch wildfowl in Britain, as large numbers congregate on our estuaries and mudflats. Many species form flocks and it is not uncommon to see three or four different species feeding side by side.

male

TEAL

female

PALE-BELLIED BRENT

SHELDUCK

GOLDENEYE

male

female

male

RED-BREASTED MERGANSER

The montage shown here illustrates the range of common species that might be seen on a typical estuary from November to February.

WIGEON

male

female

PINTAIL

female

male

DARK-BELLIED BRENT

GOLDENEYE

SHOVELER

females

males

MALLARD

female

male

WILDFOWL IN FLIGHT – FRESH WATERS IN WINTER

Freshwater wetlands offer splendid opportunities for observing wildfowl during the winter months. Although the range of species seen overlaps to a degree with those observed on the coast, there are a number of ducks in particular that favour these habitats. Many are diving species whose specialist diets are linked to freshwater food.

SHOVELER

GOLDENEYE
male

female

female

male

SMEW

TEAL

male

male

PINTAIL

female

male

male

MALLARD

The montage shown here illustrates the range
of common freshwater species that might
be seen from November to February.

male

female

TUFTED DUCK

POCHARD

male

female

male

GADWALL

male

female

GOOSANDER   male

POCHARD

Aythya ferina | PO | LENGTH 42–49cm

Bulky diving duck with a proportionately long bill, curving forehead and peaked crown. All birds have a dark bill marked with a pale grey transverse band. Sexes differ.

MALE

male's bill pattern is striking and diagnostic

colours on head and back make identification of male straightforward

MALE

contrast between white belly and black neck and rear end is striking in flight

wings of females look rather pale silvery grey in flight

FEMALE

'spectacle' around eye usually shows up well

FEMALE

Adult male has a reddish-orange head, black breast, finely marked grey flanks and back, and black rear. In eclipse plumage, black elements of plumage are sooty brown. Adult female has a brown head and breast, and grey-brown on back and flanks; pale 'spectacles' usually surround the eyes. Juvenile resembles adult female but plumage is more uniformly brown. In flight, all birds have rather grey, uniform wings with a dark trailing edge to outer flight feathers. **VOICE** Mostly silent. **HABITS** In winter, forms flocks, sometimes in loose association with Tufted Ducks and Coots. Dives, and feeds on both plants and invertebrates. **STATUS AND HABITAT** Around 500 pairs nest in the UK. Birds from mainland Europe arrive in autumn and the winter non-breeding UK population numbers around 38,000. A classic species of flooded gravel pits, reservoirs, and larger lochs and lakes.

TUFTED DUCK

Aythya fuligula | TU | LENGTH 40–47cm

26

Common diving duck with a tufted crown, this
feature more distinctive in males than females.
Sexes are dissimilar in appearance.

FEMALE

MALE

white wingbars are
striking in flight

MALE

Adult male has a black body with white flanks;
dark head shows a purplish sheen in good light. Has
a beady yellow eye and black-tipped blue-grey bill. In eclipse
plumage, white elements of plumage become buffish brown. Adult female has essentially
brown plumage, palest on flanks and belly. Also has a small amount of white at base of bill
(cf. female Scaup), yellow eye and black-tipped blue-grey bill. Juvenile is similar to adult
female but with duller eye and plumage colours. In flight, all birds show a striking white
wingbar. **VOICE** Male utters a soft peeping call. **HABITS** Forms large flocks in winter,
often with other diving duck species, as well as Coots. Dives, and feeds on both plants
and invertebrates. **STATUS AND HABITAT** Common year-round resident. Around 17,000
pairs breed in the UK, favouring lakes, reservoirs and flooded gravel pits with marginal
vegetation. In winter, the UK population is boosted with arrivals from mainland Europe;
peak numbers reach around 110,000, with birds occurring on
a wider range of freshwater bodies than in summer.

FEMALE

male's head tufts are obvious
but purplish sheen can be hard
to discern in poor light

extent of white on female's head is variable

MALE

SCAUP

Aythya marila | SP | LENGTH 42–51cm

Rather bulky diving duck with a rounded head, lacking the 'tufts' seen in the smaller yet superficially similar Tufted Duck. Sexes are dissimilar in appearance.

Adult male has a green-glossed head and dark breast (can look black in poor light). Belly and flanks are white, back is grey and rear is black. Has a yellow eye and dark-tipped grey bill. Eclipse plumage male is similar but dark elements of plumage are buffish brown. Adult female has essentially brown plumage, palest and greyest on flanks and back. Note the striking white patch at base of bill. Juvenile is similar to adult female but white patch on face is less striking. In flight, all birds show a striking white wingbar. **VOICE** Generally silent. **HABITS** Forms flocks outside the breeding season, when most records occur. Dives for bottom-dwelling invertebrates, notably molluscs. **STATUS AND HABITAT** In most years, a few pairs are suspected of breeding, usually in Scotland. Around 5,000 birds winter in the UK, arriving from breeding grounds in Iceland and Scandinavia. Most favour estuary mouths, large bays and firths. Occasionally occurs inland, on reservoirs, lochs and flooded gravel pits.

MALE

white wingbar is obvious in flight

FEMALE

compared to female Tufted Duck, head is rounded and lacks tufts, and white markings are better defined

FEMALE

MALE

compared to male Tufted Duck, head is rounded and lacks tufts; bill is more substantial with smaller extent of black on tip

EIDER

Somateria mollissima | E. | LENGTH 50–70cm

Bulky sea duck that dives frequently and for long
periods. Large wedge-shaped bill creates a distinctive
profile. Sexes differ, the male being boldly marked, the
female with rather uniform plumage.

FEMALE

FEMALE

MALE

proportionately large head and
bill, and triangular outline, are
obvious even at a distance

colours on nape and
bill can be hard to
discern in poor
light

MALE

Adult male has mainly black underparts and white upperparts, except for black cap,
lime-green nape and pinkish flush on breast. In flight, looks black and white. In eclipse
plumage, male is mixture of brown and black, with some white on back and a pale stripe
above eye. Adult female is brown with darker barring; plumage provides good camouflage
when bird is nesting. In flight, looks mainly dark. Juvenile is similar to adult female but with
a pale stripe above eye. **VOICE** Male utters characteristic and endearing, cooing *ah-whooo*,
while throwing head back in a distinctive manner. Female utters a variety of deep, throaty
calls. **HABITS** Gregarious, forming variable-sized flocks. Dives for invertebrate prey,
particularly mussels. In summer, several females may band together, accompanied by a
'crèche' of youngsters. **STATUS AND HABITAT** Coastal resident, nesting close to the
seashore and feeding in inshore waters. Favours estuaries and rocky shores. Commonest
around coasts of Scotland and NE England, and on the N coast of Ireland; around 26,000
pairs breed in the UK. In winter, its range extends to S England and the winter population is
around 60,000 birds. A few birds linger year-round at southerly outposts.

LONG-TAILED DUCK

Clangula hyemalis | LN | LENGTH 40–47cm

Small, elegant diving duck, at home among raging seas and breaking waves. Dives frequently. Sexes differ: only the male sports the long tail.

female is small and compact by comparison with male; white face and relatively stubby bill help with identification

FEMALE

rides the waves in a buoyant manner

MALE

MALE, SUMMER

FEMALE, WINTER

wings are relatively long and narrow, and flight is rapid

Adult male in winter and spring is black, grey and white with a buffish patch around eye and a pink band on bill. In summer and eclipse plumages (seldom seen here), adult male is mainly brown and black, with white on belly and flanks, and a pale buff patch around eye; bill is dark. Adult female in winter has mainly brown and white plumage; face is white except for a dark cheek patch and crown. Adult female in summer is similar, but face is mainly brown with a pale patch around eye. Juvenile is similar to adult female in summer but browner overall. In flight, all birds show dark wings and mainly pale underparts. **VOICE** Male utters a characteristic nasal *ow-owlee*. **HABITS** Dives after bottom-dwelling invertebrates. In winter, usually seen in small flocks. **STATUS AND HABITAT** Winter visitor. Around 11,000 birds are present in the UK mainly in Dec–early Mar, coming from breeding grounds in Iceland and Norway. Favours gently shelving, often sandy beaches; commonest around Orkney, Shetland and the NE coast of Scotland.

COMMON SCOTER

Melanitta nigra | CX | LENGTH 44–54cm

Bulky, dark-looking duck. The relatively long tail is sometimes elevated when swimming. Sexes differ.

FEMALE

pale cheeks usually show up well

tail is sometimes cocked up

MALE

flocks are often seen flying in long lines

WINTER FLOCK

Adult male has uniformly black plumage. In good light, head acquires an oily sheen. Bill is mainly dark with a striking yellow ridge and bulbous base. Plumage in 1st-winter male is similar but subtly browner, and bill is uniformly dark. Adult female is mainly dark brown but with pale buff cheeks. Juvenile resembles adult female. In flight, all birds look mainly dark, although paler flight feathers can sometimes be discerned in good light. **VOICE** Mostly silent, although displaying males utter piping calls. **HABITS** Secretive and unobtrusive in the breeding season. Gregarious at other times and usually seen in flocks, these sometimes numbering thousands of birds. **STATUS AND HABITAT** Around 50 pairs usually breed in the UK, favouring northern lakes and lochs; nests among waterside vegetation. Outside the breeding season, almost exclusively coastal, favouring areas with sandy seabeds. Sizeable flocks gather in favoured locations and around 100,000 birds winter here. Also seen on passage, heading to and from breeding grounds in Scandinavia and wintering areas such as the Bay of Biscay.

VELVET SCOTER

Melanitta fusca | VS | LENGTH 51–58cm

Larger than Common Scoter. Both sexes show a white innerwing, easily seen in flight. White markings on male's head and female's facial markings are good identification features.

Adult male has mainly black plumage, with a striking white patch below the pale eye. Areas of white are sometimes glimpsed on closed wings in swimming birds. Bill has yellow sides and a black ridge (opposite of Common Scoter). In similar 1st-winter male white under eye is absent. Adult female has mainly dark sooty-brown plumage, with pale patches on cheek and at base of bill; bill is dark. **VOICE** Mainly silent. **HABITS** Often associates with Common Scoter flocks. Dives frequently for molluscs and other invertebrates. **STATUS AND HABITAT** A non-breeding visitor to Britain and Ireland from Scandinavian nesting grounds; around 2,500 birds are usually present in the UK in Oct–Mar. Favours coastal areas with sandy seabeds. Occasionally turns up inland on lakes or reservoirs.

white on wings shows up at a considerable distance in flying birds

MALES

white facial markings are striking

FEMALE

FEMALE

white patch under eye is striking at a distance

MALE

GOLDENEYE

Bucephala clangula | GN | LENGTH 42–50cm

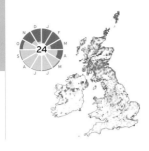

Compact diving duck. Sexes differ and both are
striking and easy to recognise; males have
particularly attractive markings.

FEMALE

**rounded head, pale eye, and white line along top
of flanks make identification straightforward**

**white on innerwing
is obvious in flight**

FEMALE

MALE

Adult male has mainly
black and white plumage.
The rounded, peaked
head is green-glossed
in good light; note the
beady yellow eye and
striking white oval patch
at base of bill. In flight,
shows white on inner
half of wings. In eclipse
plumage, male resembles
adult female but retains
his more striking white
wing pattern. Adult female
has mainly grey-brown
body plumage, separated
from dark brown head by
pale neck. Note the beady yellow eye. In flight, white on inner half of wings is less extensive
than in male. Juvenile is similar to adult female but has a dark eye. **VOICE** Displaying male
utters squeaky calls and a Garganey-like rattle. **HABITS** Goldeneyes dive frequently, and for
relatively long periods, in search of invertebrate food. Nests in tree-holes and also uses nest
boxes. **STATUS AND HABITAT** Around 200 pairs of Goldeneyes breed here, using large
lakes and lochs mainly in the north. A non-breeding influx from Scandinavia and further
east swells numbers. Around 20,000 birds are usually present in the
UK in Nov–Mar, favouring estuaries and coastal bays, as well as
freshwater habitats.

**white facial patch and beady
yellow eye are striking**

MALE

**often swims low in the water and spends
a minimal amount of time at the
surface before diving**

SMEW

Mergellus albellus | SY | LENGTH 38–44cm

Elegant little diving duck. Male is stunning and unmistakable. More sombre female could perhaps be confused with a grebe in winter plumage.

Adult male looks pure white at a distance; a closer view reveals a black patch through eye and black lines on breast and back. In flight, shows extensive white on innerwing. In eclipse plumage (not seen here) male resembles adult female but retains more extensive white on wing. Adult female, juvenile and 1st-winter birds (collectively known as 'Redhead' Smew) have an orange-red cap and nape contrasting with white on cheeks and throat; body plumage is grey-brown. Females of all ages show less white in wing than male. **VOICE** Silent. **HABITS** Can occur singly but more often found in small flocks. Sex ratio of flocks is very variable, females often more frequent than males. **STATUS AND HABITAT** Unpredictable winter visitor to Britain and Ireland, with around 150 UK records in most years. Its appearance usually follows the onset of severe weather at its nearest traditional wintering grounds in the Netherlands. Most records occur in SE England, with birds turning up on fish-rich flooded gravel pits, reservoirs and lakes.

MALES

'redhead' birds in particular can look rather grebe-like

FEMALE

mainly white plumage makes identification of male straightforward

MALE

RED-BREASTED MERGANSER

Mergus serrator | RM | LENGTH 52–58cm

Distinctive slim diving duck. Both sexes have
a shaggy, spiky crest on the back of the head.
In other regards, sexes are dissimilar.

FEMALE

rather straggly crest
often gets ruffled
by the wind

MALE

MALE

white on upperwing is
confined to trailing
half of innerwing

FEMALE

Adult male has a long, narrow red bill, green head (looks black in poor light), white neck
and orange-red breast. Flanks are grey and back is black. In eclipse plumage, male is similar
to adult female but retains extensive white on wing. Adult female has a red bill, dirty orange
head and nape, and pale throat; body plumage is otherwise greyish buff. Juvenile resembles
adult female. In flight, all birds show white on upper surface of innerwing; extent is greater
in males than females. **VOICE** Mostly silent, although displaying males sometimes utter soft
grunting calls. **HABITS** Dives frequently in search of fish. Nests on the ground, in waterside
vegetation. **STATUS AND HABITAT** Around 2,200 pairs breed in the UK, favouring fish-
rich lakes and rivers. Scotland is their stronghold; also found in N England, N Wales and parts
of Ireland. Outside the breeding season, more than 8,000 UK birds are present thanks to an
influx from N Europe. In winter, it is almost exclusively coastal, particularly favouring estuaries.

GOOSANDER

Mergus merganser | GD | LENGTH 58–66cm

Large, elegant diving duck that swims with a stately posture. In flight, all birds show a considerable amount of white on the wings. Sexes differ.

FEMALE

green gloss on head is not obvious in poor light

compared to female Red-breasted Merganser, note clear demarcation between the reddish head and neck, and greyish body plumage

MALE

pink flush on white underparts is variable in intensity and often hard to discern

Adult male is unmistakable, with a bright red bill, green-glossed head (looks dark in poor light), white body and black back. In good light, white elements of plumage appear flushed pale salmon pink. In flight, upper surface of innerwing is white. In eclipse plumage, male resembles adult female but retains his white wing pattern. Adult female has a reddish bill and orange-red head with a shaggy, drooping crest. Body plumage is greyish, palest on breast; chin is white. In flight, white on innerwing is restricted to trailing edge. Juvenile resembles adult female but with duller plumage colours. **VOICE** Displaying males utter ringing calls. **HABITS** Dives frequently in search of fish. Nests in tree-holes. Outside the breeding season, usually seen in groups. **STATUS AND HABITAT** Associated with freshwater habitats. Around 3,500 pairs nest in the UK, beside wooded upland rivers, mostly in Scotland, N England and central Wales. In winter, birds from mainland Europe boost the UK population to around 12,000 birds; favours reservoirs, lochs and flooded gravel pits.

FEMALE

in flight, all birds show extensive white on innerwing

MALE

MALE

RED GROUSE

Lagopus lagopus | RG | Length 37–42cm

Iconic gamebird, associated with upland moors.
The subspecies *scoticus* is unique to Britain and
Ireland. Sexes are dissimilar and separable with care.

Adult male has essentially chestnut-brown plumage with fine markings on the body visible at close range; has a striking red wattle over eye (lacking in female). Adult female has paler, more buffish-grey and marbled plumage than male; provides excellent camouflage when sitting on the nest. Juvenile resembles adult female but with less distinct plumage markings. In flight, all birds have uniformly dark wings and a blackish tail. **VOICE** Utters a nasal call that is sometimes described as 'go-back, go-back, go-back'. **HABITS** If alarmed, takes flight explosively: pattern comprises bouts of rapid wingbeats interspersed with long glides on bowed wings. **STATUS AND HABITAT** Restricted to areas of heather moorland. Feeds primarily on shoots of Heather (*Calluna vulgaris*) and related plant species; large tracts of land are managed (e.g. by selective burning) by shooting interests to encourage fresh plant growth. Around 230,000 pairs breed in the UK in most years. Hundreds of thousands of birds are shot each year. Irish birds are generally paler than their British counterparts and are sometimes assigned subspecies status (ssp. *hibernicus*); genetic studies appear not to support this contention.

MALE

female's plumage provides good camouflage amongst moorland vegetation

FEMALE

MALE

PTARMIGAN

Lagopus muta | PM | Length 34–36cm

Hardy mountain gamebird. In flight, all birds reveal striking white wings and an obvious black tail. Plumage varies throughout the year but sexes are separable at all times.

Adult winter male is white except for dark eye, lores and bill; at other times, plumage is marbled greyish-buff above, with white element decreasing as season progresses; underparts are white at all times and striking red wattle fades by midsummer. Adult winter female is white except for black eye and bill; in spring and summer, has finely barred buffish-grey upperparts; white on back decreases as season progresses. Juvenile resembles a uniformly brown female. **VOICE** Rattling *kur-kurrrr* call. **HABITS** Not unduly wary, but unobtrusive and well-camouflaged. Feeds on plant shoots. Forms small flocks in winter. **STATUS AND HABITAT** Confined to the Scottish Highlands, favouring rocky ground usually above 1,000m but at lower altitudes further north. Around 8,500 pairs breed here.

FEMALE, SUMMER

in spring and summer, compared to female Red Grouse, note the greater extent of white on underparts, and white in wings when flying

MALE, WINTER

white winter plumage provides excellent camouflage in snow, but renders birds conspicuous in mild winters

MALE, SUMMER

MALE, SUMMER

proportion of brown to white in male's plumage varies throughout spring and summer; this individual was photographed in May

BLACK GROUSE

Tetrao tetrix | BK | Length 40–45cm

Bulky moorland gamebird. Sexes are dissimilar in appearance and males are larger than females.

MALE

often fans tail in flight

white wingbar on upperwing and white underwing coverts are striking in flight

MALE

FEMALE

female's plumage is a match for moorland vegetation

Adult male has mainly blackish plumage; at close range, note the red wattle above the eye. Displaying birds reveal and fan white undertail coverts and elevate and spread tails, which then look lyre-shaped. In flight, tail looks proportionately long and forked, and wings reveal striking white bars. Adult female has orange-brown plumage, finely marked with dark bars. In flight, wings show a narrow white bar. Juvenile resembles a small female with subdued markings. **VOICE** Displaying males utter a bubbling, cooing call. **HABITS** Well known for its lekking behaviour: displaying males gather at traditional sites, early in the morning, to win the favours of onlooking females. **STATUS AND HABITAT** Associated with moorland where a mosaic of grassland, heather moorland, bilberry stands and adjacent woodland occur. Numbers are in decline, as is the species' range; annually there are around 5,000 lekking males in the UK.

glossy blue sheen is seen in good light

MALE

CAPERCAILLIE

Tetrao urogallus | CP | Length 60–90cm

Huge, impressive gamebird. Male is almost half as big again as female and sexes are markedly dissimilar in appearance.

Adult male looks all dark at a distance but a closer view reveals a greenish sheen on breast, brownish wings and a red wattle above eye. Note the rounded white spot at the base of the folded forewing. When displaying, tail is fanned out and elevated. Adult female has finely barred grey-brown plumage, except for plain orange-brown patch on front of breast. Juvenile resembles a small, dull female. **VOICE** Male utters a bizarre sequence of clicking sounds followed by a noise likened to a cork being pulled from a bottle. **HABITS** If disturbed from cover, sometimes 'explodes' into flight, revealing its all-dark, proportionately long wings and tail. Males display at traditional leks in late winter and early spring. **STATUS AND HABITAT** Restricted to areas of mature Scots Pine (*Pinus sylvestris*) – both relict areas of native Caledonian pinewoods and long-established plantations. Became extinct here in the 18th century but was reintroduced to some of its former haunts in the 19th century. Current population numbers around 1,300 birds.

immense size and precise habitat requirement makes recognition easy

some displaying males are bold and aggressive towards people

fans tail when displaying

despite their size, females are surprisingly unobtrusive, and usually harder to spot than males

MALE

FEMALE

QUAIL

Coturnix coturnix | Q. | Length 16–18cm

Tiny, secretive gamebird. Extremely hard
to see but its presence is easily detected
by hearing the distinctive call. Sexes
are separable with care.

beware the potential for confusion
with juvenile Grey Partridge, which
is more uniformly streaked brown,
and has red outer tail feathers

often creeps low to the ground if nervous

best chances of observation come by pinpointing
a territory and waiting silently at a safe distance
in the hope a bird will emerge from cover

Adult male has streaked, mainly brown
plumage, palest and unmarked on belly.
Head is adorned with dark stripes; pale
throat has a black centre and is defined
by dark lines. Adult female is similar
to male but has a pale throat. Juvenile
is similar to adult female. If flushed (a
rare event), all birds fly on relatively
long, bowed wings. **VOICE** Song is a
diagnostic, liquid, trisyllabic *whit-we-whit*
phrase. **HABITS** Hardly ever ventures
from the cover of vegetation. Sometimes
glimpsed running between strips of arable
crops. Feeds on a mixture of seeds and
invertebrates. **STATUS AND HABITAT**
Migrant summer visitor from wintering
grounds in Africa; also seen on migration.
Numbers vary from year to year: in a
typical season, there might be 400–500
calling males in the UK; in 'invasion'
years there could be 1,000 or more.
Arable farmland is the preferred
habitat for the species.

PHEASANT

Phasianus colchicus | PH | Length, 65–90cm (♂), 55–70cm (♀)*

* including tail

Colourful, introduced gamebird. Sexes are strikingly dissimilar: male unmistakable and female hard to confuse.

wings are broad and rounded

FEMALE

MALE

flight involves rapid wingbeats to get airborne, followed by a long glide on bowed wings

Adult male has orange-brown body plumage, blue-green head with a sheen in good light, large, striking red wattle, and long barred tail; some birds have a white collar. Other captive-bred forms are sometimes seen (e.g. birds with essentially violet-blue plumage). Adult female is mottled buffish brown with a shorter tail than male. Juvenile resembles a small, short-tailed female. **VOICE** Territorial male utters a loud, shrieking *coo-cukk* call, which is followed by a bout of vigorous wingbeating. In alarm, a loud *ke-tuk, ke-tuk, ke-tuk* is uttered as the bird flies away. **HABITS** Feeds on arable farmland and in open woodland, on invertebrates and seeds. Roosts in trees. **STATUS AND HABITAT** Originates in Asia and introduced here repeatedly since the 11th century. Now widespread and associated with a mosaic of farmland and wooded habitats. Although around 3–4 million birds may form the core of a stable breeding population across the UK, the species' exact status is hard to assess with any certainty: around 38 million are released each autumn for the shooting season.

male's gaudy, colourful plumage makes it easy to identify

MALE

female's plumage provides good camouflage in woodland habitat

FEMALE

RED-LEGGED PARTRIDGE

Alectoris rufa | RL | Length 32–34cm

Dumpy, well-marked gamebird. Usually seen in small parties (covies) outside the breeding season. Sexes are similar.

wings are rounded and wingbeats are rapid

white throat and black and white barring on flanks allow separation from Grey Partridge

red legs and bill are diagnostic

Adult has a red bill and legs, and a white throat bordered with a gorget of black spots. Plumage is otherwise mainly blue-grey and warm buff except for black and white barring on flanks. Juvenile has grey-buff plumage with hint of adult's dark markings; they are seldom seen unaccompanied by adults. **VOICE** Utters a loud *ke che-che, ke che-che, ke che-che…* call. **HABITS** Widely hunted and generally wary. Prefers to run from danger but, when forced to take to the air, flies low on stiffly held wings. **STATUS AND HABITAT** Typically found on arable farmland with mature hedgerows and scattered woods, but also occurs on heathland and coastal grassland. Introduced here for hunting; current population is maintained at artificially high levels by release (by shooting interests) of captive-bred birds each autumn, many of which are subsequently shot. The species' true population is hard to assess, but around 80,000 territories are held in the UK in most years.

GREY PARTRIDGE

Perdix perdix | P. | Length 29–31cm

Our native partridge species. Often seen in small parties that prefer to run from danger rather than fly. Sexes are separable.

MALE

Adult male has finely marked, mainly grey plumage with an orange-buff face, chestnut patch on belly, maroon stripes on flanks and streaked back. Adult female is similar to male but marking on belly is small and indistinct. Juvenile is grey-buff with a hint of adult's dark markings. **VOICE** Utters a harsh, choked *kierr-ikk* call. **HABITS** Generally wary, a trait that aids its survival in areas where it is hunted. Feeds on a wide variety of plant and invertebrate material, but chicks need insects for at least the first 2 weeks of life. **STATUS AND HABITAT** Favours open grassland and traditional arable farmland with mature hedgerows. Once abundant, it has declined dramatically over the last 50 years or so, as a direct consequence of modern farming methods. The impact of modern herbicides on plant diversity, and pesticides on insect diversity, has been catastrophic. Currently there are around 43,000 territories in the UK.

MALE   FEMALE

RED-THROATED DIVER

Gavia stellata | RH | Length 55–65cm

Elegant waterbird. Swims low in the water, typically holding its head and bill tilted upwards. Sexes are similar.

head and neck sometimes droop in flight

WINTER

Summer adult has blue-grey on face and sides of neck. Red throat can look dark at certain angles. Has black and white lines on back of neck and, lower down, on sides of neck too.

Upperparts are otherwise brownish grey while underparts are whitish. Winter adult has grey upperparts, delicately spangled with small white spots. Underparts, including sides to neck and face, are white. Shows a diagnostic white crescent around front of eye. Juvenile is similar to winter adult but upperparts are browner and underparts appear grubby white. In flight, all birds hold head and neck outstretched while feet and legs trail behind. **VOICE** On breeding grounds, utters a goose-like *kaa-kaa-kaa* in flight. Silent in winter. **HABITS** Dives frequently for fish, submerging in a 'gliding' manner rather than leaping like Shag, for example. **STATUS AND HABITAT** Nests beside small pools and flies to sea to feed; the UK breeding population is around 1,300 pairs. Outside the breeding season (Aug–Mar), almost exclusively restricted to coastal seas, but individuals can occur inland on reservoirs and gravel pits. Influx from N Europe boosts the UK winter population to around 17,000 birds; most numerous on eastern coasts of England and Scotland.

narrow, uptilted bill is diagnostic

WINTER

SUMMER

red patch on throat can look dark in poor light

BLACK-THROATED DIVER

Gavia arctica | BV | Length 60–70cm

Robust waterbird that swims buoyantly, typically holding its bill horizontally. Sexes are similar.

WINTER

compared to winter plumage Great Northern, note the more dainty bill, rounded head, and absence of partial neck collar

WINTER

white patch at rear end in swimming birds is usually obvious

Summer adult is stunning, with a blue-grey nape and head and black throat; sides of neck are adorned with black and white lines. Blackish back is marked with a chequer-board of white spots, while underparts are white. Winter adult has mainly grey-black upperparts and whitish underparts; a striking white patch is often visible on flanks at water level in swimming birds. Juvenile is similar to winter adult but upperparts are browner and underparts appear slightly grubby. In flight, all birds hold head and neck outstretched while feet and legs trail behind. **VOICE** On its breeding territory, utters croaking and wailing calls. Silent in winter. **HABITS** Dives frequently for fish, submerging in a 'gliding' manner rather than leaping like Shag, for example. **STATUS AND HABITAT** Rare breeding species that nests beside large lochs, where it also feeds; around 200 pairs breed each year. More widespread in winter thanks to an influx from Scandinavia: 500–600 birds are probably present in most years in the UK. Outside the breeding season, mainly coastal but individuals occasionally occur inland on reservoirs and flooded gravel pits.

pattern on throat and neck is diagnostic

SUMMER

GREAT NORTHERN DIVER

Gavia immer | ND | Length 75–85cm

Large, robust waterbird. Swims buoyantly with its massive bill held horizontally or very slightly elevated. Sexes are similar.

note partial half-collar on neck

WINTER

unmistakable in summer plumage with striking white banding on otherwise dark head and neck

SUMMER

SUMMER

often roll-preens and wing-stretches revealing white belly and underwings

Summer adult has a black neck (sheen visible in good light) marked with 2 rows of white stripes. Upperparts are blackish, with a chequerboard of white spots on mantle and smaller white spots elsewhere. Underparts are gleaming white. Bill is dark. Winter adult has dark grey upperparts and whitish underparts, including throat and front of neck; note the dark half-collar on neck. Bill is greyish with a dark culmen. Juvenile is similar to winter adult but upperparts are brownish grey and underparts are grubby white. Steep forehead is obvious in all ages. In flight, head and neck are held outstretched while feet and legs trail behind. **VOICE** Wailing, evocative 'song', uttered on breeding territory, is seldom heard in Britain. Silent in winter. **HABITS** Dives frequently for fish and crabs, submerging in a 'gliding' manner rather than leaping like Shag, for example. **STATUS AND HABITAT** Non-breeding visitor to Britain and Ireland, with perhaps 2,500 birds present in the UK in most years. Favours inshore seas; widespread off coasts of Scotland, Ireland and SW England. The diver most frequently found on inland water bodies. Occasionally lingers in northern waters into summer (in breeding plumage), creating the suspicion of nesting.

The open sea is a seemingly inhospitable environment for a bird. Nevertheless, several different groups make it their home, exploiting its biological richness as a food resource. Watching seabirds brings with it its own challenges: observation from land often means that the birds are distant, while observation from a boat introduces inherent instability. Get to know the main groups – partly by appearance but also by flight pattern – to help refine the process of identification.

SKUAS Superficially gull-like seabirds with mainly dark plumage and white flashes on wings. Have predatory and scavenging habits, either killing smaller seabirds or harassing larger ones for food. Four species are seen regularly.

TERNS Elegant and slim-bodied when compared to gulls. Long, pointed wings give them a buoyant and powerful flight. Plunge-dive after fish. Several common species.

SHEARWATERS Fly with stiffly held wings low over the water, banking and revealing alternate views of their dark upperside and white underside. The Manx Shearwater is the only shearwater that breeds in our region.

FULMAR Glides on stiffly held wings, seldom flapping them.

AUKS Mainly black and white seabirds whose wingbeats are fast and whirring. Spend long periods bobbing around on the sea; dive for extended periods in search of fish. Five species are seen regularly.

GULLS Range from small to large birds with mainly white adult plumage. Some species are true seabirds, while others are more coastal. Wings are comparatively long and narrow, affording them powerful flight. Several common species.

STORM-PETRELS Tiny, all-dark seabirds with a white rump and fluttering flight. Food is picked from the sea's surface. Two species are seen regularly.

GANNET Glides on stiffly held wings, and has deep wingbeats during direct flight. Plunge-dives after fish.

EUROPEAN STORM-PETREL

Hydrobates pelagicus | TM | Length 14–16cm

Britain's smallest seabird; looks improbably tiny when dwarfed by waves in a rough sea. Dark plumage and white rump recall House Martin. Sexes are similar.

upperwings are rather uniformly dark and lack the pale bar seen in Leach's Storm-petrel

square-ended rump and relatively narrow white rump band allow separation from Leach's Storm-petrel

FEEDING GROUP

Adult appears all dark at a distance except for the white rump. At close range, plumage is seen to be dark sooty brown. In flight, note the square-ended tail, white rump and white bar on underwing. Juvenile is similar to adult but 1st-autumn typically shows a pale wingbar on upperwing. **VOICE** Silent at sea but at breeding colonies utters strange gurgling and purring calls from nesting burrows. **HABITS** Consummate seabird, seemingly unaffected by even gale-force winds. Its 'bat-like' flight is strong and direct. When feeding, flutters low over the water with dangling feet. Sometimes seen from ferry crossings in summer. Otherwise observed in autumn migration when gales force birds close to land. **STATUS AND HABITAT** Seldom comes close to land willingly except during the breeding season, and then only at night. Colonies are on remote islands. Nests in burrows, rock crevices and cavities on old stone walls. Around 26,000 pairs breed in the UK.

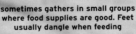

sometimes gathers in small groups where food supplies are good. Feet usually dangle when feeding

LEACH'S STORM-PETREL

Oceanodroma leucorhoa | TL | Length 16–18cm

Considerably larger than European Storm-petrel, and a more robust-looking bird with longer wings. Its flight pattern is also distinctly different. Sexes are similar.

Adult plumage is sooty grey but often looks all dark at a distance, except for pale bar on upperwing coverts. Tail is forked but this feature is not always easy to discern; pale grey line that divides rump is seen only at very close range. Underwings are all dark. Juvenile is similar to adult. **VOICE** Silent at sea, but at breeding colonies birds utter a bizarre-sounding gurgling rattle, likened to a pixie chuckling and being sick! **HABITS** Flight appears ever-changing in terms of direction, with powerful wingbeats and interspersed glides. Seldom seen except on autumn migration, mainly off western coasts, when severe gales force birds close to land. **STATUS AND HABITAT** An oceanic species that seldom comes close to land except in the breeding season, and then only at night. Around 48,000 pairs nest in the UK but all are found on remote and inaccessible islands.

grey central line to white rump can be tricky to observe

forked tail is a reliable diagnostic feature

underwings are uniformly dark and lack the white bar seen in European Storm-petrel

flight pattern is erratic and variable, except when battling against severe winds, when flight tends to be more direct

MANX SHEARWATER

Puffinus puffinus | MX | Wingspan 70–85cm

The only common shearwater in British waters. Gathers in groups and invariably seen at sea flying low over the water. Sexes are similar.

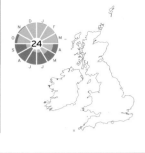

24

flight pattern comprises extended periods of gliding with occasional bouts of rapid wingbeats

underparts, including underwings, are mainly white and contrast with dark upperparts

Adult has blackish upperparts, although these can look dark reddish brown in evening light. Underparts are mainly white but wing margins are dark. Bill is dark and has slender tube nostrils at its base; legs and feet are pinkish. Juvenile is similar to adult. **VOICE** Silent at sea, but nesting birds at breeding colonies utter weird, strangled coughing calls after dark. **HABITS** Flies on stiffly held wings, alternately revealing contrasting dark upperparts and mainly white underparts as it banks and glides. Seen on land only at breeding colonies, and then after dark. Legs are incapable of supporting its weight properly and birds have to shuffle along, making them vulnerable to predation. **STATUS AND HABITAT** Typically a summer visitor to the region, present in Apr–Sep. Spends most of its life at sea and visits land only to breed. Nests in burrows on offshore islands. Around 300,000 pairs breed in the UK.

FULMAR

Fulmarus glacialis | F. | Wingspan 105–110cm

Gull-like relative of shearwaters and petrels.
Distinguished by its tube nostrils and
'stiff-winged' gliding flight pattern.
Sexes are similar.

DARK PHASE

uniformly dark
'blue' Fulmars are
scarce in British
waters but least
so in the north

Adult typically has blue-grey upperwings and back. Head,
underparts and tail are white; note the dark smudge around
eye. The so-called 'Blue Fulmar' (visitor from
Arctic) is seen occasionally; white elements of
plumage are blue-grey. Juvenile is similar to
adult, once the chick's fluffy white down has
been lost. In all birds, bill is chunky, with striking
tube nostrils at its base. **VOICE** Various gurgling
cackles and grunts are uttered at colonies.
Otherwise silent. **HABITS** Flies on stiffly
held wings with effortless gliding action.
White head is surprisingly obvious even
at a great distance. Swims buoyantly and
often gathers in groups where feeding
is good (e.g. around fishing boats).
Typically indifferent to people.
Can regurgitate oily, smelly
crop contents in a projectile
fashion over an intruder
if alarmed. **STATUS AND HABITAT** Nests on
ledges on sea cliffs and often colonial. Otherwise,
seen gliding over the sea. Until the end of the 19th
century, Fulmars were restricted as a breeding species
to St Kilda. Now widespread, with around 500,000
pairs breeding in the UK.

stiff-winged flight pattern
allows separation from gulls

bill is heavy and
hook-tipped, with
pronounced tube
nostrils

swims buoyantly, and often approaches fishing boats

CORMORANT

Phalacrocorax carbo | CA | Length 80–100cm

Large, dark waterbird with a heavy, hook-tipped
bill. Associated mainly with coastal waters,
but increasingly also freshwater sites
inland. Sexes are similar.

IMMATURE

Summer adult appears mainly dark. In good light, note the plumage's
oily sheen and black-bordered brownish wing feathers. Green eye is
surrounded by bare skin, and skin at base of bill is yellow,
grading to white. In breeding plumage, has a white
thigh patch and white on head and neck; winter adult
loses this white feathering. Juvenile has brown upperparts
and whitish underparts; it takes 2 years to acquire adult
plumage. **VOICE** Utters nasal and guttural calls at breeding colonies
but otherwise silent. **HABITS** Swims low in the water using large
webbed feet for propulsion; dives (with a noticeable leap) for fish.
Flies with head and neck held extended. Often perches
on rocks or posts with wings
outstretched. **STATUS
AND HABITAT**
Resident, found mainly
around coasts but
increasingly on rivers and flooded
gravel pits, especially in winter. Breeds
colonially; large twig and seaweed
nests are usually built on sea-cliff
ledges but occasionally in trees; around
8,400 pairs nest in the UK. Outside the
breeding season, the UK population
numbers around 35,000 birds.

**in flight, looks
appreciably bulkier
than Shag, with
longer wings**

**white thigh
patches are
most obvious
in flight**

SUMMER

**feather markings
create a 'scaly'
look to the back**

SUMMER

**swims low in the water
and dives frequently**

WINTER

SHAG

Phalacrocorax aristotelis | SA | Length 65–80cm

Similar to Cormorant but appreciably smaller. Its hook-tipped bill is noticeably more slender than that of its cousin. Sexes are similar.

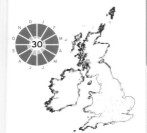

flies with head and neck extended

tail is relatively long

JUVENILE

Summer adult often looks all dark but, in good light, note the plumage's oily green sheen. Emerald-green eye is surrounded by feathering. Has a yellow patch at base of bill and a prominent crest. Winter adult loses crest and colours at base of bill are more subdued. Juvenile has dark brown upperparts and buffish-brown underparts with a pale throat. Crown peaks on forehead (in juvenile Cormorant, peak is at rear of crown). **VOICE** Utters various harsh grunting calls at breeding colonies but otherwise silent.

WINTER

like Cormorant, usually swims with bill slightly tilted upwards

HABITS Swims low in the water using its large webbed feet for propulsion; dives (with a noticeable leap) for fish. Flies with head and neck outstretched. Often seen perched on rocks with wings held outstretched. **STATUS AND HABITAT** Exclusively marine resident that favours rocky shores and tolerates rough seas. Nests colonially on sea-cliff ledges and commonest on western and northern coasts; around 27,000 pairs breed in the UK. In winter, most remain at sea, in the general vicinity of nesting colonies. Some immature birds disperse, very occasionally turning up inland. Overall the winter UK population numbers around 110,000 birds.

in poor light, plumage's green sheen can be hard to discern

SUMMER

GANNET

Morus bassanus | GX | Wingspan 165–180cm

Our largest seabird. Recognised in flight by its cigar-shaped body and long, narrow wings. Sexes are similar.

3RD CALENDAR YEAR

flies on long, narrow wings and often glides for extended periods

2ND CALENDAR YEAR

JUVENILE

yellowish flush on head and neck is only obvious at close range

plumage is mostly gleaming white with contrasting black wingtips

Adult is mostly white with black wingtips and a buffish-yellow wash to head. Bill is large and dagger-like. Juvenile has dark brown plumage, speckled with white dots. Adult plumage is acquired over a 5-year period. Plumage in 2nd-winter is similar to juvenile but underparts are mainly white; typically, head and neck are white except for dark cap. In 3rd-winter back and innerwings show extensive dark feathering. Plumage in 4th-winter resembles that of adult but some inner secondaries are dark. **VOICE** Silent at sea but nesting birds utter harsh, grating calls. **HABITS** Flies with deep, powerful wingbeats but glides on stiffly held wings in strong winds. Groups of birds plunge-dive after fish from a considerable height. **STATUS AND HABITAT** Found at sea, apart from when nesting. Nests on steep, inaccessible sea cliffs. The dozen or so important British colonies hold more than 220,000 pairs (nearly three-quarters of the world population). Passes close to headlands during strong onshore winds but otherwise occurs offshore, though with occasional inland records following storm winds. In winter, most birds move south to the west coast of Africa, but small numbers remain year-round.

BITTERN

Botaurus stellaris | BI | Length 70–80cm

Despite its large size, hard to see because of its shy nature and superb camouflage in its favoured reedbed habitat. Sexes are similar.

extremely long neck is only obvious when bird is nervous

Adult has brown plumage with intricate, fine streaks and barring that create excellent camouflage. Has a dark moustache and cap. Bill is dagger-like, and legs and feet are long and powerful. Superficially owl-like in flight, but note the outstretched head and neck and trailing legs. Juvenile is similar to adult but crown and moustache are brown. **VOICE** Territorial males utter deep, booming *whummp* calls in spring, mostly at night. **HABITS** Typical posture is hunched and dumpy; if alarmed, head and neck are held outstretched, pointing skywards. Feeds on fish and amphibians, relying on stealth and patience to catch prey. **STATUS AND HABITAT** In the breeding season, favours extensive reedbeds with areas of shallow water for feeding. Around 80 territorial (booming) males are noted in most years in the UK. Outside the breeding season, birds occasionally turn up in more open wetland areas, particularly in harsh weather. In winter, numbers are boosted slightly by birds from mainland Europe, when the population reaches around 600 individuals.

in flight, note the large, broad wings and hunched up head and neck

plumage is a good match for wetland vegetation

GREY HERON

Ardea cinerea | H. | Length 90–98cm

Familiar large wetland bird. Often stands motionless for long periods. Sexes are similar but adult and juvenile birds are separable.

Adult has a whitish-grey head, neck and underparts with dark streaks on front of neck and breast; note the pure white forecrown and black sides to crown leading to black nape feathers. Back and upperwings are blue-grey with contrasting black flight feathers. Dagger-like bill is yellowish and long legs are yellowish grey. In flight, note the broad wings and slow, flapping wingbeats; neck is held in a hunched 'S' shape and legs and feet trail behind. Juvenile is similar to adult but plumage is more uniform and bill is duller. **VOICE** Utters a harsh and distinctive *krrarnk*, typically in flight. **HABITS** Usual feeding tactic is to wait for fish and amphibian prey to pass within striking range. Sometimes engages in active pursuit. Often stands on one leg. **STATUS AND HABITAT** Fairly common resident of rivers, lakes and marshes; also found on estuaries and coasts, especially in winter. Around 12,000 pairs breed in the UK; nests colonially, constructing large twig nests, usually in trees but sometimes in reedbeds. Influx from mainland Europe can boost numbers in winter to around 60,000 birds.

head and neck are held hunched up in flight

resting birds often adopt hunched up appearance

massive bill

juvenile lacks striking head markings

extremely long legs

JUVENILE

LITTLE EGRET

Egretta garzetta | ET | Length 55–65cm

Elegant, pure white heron-like bird with a dagger-like black bill and long neck. Sexes are similar.

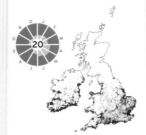

pure white plumage

flight is buoyant, on broad, rounded wings

yellow feet are diagnostic

Adult has essentially pure white plumage, a striking yellow eye and blue-grey lores. In breeding plumage, sports elongated nape plumes and briefly reddish lores. Long black legs contrast with bright yellow toes, the latter features often hard to see in wading birds. In flight, note the trailing legs; neck is held in a curved 'S' shape. Juvenile is similar to adult. **VOICE** Generally silent, but coarse, grating calls are sometimes uttered between rivals. **HABITS** Feeds actively in water, often chasing small fish and stabbing at them with vigour. When resting, adopts a hunched posture with the bill often hidden from view. **STATUS AND HABITAT** Classed as a rarity in Britain until recently. Nowadays, a common resident on estuaries and coastal rivers in S Britain, and increasingly seen inland. Around 700 pairs breed and the winter population numbers around 4,500 individuals.

SPOONBILL

Platalea leucorodia | NB | Length 70–80cm

Large wetland bird. Unmistakable when its bill is seen: it is flattened, with a spoon-shaped tip. Sexes are similar.

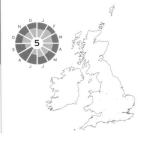

Breeding adult has mainly white plumage, with base of bill and breast flushed yellow. Has a crest of bushy feathers on nape. Bill is black with a yellow tip. Non-breeding adult is similar but yellow flush and crest are absent. Juvenile is similar to non-breeding adult but legs and bill are dull pinkish and wingtips are black. All birds fly with head and neck extended and legs trailing. **VOICE** Generally silent. **HABITS** Feeds by wading through shallow water, sweeping bill from side to side to catch small fish and crustaceans. Often stands with bill tucked under wings, leading to confusion with a sleeping Little Egret. **STATUS AND HABITAT** Very rare breeding resident and scarce non-breeding visitor to Britain (around 75 records each year). Mostly coastal, favouring extensive areas of shallow water (both fresh and brackish) for feeding.

head and neck are held extended in flight

IMMATURE

subtle black wingtips are only visible in flight

plumage is mostly pure white

bill shape is diagnostic

LITTLE GREBE

Tachybaptus ruficollis | LG | Length 25–29cm

Small, dumpy, buoyant bird, and Britain's smallest grebe. Sexes are similar but summer and winter plumages differ.

SUMMER

white underwing seen when wing-flapping and in flight

WINTER

powderpuff of feathers at rear end

Summer adult has mainly brownish plumage but neck and cheeks are bright chestnut. White-tipped dark bill has a lime-green spot at base. Swimming birds show whitish powderpuff of feathers at rear end. Winter adult has mainly brown upperparts and buffish underparts. Juvenile recalls winter adult but note the pale throat and black stripes on face. In all plumages shows a dark cap from base of bill to nape. In flight (seldom seen), all birds hold head and neck extended with legs trailing; wings are rounded and uniform grey-brown. **VOICE** Utters a characteristic whinnying call. **HABITS** Dives frequently for fish and aquatic invertebrates. **STATUS AND HABITAT** Widespread and fairly common resident of freshwater habitats, from ponds to lakes and slow-flowing rivers; around 5,300 pairs breed in the UK. Some dispersal takes place outside the breeding season and birds turn up on sheltered coasts and estuaries; the winter population numbers some 16,000 individuals across the UK.

SUMMER

pale tip to bill and lime-green spot at base of bill both show up well

bobs around buoyantly in the water

GREAT CRESTED GREBE

Podiceps cristatus | GG | Length 46–51cm

Britain's largest grebe. Elegant, graceful waterbird
with a slender neck and dagger-like bill. Sexes
are similar but summer and
winter plumages differ.

WINTER

WINTER

extensive patches of
white on innerwing

Summer adult has grey-brown upperparts, including nape. Underparts, including front of neck,
are whitish, flushed buffish orange on flanks. Head has a black cap and crest, with a striking
orange-buff ruff bordering paler cheeks. Bill is pink and eye is red. Winter adult has rather drab
grey-brown upperparts and a clean white neck and flanks; ruff is lost but it retains dark cap
and hint of a crest. Bill is dull pink. Juvenile recalls winter adult but has striking dark stripes on
cheeks. All birds fly with head and neck outstretched and legs trailing; note the striking white
panels on wings. **VOICE** During the breeding season utters a range of wailing, croaking
calls. **HABITS** Swims buoyantly and dives frequently, sometimes for long periods, in search of
fish. Builds a floating nest of compacted water plants. In spring, pairs perform elaborate ritual
'head-shaking' displays. **STATUS AND HABITAT** Widespread and locally common breeding
species; around 4,600 pairs nest in the UK. Favours large, fish-rich lakes, reservoirs and flooded
gravel pits. Winter influx from mainland
Europe boosts numbers (up to 19,000
birds may be present), when it also occurs
on inshore coasts.

dark stripes on head
are striking

ruff and crest are only
present in summer
months

JUVENILE

beady
red eye

SUMMER

RED-NECKED GREBE

Podiceps grisegena | RX | Length 40–45cm

Smaller and more stocky than Great Crested Grebe, and with a diagnostic yellow-based bill in all plumages. Sexes are similar but summer and winter plumages differ.

WINTER

white on trailing edge of innerwing

Summer adult has greyish-brown upperparts, including nape. Underparts are whitish, with grey streaking on flanks. Neck and upper breast are brick red. Head has white-bordered pale grey cheeks, a black cap and hint of a crest. Winter adult loses neck colours but often retains a subtle reddish collar. Cheek pattern is less well defined and ear coverts are grubby-looking. Juvenile recalls winter adult but shows more extensive red on neck; note the striking dark stripes on cheeks. All birds fly with head and neck outstretched and legs trailing; note the white wing panels. **VOICE** During the breeding season, utters various wailing and grunting calls; otherwise silent. **HABITS** Swims buoyantly but low in the water and dives frequently for fish. **STATUS AND HABITAT** Best known as a scarce winter visitor with perhaps 50–100 birds present Sep–Mar, favouring sheltered inshore seas and estuaries. Occasionally turns up on inland lakes and reservoirs. A few pairs sometimes linger on large, well-vegetated lakes during the summer, especially in N Britain, giving rise to speculation about possible breeding.

always shows some yellow on base of bill (never seen in Great Crested)

WINTER

SUMMER

centre of pale cheeks is greyish

red on neck can look rather dark in poor light

SLAVONIAN GREBE

Podiceps auritus │ SZ │ Length 31–38cm

Small, elegant waterbird. Sexes are similar
but summer and winter plumages differ;
beady red eye is seen at all times.

WINTER

looks black and white in flight

extensive
white on
trailing half
of innerwing

Summer adult has a reddish neck and
flanks. Back is black and black head has
golden-yellow plumes. Winter adult has mainly
black upperparts and white underparts. Note the clear
demarcation between black cap and white cheeks. Juvenile is
similar to winter adult. In all birds, flattish crown and bill shape (both
mandibles are curved) allow separation from similar Black-necked Grebe; note also the bill's
white tip. In flight, wings show white patches on both leading and trailing edges. **VOICE**
Territorial calls include various rattling trills and squeals. **HABITS** Swims buoyantly and
dives frequently in search of small fish and aquatic invertebrates. **STATUS AND HABITAT**
Most numerous in winter, when 1,000 or more birds are found in
sheltered UK coastal waters. Around 30 pairs breed in Scotland
each year, favouring shallow lochs with abundant sedges.

WINTER

**compared to Black-necked, note the shallow-sloping
forehead, flattish crown and evenly curved bill**

**elegant yellow plumes
contrast with otherwise
black head**

beady
red eye

SUMMER

pinkish line
from base of
bill to eye

BLACK-NECKED GREBE

Podiceps nigricollis │ BN │ Length 28–34cm

Small yet distinctive waterbird. Recognised at all times by its uptilted bill and steep forehead. Sexes are similar but summer and winter plumages differ.

WINTER

black on head extends to cheeks (which are white in Slavonian)

bill has straightish upper mandible and upcurved lower mandible (both mandibles are evenly curved in Slavonian)

beady red eye

SUMMER

neck is black (reddish in Slavonian)

Summer adult has a blackish head, neck and back, the face with golden-yellow tufts. Flanks are chestnut and it has a beady red eye. Winter adult has mainly blackish upperparts and white underparts. At this time, it is distinguished from similar Slavonian Grebe by more rounded head shape and greater extent of black on cheeks. Juvenile is similar to winter adult but white elements of plumage are buffish. In flight, all birds show a white patch on trailing edge of wing only. **VOICE** Calls include various whistles and squeaks; silent in winter. **HABITS** Swims buoyantly and dives frequently. **STATUS AND HABITAT** Best known as a scarce winter visitor to sheltered coasts, with around 130 records in the UK each year; occasionally turns up on inland freshwater lakes and reservoirs. Around 40 pairs breed here, favouring shallow, well-vegetated lakes.

RECOGNISING RAPTOR FAMILIES IN FLIGHT

Birds of prey (also known as raptors) are frequently seen in flight. They can be a challenge to identify, especially because absolute size is often hard to judge accurately when birds are distant, and because birds often appear in silhouette. However, if you study the shape and proportions of the wings and tail, as well as the bird's behaviour, you can usually assign it to a raptor family, which is a step in the right direction when it comes to identification. The following is a guide to some of the more useful identification pointers.

KITES Graceful and aerobatic raptors (one common British species) identified in flight by the deeply forked tail (twisted to aid flight control) and long, bowed wings.

HARRIERS Long-winged and long-tailed raptors; flight is slow and buoyant with relatively infrequent wingbeats. When hunting, harriers fly within a few metres of the ground scanning for prey. Three species are seen regularly.

OSPREY A 'one-off' raptor with no close allies; invariably associated with water. Can look gull-like in flight but its fishing technique is unmistakable: hovers, then plunges talons-first into water.

FALCONS Small to medium-sized raptors with rather pointed wings and agile, rapid flight; some species hover. Most falcons catch their prey in flight and some are capable of extraordinary bursts of speed. Four species are seen regularly.

HONEY-BUZZARD Superficially similar to *Buteo* buzzards, this 'one-off' summer visitor has a proportionately longer tail, smaller head and longer neck than its cousins. Taken in combination, the outline in flight is subtly distinctive.

BUZZARDS Broad-winged raptors, adept at soaring; relatively short tail is sometimes fanned out to increase lift or aid manoeuvring. Head is relatively large and neck is rather short. Two species are seen regularly.

EAGLES Large, broad-winged raptors, represented in our region by two rather different species (White-tailed and Golden eagles). Both are adept at soaring but capable of active and aerobatic flight when hunting. In both species, head is relatively large.

HAWKS Dashing raptors and active predators, adapted to hunt flying birds, as well as mammals in the case of the larger of our two species (Goshawk). Both it and Sparrowhawk have relatively broad, rounded wings and long tails; tail is sometimes fanned in soaring birds. Two species are seen regularly.

OSPREY

Pandion halieaetus | OP | Wingspan 145–160cm

Large, pale-looking, narrow-winged bird of prey,
and the classic fish-eating raptor, almost always
seen near water. Sexes are similar.

JUVENILE

looks very black
and white when seen
from below in flight

wings are swept back during
the initial stages of a dive

Adult has mainly brown upperparts, except for pale crown, while underparts
are whitish with a dark chest band. In flight and from below, looks rather pale
but note dark carpal patch, dark band along base of flight feathers and
dark terminal band on barred tail. Juvenile is similar to adult but
darker markings (notably dark tip to tail and dark line at base of
flight feathers) are less distinct. In soaring flight, all
birds show long, narrow wings and can look
rather gull-like. **VOICE** Utters various
mournful, whistling calls. **HABITS**
Unmistakable when fishing:
often hovers and then
plunges, talons-first,
into the water.

staring
yellow eye

feet texture is
designed to hold
slippery fish

STATUS AND HABITAT Migrant visitor, present
mainly Apr–Sep; winters in Africa. Usually seen near
water and even migrants gravitate towards fish-rich
reservoirs and lakes on passage. During the breeding
season, large water bodies are its favoured haunt. Around
200 pairs breed here and Scotland remains the stronghold.

MARSH HARRIER

Circus aeruginosus | MR | Wingspan 110–125cm

A graceful raptor, typically associated with
wetland habitats. Easiest to observe in
flight. Sexes differ.

Adult male is reddish brown except for blue-grey head and unbarred grey tail. In flight, note
the grey and reddish-brown areas on wings and black wingtips. Adult female is mainly dark
brown except for pale leading edge to wings and diagnostic pale cream cap and chin. Tail is
reddish brown. Juvenile is similar to adult female but tail is dark brown. **VOICE** Mainly
silent, but displaying birds sometimes utter thin, piping, whistling calls. **HABITS** Usually seen
quartering low over the ground at a slow pace, occasionally stalling and dropping into
vegetation to catch prey. **STATUS AND HABITAT** Classic wetland raptor, usually associated
with extensive reedbeds and marshes in the breeding season. On migration, sometimes seen
over open-country habitats. Around 400 pairs attempt to breed each year, most in East
Anglia. In autumn, most migrate to the Mediterranean region and
further south; a handful remains here year-round.

MALE

sometimes adopts a rather
upright posture when perched

flight is buoyant
and leisurely

MALE

MALE

FEMALE

seen side-by-side, female is
noticeably bulkier than male

FEMALE

HEN HARRIER

Circus cyaneus | HH | Wingspan 100–120cm

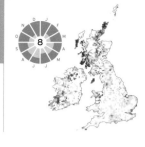

Distinctive raptor, typically seen gliding slowly, low over the ground. Sexes differ.

FEMALE

MALE

white rump is a feature of all birds

wings are proportionately broader than in superficially similar Montagu's Harrier

FEMALE

Adult male has pale blue-grey plumage except for white belly, white rump and black wingtips. Adult female is brown with darker barring on wings and tail, streaking on body underparts, and a distinctive narrow white rump. Juvenile is similar to adult female but breast and underwing coverts are more reddish, and upperwing coverts are brighter and show more contrast. **VOICE** Mainly silent. **HABITS** Usual flight pattern is seemingly effortless gliding; in direct flight, wingbeats are deep and powerful. Confusion with corresponding plumages of Montagu's Harrier is possible. The time of year and habitat are useful pointers; only Hen Harrier is likely to be seen in open country in winter. **STATUS AND HABITAT** In the breeding season, associated with upland and northern heather and grass-covered moors. Around 500–600 pairs probably attempt to nest each year in the UK but many are still persecuted illegally. In winter, moves to low-lying areas, particularly heaths and coastal grassland.

MALE

in some lights, looks almost uniformly pale

MONTAGU'S HARRIER

Circus pygargus | MO | Wingspan 100–115cm

Graceful raptor with a slow, buoyant flight.
Usually flies low over the ground, scanning
for prey. Sexes differ.

male's wing markings are
most obvious in flight

MALE

Adult male has mainly blue-grey plumage with
a smaller extent of white on rump than male
Hen Harrier. In flight, note the black wingtips,
single dark bar across upperwing and 2 dark
bars on underwings; at close range, chestnut
barring on underwing coverts and streaking on
belly are visible. Adult female has pale brown
plumage with darker barring on wings and tail,
streaking on body underparts and a narrow
white rump. Juvenile recalls adult female but
underparts and underwing coverts are orange-
red and unstreaked. In flight, all birds show a
proportionately narrower 'hand' and longer
wings than Hen Harrier. **VOICE** Mainly
silent. **HABITS** Usually quarters the ground,
occasionally plunging into cover after prey. **STATUS AND HABITAT** Migrant
summer visitor that winters in Africa. Around 15 pairs nest in the UK each year,
usually favouring arable farmland or heathland. Passage migrants are also
seen in spring and autumn.

FEMALE

sometimes
hovers briefly
if potential
prey is
located

eye 'crescents'
obvious

intensity and hue of female's
brown coloration varies
between individuals

FEMALE

dark bars on wings are
not always obvious
in standing birds

MALE

RED KITE

Milvus milvus | KT | Wingspan 145–165cm

Elegant and graceful raptor. Easily identified in flight by its deeply forked tail, constantly twisted to aid control. Sexes are similar.

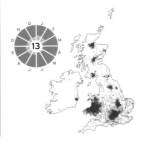

Adult has a pale grey head but otherwise looks overall reddish brown when perched. At close range, note the yellow eye, base of bill and legs. Seen from below in flight, note the reddish-brown body and underwing coverts, silvery-grey tail and patch on primaries, and otherwise dark wings. From above, tail appears red while reddish-brown back and wing coverts contrast with the dark flight feathers. Juvenile resembles adult but has subdued colours, and pale tips to wing coverts. **VOICE** Utters shrill calls in flight, not unlike somebody whistling for their dog. **HABITS** Seldom spends much time on the ground, except when hunting earthworms. **STATUS AND HABITAT** Until the 1980s, a relict population was confined to wooded valleys in central Wales. Reintroduction programmes in England and Scotland have since expanded its range and numbers dramatically, and around 1,600 pairs now breed in the UK. Favours open farmland with scattered woodland.

frequently calls in flight

perched birds often adopt a rather upright posture

forked tail is not always noticeable in perched birds

forked tail is flexed as an aid to flight control

HONEY-BUZZARD

Pernis apivorus | HZ | Wingspan 135–150cm

Buzzard-like raptor. Differs from Buzzard in its proportionately longer tail and wings, and rather small, almost Cuckoo-like head.
Sexes separable with care.

MALE

MALE

FEMALE

underwing markings
in particular are
extremely variable

Adult is very variable but typically has brownish upperparts, pale underparts and a grey head. Female generally separable from the male by strongly barred underparts. At close range, note the yellow eye and rather long, narrow bill. In flight and from below, note the 3 even bars on the grey tail, dark carpal patch, conspicuous barring on underwing and 'pinched-in' wings. Juvenile is similar to adult but usually browner overall, with less distinct barring on underwing coverts. **VOICE** Mainly silent. **HABITS** Soars with wings held slightly downcurved. Raids nests of bees and wasps, and feeds on larvae and adults of these insects. Generally shy and secretive. **STATUS AND HABITAT** Breeding summer visitor that winters in Africa. Associated with areas of large and relatively undisturbed woodland where its insect prey are numerous. Around 100 pairs breed in most years. Also seen on migration; in some autumns, a steady trickle of birds passes during periods of easterly winds.

head and
bill shape
are subtly
different
from that of
Buzzard, and
neck is longer

MALE

long toes and claws are
adapted to digging out
bee and wasp nests

BUZZARD

Buteo buteo | BZ | Wingspan 115–130cm

Broad-winged raptor and our commonest medium-sized bird of prey. Plumage variability means sexes are hard to tell apart, although females are larger than males.

PALE FORM

pale birds could be confused with male Rough-legged Buzzard

TYPICAL FORM

Plumage is variable but most adult birds are brown overall (extreme individuals range from all dark to virtually white). Seen perched, typical bird has a finely barred breast, usually paler than throat or belly. In flight and from below, carpal patch is generally the darkest feature. Flight feathers and tail are grey and barred; note the dark trailing edge to wings and dark terminal band on tail. Body and underwing coverts are contrastingly dark, and a pale breast band and pale band on underwing coverts can sometimes be seen. Juvenile is similar to adult but lacks terminal dark band on tail and obvious dark trailing edge to wings. **VOICE** Distinctive mewing *pee-ay* call often attracts attention, even with distant birds. **HABITS** Soars effortlessly, often with broad, rounded wings in a shallow 'V' and tail fanned out. **STATUS AND HABITAT** Locally common resident. Once persecuted and affected by pesticide contamination, it has returned to much of the region. Around 67,000 pairs now breed in the UK in most years. Territorial residents favour open country (including farmland) with scattered woodland for nesting. Juvenile birds tend to wander in winter.

DARK FORM

in a typical bird, pale throat, chest band and undertail coverts are striking

some birds have extremely dark body plumage

ROUGH-LEGGED BUZZARD

Buteo lagopus | RF | Wingspan 125–140cm

Medium-sized raptor, with proportionately longer wings than similar Buzzard, and subtly different plumage and behaviour. Sexes are separable with care.

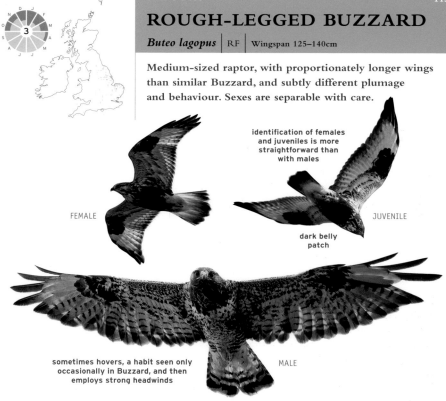

identification of females and juveniles is more straightforward than with males

FEMALE

JUVENILE

dark belly patch

sometimes hovers, a habit seen only occasionally in Buzzard, and then employs strong headwinds

MALE

Adult male has brown upperparts, except for white tail, which has a dark terminal band and smaller 2nd bar. From below, underparts appear pale except for dark head, carpal patches, wingtips and trailing edge to wing; pale tail is tipped with 2 dark bands. Adult female is similar to adult male but has a dark belly and single dark terminal band on tail. Juvenile is similar to adult female but dark markings (especially on tail) are indistinct. In flight and from above,

sometimes feeds on carrion in harsh winters; white base to tail

FEMALE

all birds look white-rumped due to pale tail-base. **VOICE** Mainly silent. **HABITS** Birds hover more frequently than Buzzards, often surprisingly low over the ground. **STATUS AND HABITAT** Scarce autumn passage migrant and winter visitor from mainland Europe. In most years, 20-plus are recorded, mainly from east coast locations. In exceptional years, more than 100 birds have occurred. Favours open habitats, including coastal marshes and grassland.

GOLDEN EAGLE

Aquila chrysaetos | EA | Wingspan 190–225cm

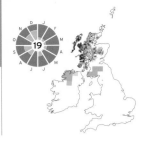

Majestic raptor. Told from a soaring Buzzard by its much larger size; relatively longer, narrow-based, 'pinched-in' wings; and longer tail. Sexes are similar but age differences can be discerned.

in flight, proportions are very different from Buzzard, particularly the relatively longer wings and tail

1ST-WINTER

golden 'mane' is striking in perched adults

Adult has mainly dark brown plumage with paler margins to feathers on back and golden-brown feathers on head and neck. Tail is dark-tipped and barred, but in flight and against the sky it can look uniformly dark. Juvenile is similar to adult but note the striking white patches at base of outer flight feathers; tail is mainly white with a broad, dark tip. Sub-adult gradually loses white elements of juvenile plumage by successive moults over several years.

seen from above in flight, pale head and base of tail contrast with rest of plumage

VOICE Mainly silent. **HABITS** Catches live prey such as Mountain Hares (*Lepus timidus*) and Red Grouse, but also feeds on carrion, especially in winter. Soars effortlessly and stoops on prey at speed. Males perform aerial displays in spring. **STATUS AND HABITAT** Resident of remote uplands in N and NW Britain. Scotland remains its stronghold, with 400 or so pairs present, but it has a toehold in N England too. In winter, immature birds disperse and occasionally wander south.

WHITE-TAILED EAGLE

Haliaeetus albicilla | WE | Wingspan 190–240cm

Immense raptor, larger and longer-winged than Golden Eagle. In flight, note the long, broad and parallel-sided wings, and short, wedge-shaped tail. Sexes are similar but adults and juveniles are separable.

in flight, has been likened to a flying 'barn door'

IMMATURE

despite its size, surprisingly agile in flight when in pursuit of prey

Adult has mainly brown plumage, palest on head and neck. At rest, white tail is often obscured by wings. At close range, yellow legs and huge bill can be discerned. In flight and from below, looks mainly dark except for paler head and neck, and white tail. Juvenile is similar to adult but appears darker overall and tail is uniformly dark. Sub-adult acquires adult plumage over successive moults; last immature feature to disappear is the dark terminal band on tail. In flight, neck looks rather long in all birds. **VOICE** Utters loud, mournful whistling calls. **HABITS** Despite its size, the raptor is surprisingly manoeuvrable, capable of catching fish and waterbirds while hunting low over the water. **STATUS AND HABITAT** Formerly a rare visitor from mainland Europe, with mostly immature birds present in winter. Now reintroduced successfully to some former Scottish haunts, mainly on west coast islands; around 40 pairs breed in most years. Immatures wander in winter.

note the massive bill

standing birds look very compact and the tail is barely noticeable

GOSHAWK

Accipiter gentilis | GI | Wingspan 100–115cm

Buzzard-sized raptor. In flight, shows broad wings and a long, broad-based, barred tail. Sexes are similar but males are smaller than females.

compared to Sparrowhawk in flight, note the relatively longer inner section of the wing

in flight, looks relatively deeper bodied and larger headed than Sparrowhawk

1ST-WINTER

1ST-WINTER

Adult has mainly grey-brown upperparts and pale underparts that have fine, dark barring. A close view reveals orange eye, yellow legs and feet, and striking pale supercilium. Juvenile has brown upperparts and buffish underparts, the latter heavily marked with teardrop-shaped dark spots. In flight, compared to Sparrowhawk, all birds show relatively longer, more pointed wings with a longer inner section ('forearm'), and a relatively longer tail that is rounded (not square-cut) at tip.

VOICE Utters a harsh *kie-kie-kie* during the breeding season; otherwise silent.

HABITS Rather secretive and spends long periods sitting in tree cover. Easiest to see in spring, when males perform aerial displays. Circling and soaring birds fan their tail, which appears rounded; the fluffy white undertail coverts are seen at such times. **STATUS AND HABITAT** Resident breeder that has staged a comeback in recent decades. Around 400 pairs now breed in the UK. Territories centre on wooded habitats; birds hunt along their margins and over nearby open country for birds the size of Woodpigeons.

feet and legs look large and powerful; in Sparrowhawk they are rather spindly by comparison

SPARROWHAWK

Accipiter nisus | SH | Wingspan 60–75cm

One of our commonest raptors, but generally unobtrusive and seen rather infrequently compared to Kestrel. Male is smaller than female and separable on plumage details as well as size.

soars when displaying at start of breeding season, but otherwise usually seen in fast low-level flight

MALE

1ST-WINTER

MALE

male is colourful and surprisingly small when compared to other birds of prey

1ST-WINTER

toes are extremely long (central one in particular) and used to grab small birds in flight

Adult male has blue-grey upperparts, and pale underparts that are strongly barred and reddish brown on body and underwing coverts. Adult female has grey-brown upperparts and pale underparts with fine, dark barring. 1st-winter has brownish upperparts and pale underparts, strongly marked with broad brown barring. In flight, all birds have relatively short, rounded wings, a long, barred tail (with a square-cut end), long yellow legs; eyes are yellow in female, orange-yellow in male. **VOICE** Utters a shrill *kew-kew-kew* in alarm.

HABITS Common raptor that catches small birds in flight in surprise low-level attacks. **STATUS AND HABITAT** Common breeding resident. Favours wooded habitats, both rural and suburban. Builds a twig nest in a tree. Hunts within woodland, along hedgerows in farmland and in gardens. Established birds are typically resident, while juveniles tend to wander in autumn and winter. Around 33,000 pairs breed in the UK. In autumn, the year's young boost that number considerably.

KESTREL

Falco tinnunculus | K. | Wingspan 65–80cm

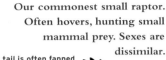

Our commonest small raptor.
Often hovers, hunting small
mammal prey. Sexes are
dissimilar.

FEMALE

tail is often fanned
when hovering or
banking, but not
in direct flight

MALE

Adult male has a spotted orange-brown back, blue-grey head and blue-grey tail with a black terminal band. Underparts are creamy buff with bold black spots on body. In flight and from above, dark outerwing contrasts with orange-brown innerwing and back. Adult female has barred brown upperparts and pale creamy-buff underparts adorned with dark spots. In flight and from above, contrast between brown innerwing and dark outerwing is less distinct than in male, and brown tail is barred. Juvenile resembles adult female but upperparts are more reddish brown. **VOICE** Utters a shrill and insistent *kee-kee-kee…* **HABITS** Frequently seen hovering over roadside verges. **STATUS AND HABITAT** Widespread and common resident breeder. Favours open grassy places, from lowland grassland to moorland. Diet includes small mammals as well as small birds and insects. Nests in tree-holes and on cliff ledges, as well as in man-made structures. In most years, around 50,000 pairs usually breed in the UK. Upland breeding birds usually move to lower-lying regions in winter.

rows of dark spots
create a barred effect
on otherwise brown
plumage

often perches on
posts, scanning
ground below
for prey

MALE

FEMALE

MERLIN

Falco columbarius | ML | Wingspan 60–65cm

Our smallest raptor. Usually seen in low, dashing flight in pursuit of prey such as Meadow Pipits. Sexes are dissimilar.

Adult male has blue-grey upperparts and streaked and spotted buffish underparts. In flight and from above, note the contrast between the blue-grey back, innerwings and tail with dark wingtips and dark terminal band on tail. Adult female has brown upperparts and pale underparts adorned with large, brown spots. In flight and from above, upperparts look uniformly brown with numerous bars on wings and tail. Juvenile closely resembles adult female. **VOICE** Mainly silent, although a shrill *kee-kee-kee…* is uttered in alarm near the nest. **HABITS** Sometimes perches for extended periods on lookout, using fenceposts or rocky outcrops. Soaring bird could be confused in silhouette with a small Peregrine; in low, dashing flight, it is vaguely reminiscent of a Sparrowhawk. **STATUS AND HABITAT** Local breeding species and migrant visitor. Nesting birds favour upland moorland and target prey such as Meadow Pipits and Skylarks; around 1,100 pairs breed in the UK. In winter, moves to lower-lying districts, often near coasts. Outside the breeding season, numbers are boosted by visitors from Iceland.

FEMALE

in flight, note the streaked underparts and barred tail

MALE

often perches on fenceposts

FEMALE

female's coloration blends in well with moorland vegetation

HOBBY

Falco subbuteo | HY | Wingspan 70–85cm

Elegant Kestrel-sized raptor and a consummate aerial
predator of small birds and insects. Sexes are similar.

often dismembers
and eats insect
prey on the wing

wings are relatively
narrow and pointed

apart from reddish-orange
'trousers' plumage can look
rather black and white

Adult has blue-grey upperparts and pale, dark-streaked underparts. At close range, note the
dark moustachial markings, white cheeks and reddish-orange 'trousers'. Juvenile is similar to
adult but lacks reddish 'trousers', and underparts look buffish overall. Upperpart feathers are
narrowly tipped pale. **VOICE** Utters a shrill *kiu-kiu-kiu…* in alarm. **HABITS** Unobtrusive
when nesting. Sometimes seen in stooping pursuit of prey or in soaring flight. Often targets
colonies of House Martins, or groups of feeding hirundines. In silhouette, has longer,
narrower wings, and a longer tail, than Peregrine. At times, can also recall an outsized Swift.
STATUS AND HABITAT Migrant summer visitor that winters in Africa; present here late
Apr–Sep; nesting birds favour heathland and farmland with scattered woods. Around 2,800
pairs nest in most years. Also seen on migration on coasts, and passage birds sometimes linger
in autumn.

PEREGRINE

Falco peregrinus | PE | Wingspan 95–115cm

Impressive stocky falcon. Often associated with dramatic windswept locations on coasts and mountains, but more recently also in towns and cities. Sexes are similar.

Adult has dark blue–grey upperparts and pale, barred underparts. Note the dark 'mask' on the face and powerful yellow legs and feet. In flight and from above, looks rather uniform in colour, although rump may appear paler. From below, pale underparts are distinctly barred, and contrast between pale cheeks and throat, and dark moustache, is usually striking. Juvenile is similar to adult but upperparts are brownish while paler underparts are suffused with buffish orange. In flight and from below, birds are typically anchor-shaped. **VOICE** Loud and distinctive *kek-kek-kek…* **HABITS** Soars with ease, its wings sometimes looking rather broad and bowed. Stoops at phenomenal speed on prey such as pigeons. **STATUS AND HABITAT** Widespread breeding resident in W and N Britain, and in parts of Ireland. Nests at lower densities in lowland areas and upland birds often move to lower-lying districts in winter. Around 1,400 pairs breed in the UK.

JUVENILE

wings are relatively broad by falcon standards

usually adopts an upright posture when perched

stocky body is apparent on perched birds

WATER RAIL

Rallus aquaticus | WA | Length 23–28cm

Secretive wetland bird whose distinctive
call is heard far more frequently
than the bird itself is seen.
Sexes are similar.

red, downcurved bill is diagnostic

relatively long legs and toes allow bird to wade in water and walk on yielding wetland vegetation

Adult looks dumpy when seen side on, with long, wader-like bill; body is laterally compressed when viewed head on. Plumage is mainly blue-grey below and reddish brown above, with black and white barring on flanks. Bill is reddish. Legs are dull red. Juvenile is similar to adult but less colourful. **VOICE** Utters a piercing pig-like squeal, choking calls and distinctive *kip-kip-kip* notes, typically from cover. **HABITS** Secretive and usually hard to see. Can be seen running at speed between one clump of wetland vegetation and another. Very occasionally seen flying low, on rounded wings with trailing legs. **STATUS AND HABITAT** Resident breeder and migrant visitor; favours reedbeds and marshes with emergent vegetation. On migration and in winter, may turn up along vegetated stream margins. Around 1,100 pairs probably breed in the UK; numbers are boosted in autumn and winter by influxes from mainland Europe.

tail is often cocked up

unmarked white undertail

barred flanks are striking

SPOTTED CRAKE

Porzana porzana | AK | Length 19–22cm

Dumpy, secretive wetland bird. Its extremely long toes allow it to walk over flimsy floating vegetation. Sexes are similar.

Adult has mainly brown upperparts and blue-grey underparts, the whole adorned with white spots; note the dark-centred feathers on the back and striking barring on flanks. Face is sooty and undertail coverts are pale buff. Bill is yellow with a red base, and legs and feet are greenish. Juvenile resembles adult but lacks the dark face and throat, and blue-grey elements of the plumage are more buffish grey. **VOICE** Male's territorial call is a repetitive whiplash-like *whit*, uttered after dark. **HABITS** Typical views are of birds skulking along margins of waterside vegetation. **STATUS AND HABITAT** Migrant summer visitor. The species is a hard bird to census accurately, but around 80 pairs probably nest in the UK each year. Extensive and typically inaccessible marshy wetlands are favoured in the breeding season. Most observations are made on autumn migration, when birds sometimes turn up on much smaller wetland habitats.

body plumage is well marked with white spots

JUVENILE

bill is colourful in all birds

usually keeps to cover but sometimes feeds in the open on migration

CORNCRAKE

Crex crex | CE | Length 27–30cm

33

An elusive bird, easy to hear in the right locations but usually a real challenge to see. Sexes are similar.

bill is stout and pink

chestnut panel on innerwing is the most striking feature in flight

Adult has sandy-brown upperparts, and dark feather centres that create a rather 'scaly' appearance. Face, throat, breast and belly are blue-grey while flanks are barred chestnut and white. In flight, note the chestnut patch on innerwing and dangling legs. Juvenile is more grey-brown than adult and lacks distinctive markings. **VOICE** Territorial male utters a ceaseless *crek-crek, crek-crek…* throughout the night and sometimes in daylight hours too. **HABITS** Seldom emerges willingly from the cover of dense, grassy vegetation (often just the head and neck can be seen) and very rarely seen in flight (migrates after dark). **STATUS AND HABITAT** Scarce and local migrant summer visitor that winters in Africa. The population has declined catastrophically and the species is now restricted to traditional hay meadows and damp grassland where appropriate cutting regimes still operate. Scottish islands (Inner and Outer Hebrides in particular) are strongholds. Around 1,200 pairs probably breed in the UK in most years.

MOORHEN

Gallinula chloropus | MH | Length 32–35cm

Familiar wetland bird. Swims with jerky movements and constantly flicks its tail. Legs dangle during flight, which looks laboured.
Sexes are similar.

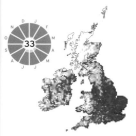

in dull light, plumage looks overall blackish except for white lines; purplish-blue and yellowish-green hues can be seen in good light

bill is extremely colourful

wings are uniformly dark in flight

uniformly brown juvenile is often seen in the company of adults

JUVENILE

Adult can look all dark. Close inspection reveals slight contrast between dark blue-grey head, neck and underparts, and brownish back, wings and tail. Has a striking yellow-tipped red bill and frontal shield on head; legs and long toes are yellow. Note the white feathers on sides of undertail and a white line along flanks. Juvenile is greyish brown with white on throat, sides of undertail coverts and along flanks. **VOICE** Utters a loud, far-carrying *kurrrk*. **HABITS** In natural surroundings, birds are usually rather wary and disappear into cover when alarmed; by contrast, in urban areas they are often rather tame. **STATUS AND HABITAT** Widespread and common resident. Favours a wide range of wetland habitats with a rich growth of submerged and emergent vegetation and associated invertebrate life. Around 260,000 pairs breed in the UK. Numbers are boosted in winter by influxes of birds from mainland Europe.

COOT

Fulica atra | CO | Length 36–38cm

Dumpy waterbird, often found in similar habitats to Moorhen. Lobed toes (seen when birds are walking on land) facilitate swimming. Sexes are similar.

Adult has blackish plumage, darkest on head and neck. Note the white bill and frontal shield on head, and beady red eye. Legs are pale yellowish. In flight, note the white trailing edge to otherwise dark, rounded wings. Juvenile has dark greyish-brown upperparts and white on throat and front of neck (can resemble the small winter-plumaged grebes). **VOICE** Utters a loud, distinctive *kwoot* call. **HABITS** Often feeds by upending or making shallow dives in water, and by grazing waterside vegetation. During the breeding season, constructs large mound nests of water plants. Forms flocks outside the breeding season. When taking off from water, typically runs along the surface, splashing its feet before finally getting airborne. **STATUS AND HABITAT** Widespread breeding resident and migrant visitor. Favours a range of freshwater wetland habitats. Around 30,000 pairs breed in the UK. In winter the population is boosted to more than 180,000 by influxes of birds from mainland Europe.

in flight, neck and legs are held outstretched

JUVENILE

juveniles are often seen being fed by attentive adults

gleaming white forehead is a diagnostic feature

CRANE

Grus grus | AN | Length 95–115cm

Large, long-legged, long-necked bird with a 'bushy' tail end. In flight, wingbeats are surprisingly shallow on broad, long wings, and neck and legs are held outstretched. Sexes are similar.

in flight, note that head and neck are held outstretched, not hunched up as with Grey Heron

posture is very upright and gait is relatively slow and stately

Adult has mainly blue-grey plumage with black and white on head and neck. Back sometimes appears rather brown and there is a patch of red on hindcrown. Juvenile is similar to adult but head is pale buffish grey, and adult's black and white markings are absent. **VOICE** Utters a loud, trumpeted, rolling *krrruu*. **HABITS** Cranes are typically extremely wary and invariably feed in wide-open spaces where potential threats can be seen from a distance. **STATUS AND HABITAT** A small group is effectively resident in Norfolk, and successful breeding occurs regularly; around 10 pairs nest in most years. Otherwise its status is that of a scarce passage migrant and very occasional winter visitor. Usually favours expansive arable and grassland fields on damp ground. In most years, there are a handful of records that do not relate to the Norfolk birds, mostly Sep–Nov or Feb–Mar. Adverse weather conditions occasionally push migrating flocks off course in mainland Europe and larger numbers arrive.

legs are extremely long

INTRODUCING WADERS

As a group, waders are attractive birds with elegant proportions and often beautifully patterned plumage. A wide range of bill sizes and shapes among the various species is reflected in the functional elegance of their feeding habits. And to add to their allure, many waders are associated with wild and untamed habitats.

PHALAROPES

Grey Phalarope feeding.

Phalaropes are extraordinary waders. Apart from a brief period on land during nesting, they spend their lives at sea. They are consummate swimmers that feed on surface plankton, and they feed on the water even during the breeding season.

BILLS, FOOD AND FEEDING

To avoid competition for food, different wader species have evolved bills and feeding habits to fill discrete ecological niches. The range of bill forms is most obvious in coastal habitats outside the breeding season, when several species can be seen feeding side-by-side.

Bar-tailed Godwit

Redshank

Ringed Plover

Food for waders: invertebrate prey from a typical estua

Typically, most waders are territorial and nest independently of others of the same species. However, outside the breeding season many form single-species flocks that feed and roost together. Working on the principle that there is safety in numbers, individual birds benefit from having an army of watchful eyes on the lookout for danger.

When the feeding is good, Knot flocks will form loose associations with other waders such as Sanderlings and Turnstones.

Curlew

Dunlin

Little Stint

INTRODUCING WADERS

NESTING AND BREEDING BEHAVIOUR

Waders often have strikingly different summer and winter plumages, with that seen in the breeding season typically more colourful. Nests are usually rudimentary, at best a small cup tucked away inside a tussock of grass, of perhaps just a bare scrape in gravel or sand. At the start of the breeding season, many wader species perform vocal displays to define their territories and attract and retain mates; some species also perform aerial displays.

TOP: Territorial Lapwing displaying.

LEFT: Many of the waders we see on our coasts in winter migrate north in order to breed, nesting well inside the Arctic Circle. A few Purple Sandpipers find remote Scottish mountain tops a suitable substitute for tundra.

FLIGHT AND MIGRATION

Waders are strong fliers and most have proportionately long wings. Their powers of flight are put to good use on a daily basis in the winter months but are essential for spring and autumn migration. Some of our wintering species breed in Greenland, Siberia or Arctic Canada, and it is thought that many individuals make at most a single stop on their journey.

Waders beginning their long migration north to Arctic breeding grounds.

TURNSTONE

Arenaria interpres | TT | LENGTH 23cm

Pugnacious little wader. Uses its short triangular bill to turn stones and tideline debris in search of seashore invertebrates. Sexes are similar.

WINTER

shows white on wings and back in flight

Summer adult has patches of orange-red on back, white underparts, and bold black and white markings on head. Male has brighter back colours than female and more distinct black head markings. Winter adult has essentially grey-brown upperparts, including head and neck. Breast has a blackish band showing clear demarcation from white underparts. Juvenile is similar to winter adult but upperparts are paler and back feathers have pale fringes. All birds have reddish-orange legs and a black and white wing pattern in flight. **VOICE** Utters a rolling *tuk-ut-ut* in flight. **HABITS** Surprisingly unobtrusive as it feeds among seaweeds and strandline debris. **STATUS AND HABITAT** Occasionally suspected of breeding in Scotland, but its status is essentially that of a common non-breeding visitor, with around 48,000 birds present in winter. Exclusively coastal, favouring beaches and rocky shores with an extensive strandline.

WINTER

striking orange legs at all times

SUMMER

orange-red coloration is more intense in male than female

OYSTERCATCHER

Haematopus ostralegus | OC | LENGTH 43cm

Distinctive wader, easily recognised
by its striking black and white
plumage and noisy alarm
call. Sexes are similar.

**bold white
wingbar is
seen in flight**

SUMMER

WINTER

WINTER

Summer adult has essentially black upperparts and white underparts with
a clear demarcation between the two on the breast. Has an orange-red bill,
pinkish legs and a beady red eye. Winter adult is similar but has a white half-collar.
Juvenile is similar to summer adult but black elements of plumage are brownish and bill and
leg colours are subdued. **VOICE** Utters a loud, piping *kleep* call. **HABITS** Uses its powerful
bill to feed on molluscs and other invertebrates. Outside the breeding season, feeding
birds are generally solitary or found in small groups; however, high-tide roosts can involve
hundreds, sometimes thousands, of birds. **STATUS AND HABITAT** Mainly a coastal bird,
often nesting on shingle, but it also breeds far inland, especially in N England
and Scotland, although seldom far from water. Around 110,000 pairs
breed in the UK in most years but non-breeding influxes of
birds from mainland Europe can boost winter numbers.
Outside the breeding season, estuaries and
mudflats are favoured habitats.

SUMMER

**Oystercatchers
are noisy birds,
especially during
the breeding
season**

AVOCET

Recurvirostra avosetta | AV | LENGTH 43cm

Distinctive wader, easily recognised by its black
and white plumage and diagnostic upcurved
bill. Sexes are broadly similar.

Adult has mainly white
plumage with black
elements on crown,
nape and wings. Legs are
long and blue, and bill is
black. Seen side-by-side,
male has a longer bill
than female and more
contrasting plumage.
Juvenile is similar to
adult but black elements
of plumage are dark
brown and less well
defined. **VOICE** Utters

looks strikingly
white and black
in flight

usually seen in
flocks outside
the breeding
season

a ringing *klueet-klueet…* call. **HABITS** Feeds by sweeping its bill from side to side through
water. Forms flocks outside the breeding season. **STATUS AND HABITAT** During the
breeding season, associated with shallow, brackish coastal lagoons; typically nests on islands
in lagoons, many of which are managed for this purpose. Around 1,500 pairs breed in most
years; East Anglia is the species' nesting stronghold. Disperses outside the breeding season;
some leave Britain but around 7,500 individuals overwinter on our estuaries, mainly on
south and east coasts of England.

feeds by sweeping
bill from side to side

blue legs

STONE-CURLEW

Burhinus oedicnemus | TN | LENGTH 38–45cm

Dry-country wader, best known for its eerie, wailing calls. Active mainly after dark, making observation a challenge. Sexes are similar.

black and white seen on outer wing in flight

relatively long tail

staring yellow eye

long yellow legs

Adult has streaked sandy-brown plumage; black and white wingbars can be discerned in standing birds but are most apparent in flight. At close range, note the white stripes on face, long yellow legs, black-tipped yellow bill and large yellow eyes. Juvenile is similar to adult but wingbars and facial markings are less distinctive. In all birds, well-marked plumage appears distinctive in isolation but in grassland its camouflage is superb. Looks rather long-winged and almost gull-like in flight, with a striking black and white pattern on upperwing. **VOICE** Utters strange Curlew-like *curleee* wailing calls, mostly at dusk and throughout the night. **HABITS** Wary and secretive, preferring to crouch and hide if perceived danger (e.g. an observer) appears. **STATUS AND HABITAT** Migrant visitor that winters in countries bordering the Mediterranean. Around 350 pairs breed in southern England. Undisturbed fragments of grazed chalk downland and Breckland heath are classic habitats, but it also nests on arable farmland where the management regime suits its needs.

DOTTEREL

Charadrius morinellus | DO | LENGTH 22cm

Rather pot-bellied mountain wader that is beautifully marked and often rather tame. Sexes are dissimilar.

Summer adult female has a striking reddish-orange breast and belly, separated from blue-grey throat by black-bordered white collar. Face is whitish and has a white supercilium above eye, and a darker cap. Otherwise upperparts are grey-brown, feathers on back having brown margins. Undertail is white and legs are yellow. Summer adult male is similar but colours are duller. Winter adult looks overall grey-buff but retains a suggestion of summer plumage patterns. Juvenile is similar to winter adult but back looks scaly, the darkish feathers having pale buff fringes. **VOICE** Utters a soft *pierrr* call. **HABITS** Exhibits role-reversal when nesting: the male, which is duller than the female, incubates the eggs. **STATUS AND HABITAT** Rare migrant visitor that winters in N Africa. Around 630 pairs nest, mostly in the Scottish Highlands. During the breeding season it is more or less confined to plateau mountain tops above 1,000m. On migration (particularly in spring), small groups of birds may linger at regular hilltop stop-off points. Autumn migrants sometimes linger on coasts.

FEMALE

dark belly patch

plumage shows a hint of pattern seen in adult

JUVENILE

yellow legs

FEMALE

dumpy-bodied appearance

GOLDEN PLOVER

Pluvialis apricaria | GP | LENGTH 28cm

Beautifully marked wader whose call is evocative of the desolate upland regions it favours in the breeding season. Sexes differ subtly in summer.

JUVENILE

WINTER

white underwing, including axillaries

usually seen in flocks outside breeding season

upperparts spangled with golden yellow

WINTER

SUMMER

extent of black on underparts is variable, differing between sexes and geographical location

Summer adult has spangled golden upperparts separated from underparts by a band of white. In males that breed in Britain, belly is black, grading to grey on neck and face. Females that breed here have far less distinct dark markings on underparts, and face is often whitish. With birds that breed further north in Europe (seen on passage), males are black on belly, neck and face, while females resemble males of British race. All races and sexes show considerable plumage variability. Winter adult loses black on underparts; head and neck become streaked golden buff while belly is white. Juvenile is similar to winter adult. In flight, all birds show white underwings, including axillaries. **VOICE** Utters a *peeoo* flight call and has a plaintive *pu-pEeoo* song. **HABITS** Forms large flocks outside the breeding season and often associates with Lapwings. **STATUS AND HABITAT** Breeds on remote upland moors; around 49,000 pairs nest in the UK. In winter, flocks are more widespread and favour grassland and arable fields. Influxes from Iceland and mainland Europe can boost wintering numbers 10-fold.

GREY PLOVER

Pluvialis squatarola | GV | LENGTH 28cm

Plump-bodied coastal wader. Best known
in winter plumage, when sexes are
similar; they are subtly dissimilar
in summer plumage.

WINTER

black 'armpits' (axillaries)
are revealed in flight

spangled grey,
black and white
plumage

Winter adult
looks overall
grey at a distance. Close view
reveals upperparts spangled
with black and white, and
whitish underparts. Legs
and bill are dark. Summer
adult male has striking black
underparts, separated from
spangled grey upperparts by a
broad white band. Adult female
has often mottled (not uniform)
black underparts. Juvenile resembles winter
adult but typically has a subtle buff wash
to plumage. In flight, all
birds reveal striking black
axillaries on otherwise white
underwings. **VOICE** Utters
a diagnostic trisyllabic
pee-oo-ee call. **HABITS**
Usually solitary outside the
breeding season. Feeds with
a typical stop–run action.

intense black on underparts,
framed by white on head
and neck

SUMMER

STATUS AND HABITAT Nests in the high Arctic and a non-breeding visitor to Britain
and Ireland. Almost exclusively coastal, favouring estuaries and mudflats; in the UK around
40,000 individuals are present in most winters.

LITTLE RINGED PLOVER

Charadrius dubius | LP | LENGTH 15–17cm

Slim-bodied little plover. Smaller than the similar Ringed Plover, but the head pattern and absence of a white wingbar and long tertials covering the primary tips are better identification features than size. Sexes are similar.

Summer adult has sandy-brown upperparts and white underparts with a black collar and breast band. Has black and white markings on head, a black bill, yellow legs and a bold yellow eye-ring. Black elements of plumage on head are duller in female than male. Juvenile has black elements of plumage replaced by sandy brown. Breast band is usually incomplete, leg and eye-ring colours are dull, and head lacks the pale supercilium seen in juvenile Ringed Plover. **VOICE** Utters a loud, short *pew* call. **HABITS** Much less gregarious than Ringed Plover and often found singly, or in small groups. Has a typical stop–start feeding action that is also shared with Ringed Plover. **STATUS AND HABITAT** Migrant breeding visitor, present mainly Apr–Sep. Usually favours inland freshwater habitats, notably margins of flooded gravel pits and other man-made sites; nests on bare ground, often on shingle. Around 1,200 pairs now breed in the UK. On migration, sometimes turns up at freshwater sites outside its breeding range and beside coastal pools.

upperwings lack
wingbar seen in
Ringed Plover

unmarked face cf.
juvenile Ringed Plover

JUVENILE

yellow eye-ring is noticeable,
even at a distance

RINGED PLOVER

Charadrius hiaticula | RP | LENGTH 17–19cm

Small, dumpy wader, associated mainly with coastal habitats. Sexes are separable with care.

JUVENILE

pale supercilium, not seen in Little Ringed Plover

JUVENILE

striking pale wingbar on upperwing

Summer adult male has sandy-brown upperparts and white underparts with a black breast band and collar. Has black and white markings on face, and a white throat and nape. Legs are orange-yellow and bill is orange with a dark tip. Summer adult female is similar but black elements of plumage on head are duller. In winter, adult black elements of plumage on head are mostly replaced by sandy brown, and there is a pale supercilium; leg and bill colours are subdued. Juvenile is similar to winter adult but breast band is small and often incomplete. All birds show a white wingbar in flight. **VOICE** Utters a soft, disyllabic *tuu-eep* call. **HABITS** Runs at speed along sand, then stands still for a few seconds before picking food items from the ground. **STATUS AND HABITAT** Nests mainly on sandy or shingle beaches. Inland gravel pit and river margins are also used. Around 5,300 pairs nest in the UK. Outside breeding season, almost exclusively coastal. Numbers are boosted by influxes from mainland Europe by up to 30,000 birds on migration.

bill is stubby and orange-yellow with a black tip

orange-yellow legs

LAPWING

Vanellus vanellus | L. | LENGTH 30cm

Distinctive wader with an obvious crest. Its broad, rounded black and white wings are striking in flight, as is the distinctive call. Sexes are usually separable in summer.

looks very black and white in flight

orange vent

broad wings, with rounded tips

crest is particularly striking in summer

Summer adult male has dark upperparts with a green and purple sheen visible at certain angles; underparts are white except for orange vent and black foreneck. Black and white markings on throat are striking. Summer adult female is similar but black markings on foreneck and throat show patches of white; crest is shorter than that of male. Winter adult is similar to summer female but throat and foreneck are white, nape is flushed with buff and feathers on back have buffish fringes. Juvenile is similar to winter adult but crest is short, and pale fringes to back feathers give it a scaly appearance. **VOICE** Utters a distinctive *pee-wit* call. **HABITS** Forms flocks outside the breeding season. **STATUS AND HABITAT** During the breeding season favours undisturbed grazed grassland, moors and spring-planted arable farmland. Around 130,000 pairs still breed in the UK despite declines due to changes in farming practices. Most British birds move to lowlands outside the breeding season and are partly nomadic. Influxes from mainland Europe boost winter numbers to around 620,000 individuals.

green gloss is seen in good light

pink legs

KNOT

Calidris canutus | KN | LENGTH 25cm

Dumpy wader (between a Dunlin and Redshank in size) with a relatively short, stout bill and legs. Lacks distinctive features in non-breeding plumage. Sexes are similar.

Adult in winter has rather uniform grey upperparts and white underparts. Bill is dark and legs are dull yellowish green. Adult in breeding plumage (sometimes seen in late spring or early autumn) has orange-red on face, neck and underparts; many back feathers have black and red centres and grey fringes. Legs and bill are dark. Juvenile resembles winter adult but has a buffish tinge, and feathers on back have pale fringes and dark sub-marginal bands, creating a scaly appearance. All birds show a white wingbar in flight, pale uppertail coverts and a plain grey tail. **VOICE** Utters a sharp *knut* call. **HABITS** In winter, forms large flocks that fly in tight formation. **STATUS AND HABITAT** Breeds in the high Arctic; its status here is that of a locally common non-breeding visitor. In winter, around 320,000 birds can be found on UK estuaries and mudflats. In autumn, newly arrived migrants (particularly juveniles) are sometimes found on atypical coastal habitats such as rocky shores.

rather plain upperwings lack obvious wingbars

WINTER

JUVENILE

legs are yellowish outside breeding season

rather uniform grey plumage

SUMMER

WINTER

beautiful orange-red plumage

SANDERLING

Calidris alba | SS | LENGTH 20cm

Small wader, invariably associated with
sandy beaches and seldom seen far from
breaking waves. Sexes are similar.

Adult in winter has rather uniform grey upperparts and white underparts. Summer adult
(sometimes seen in late spring or early autumn) has head and neck flushed with orange-
red, and shows a scattering of dark-centred feathers on back; underparts are white. Juvenile
is similar to winter adult but many back feathers have dark centres. Folded wing shows a
distinctive black 'shoulder'. All birds show a striking white wingbar in flight, and legs and
bill are black at all times. **VOICE** Utters a sharp *plit* call. **HABITS** Often seen in small flocks
running at speed, and feeding, along edges of breaking waves on sandy beaches. **STATUS
AND HABITAT** Locally common non-breeding visitor that breeds in the high Arctic.
Around 16,000 birds spend the winter in the UK in most years; almost
all favour sandy beaches and, to a lesser extent, estuary mudflats.

reddish-brown
upperparts

WINTER

striking
white
wingbar

SUMMER

gleaming white underparts

WINTER

runs at high speed
along shoreline

PURPLE SANDPIPER

Calidris maritima | PS | LENGTH 21cm

Plump-bodied wader. Generally confiding but often unobtrusive and easy to overlook. In all plumages it recalls a dark, dumpy, short-legged Dunlin. Sexes are similar.

WINTER

SUMMER

rather indistinct white wingbar

scaly-looking back

JUVENILE

Adult in winter has a blue-grey head, breast and upperparts, darkest on the back; belly is white and it has darkish streaks on flanks. Adult in breeding plumage (sometimes seen in late spring) has reddish-brown and black feathers on back; rufous crown and dark ear coverts contrast with otherwise paler, streaked grey-brown face. Juvenile recalls winter adult but back feathers, many of which are rufous, have pale margins, creating a scaly appearance; neck, breast and flanks are streaked. Legs are yellowish in all birds and long, slightly downcurved bill has an orange or yellow base. All birds show a white wingbar in flight.

purple sheen is only obvious in good light

WINTER

VOICE Utters a sharp *kwit* call in flight.

HABITS Usually found at the edge of breaking waves on rocky shores; feeding birds can often be watched at a range of just a few metres.

STATUS AND HABITAT A few pairs breed in Scotland, but best known as a non-breeding visitor. Around 13,000 birds winter in the UK, mostly on rocky shores and headlands.

yellowish legs

WADERS

LITTLE STINT

Calidris minuta | LX | LENGTH 13–14cm

Tiny wader that recalls a miniature, short-billed Dunlin. Juvenile is the most likely plumage to be seen here. Sexes are similar.

reddish-brown upperparts

SUMMER

pale feather margins align to form a white 'V' on back

dark legs

JUVENILE

Adult in breeding plumage has white underparts, reddish brown on back, and a suffusion of rufous orange on head and neck. Note the yellowish 'V' on mantle, and pale supercilium that forks above eye. Winter adult has grey upperparts and white underparts, with white lores. Juvenile has white underparts; reddish-brown and black feathers on back and wings have pale fringes, some of which align to form obvious white 'V' markings. Note the buffish-orange flush on side of breast. Head has a pale supercilium that forks above eye, pale forecrown and dark centre to crown. Legs and bill are dark in all birds. **VOICE** Utters a shrill *stip* call. **HABITS** Frantic feeding activity is a clue to its identity. Picks food items from the surface of mud, rather than probing. **STATUS AND HABITAT** Regular passage migrant, mostly juveniles in autumn. Feeds alongside Dunlins on estuaries and on drying coastal pools; occasional at inland freshwater sites. Around 750 birds are recorded in the UK in most years. Overwinters in very small numbers.

TEMMINCK'S STINT

Calidris temminckii | TK | LENGTH 14–15cm

Tiny, slim-bodied wader with short yellowish legs and a slightly downcurved bill. Sexes are similar.

compared to Little Stint, looks longer-bodied and longer-winged

SUMMER

SUMMER

scaly-looking upperparts

JUVENILE

Adult in breeding plumage has grey-brown upperparts, streaked dark grey on head, neck and breast; many back feathers have dark centres and underparts are white. Winter adult (not likely to be seen here) has grey-brown upperparts and white underparts. Juvenile has white underparts and brownish upperparts; feathers on back have pale fringes, creating a scaly appearance. All birds show a clear demarcation between dark breast and white underparts; striking white outer-tail feathers are seen in flight. **VOICE** Utters a trilling call. **HABITS** Often holds its body rather horizontally, and moves in a creeping manner. **STATUS AND HABITAT** Scarce passage migrant, with adults seen in spring and juveniles predominating in autumn; there are around 90 records each year in the UK. Migrants favour margins of shallow freshwater pools. A few pairs also breed in the Scottish Highlands in most years.

CURLEW SANDPIPER

Calidris ferruginea | CV | LENGTH 19–21cm

Elegant wader. Combination of the long, downcurved bill and white rump are reliable identification features at all times. Sexes are similar.

Summer adult has a spangled reddish-brown, black and white back, and (briefly) brick red on face, neck and underparts; latter feature often appears mottled in moulting migrants. Males are typically more colourful than females but variability means that reliable separation is challenging. Winter adult (seldom seen here) has greyish upperparts and white underparts. Juvenile (commonest plumage encountered here) has pale-edged feathers on back, creating a scaly appearance, and a white belly, buffish-peach breast and pale supercilium. **VOICE** Utters a soft *prrrp* call. **HABITS** Often seen alongside slightly smaller Dunlins but typically feeds in deeper water, with a more deliberate, probing feeding pattern. **STATUS AND HABITAT** Breeds in the high Arctic and its status here is that of a scarce passage migrant, seen mainly in autumn; around 750 birds are recorded in most years in the UK. Typically favours estuaries and coastal pools; very occasional on inland fresh waters.

JUVENILE

in flight, white
rump allows certain
separation from Dunlin

scaly upperparts and orange flush to sides of breast

JUVENILE

bill is more
noticeably
downcurved
than in Dunlin

SUMMER

most birds seen
in spring in Britain
have not yet acquired
uniform brick red plumage
seen at height of breeding season

DUNLIN

Calidris alpina | DN | LENGTH 17–21cm

Our commonest small wader and the yardstick by which to judge other species. Sexes are subtly different in summer but similar in winter.

WINTER   SUMMER

forms large flocks outside the breeding season

WINTER

Several races occur here; these are variable in terms of size and bill length. Typical summer adult has a reddish-brown back and cap, whitish underparts with a diagnostic black belly, and streaking on neck. Intensity varies according to race; males are usually more boldly marked than females. Males that breed in NE Europe and Siberia have brightest markings (and longest bills). Winter adult has uniform grey upperparts and white underparts. Juvenile has reddish-brown and black feathers on back; feathers have pale fringes, some of which align to form whitish 'V' patterns on back. Underparts are whitish but with black streak-like spots on flanks and breast; head and neck are brown and streaked. **VOICE** Utters a *preeit* call. 'Song' of displaying birds comprises a series of whistling calls. **HABITS** Forms sizeable flocks outside the breeding season. **STATUS AND HABITAT** Breeding bird, passage migrant and common winter visitor. Breeds on moorland and mountains; around 9,600 pairs nest in the UK. Outside breeding season, favours estuaries and mudflats. Very common on passage, and around 350,000 are present Oct–Mar.

all birds have dark, slightly downcurved bills

JUVENILE

SUMMER

all birds have dark legs

black belly

diagnostic dark spots on flanks

USING DUNLIN AS AN IDENTIFICATION YARDSTICK

When it comes to the identification of small waders, one of the most important steps for a birdwatcher is to get to know the Dunlin – particularly in autumn, in immature plumage. It is our most variable small wader, and three subspecies are seen regularly in Britain; each has different breeding grounds. The smallest, subspecies *schinzii*, breeds here but winters in west Africa; intermediate in size, subspecies *alpina* breeds in Siberia and winters in Britain; the largest, subspecies *arctica*, breeds in Greenland and passes through Britain on migration. The two extremes in terms of size are depicted here as autumn birds.

Both of the birds shown here are beginning to moult from juvenile into 1st-winter plumage – evidenced by the plain grey scapular feathers (on the back).

the subspecies *schinzii* is a particularly dumpy, short-winged bird

looks short-winged by comparison with subspecies *arctica*

short bill

Subspecies *schinzii* is only marginally larger than a Little Stint.

HOW AND WHY WADERS MOULT

Like other waders, a newly-fledged Dunlin has a complete set of feathers that are referred to as juvenile plumage; these feathers are not especially durable but give the bird rapid independence. Juvenile feathers are retained in the main for the first few weeks of life but then are gradually replaced by others; these eventually create an appearance known as 1st-winter plumage. The replacement feathers are much more hard-wearing than the juvenile feathers and serve the birds well during the first winter of their life.

bill length varies considerably according to subspecies – from the smallest, shortest-billed (*schinzii*) to the largest, longest-billed (*arctica*)

the subspecies *arctica* is relatively elongated and long-winged

all juvenile Dunlin, regardless of subspecies, have spots on their flanks

all juvenile Dunlin have dark legs

Subspecies *arctica* approaches Curlew Sandpiper in terms of size and bill length.

WADERS

RUFF

Calidris pugnax | RU | LENGTH 23–29cm

Very variable wader, in terms of size and appearance. The relatively small head, slightly downcurved bill and orange-yellow legs are consistent features. Sexes are dissimilar.

Male is larger than female (known as a Reeve). Summer adult male has brownish upperparts, many feathers with black tips and bars. Briefly, males acquire facial warts and variably coloured ruff and crest feathers. Each male is slightly different, but entirely black, white or chestnut ruff feathers are typical. Summer adult female has grey-brown upperparts, many feathers having dark tips and bars; underparts are pale. Winter adult has uniform grey-brown upperparts and pale underparts. Juvenile recalls a winter adult but is buff overall; feathers on back have pale fringes, creating a scaly appearance. In flight, all birds show a narrow white wingbar and broad white sides to rump. **VOICE** Mainly silent. **HABITS** In the breeding season, males display at leks. Forms flocks outside the breeding season. **STATUS AND HABITAT** During the breeding season, favours flooded meadows and marshes; a few pairs nest here. Better known as a passage migrant (commonest in autumn), seen on coastal freshwater pools. Most winter in Africa but around 800 remain in the UK.

rump is edged white

JUVENILE

indistinct pale wingbar seen in flight

FEMALE, SUMMER

MALE, SUMMER

male's plumage is variable – some have 'ruff' that is orange, in others it can be black or white

FEMALE, WINTER

legs are yellowish outside breeding season

'scaly' appearance to upperparts

JUVENILE

WOODCOCK

Scolopax rusticola | WK | LENGTH 35–38cm

Distinctive, large Snipe-like wader with a dumpy body, long bill and relatively short legs. Cryptic plumage colours and patterns afford it superb camouflage in leaf litter. Sexes are similar.

eye is set high on head

plumage is a good match for woodland leaf litter

Adult and juvenile have marbled chestnut, black and white plumage, palest and more extensively barred on underparts. Has large eyes that are located high on the head, giving it almost complete all-round vision. In flight, wings look broad and rounded, and long bill is striking. **VOICE** Male utters soft duck-like calls and explosive squeaks in a crepuscular display flight (known as roding). **HABITS** Largely nocturnal. Most encounters are by chance, when a bird is flushed, or of the flight silhouette of a displaying bird in spring. **STATUS AND HABITAT** Associated with wooded habitats. Both mixed and deciduous woodlands are favoured, and a mosaic of open areas and dense canopy cover seems important during the breeding season, with damp ground for feeding. Breeding numbers are hard to assess accurately, but around 78,000 pairs probably breed in the UK. Numbers increase in winter to around a million individuals, a result of influxes from as far away as Russia.

white tips to tail feathers

very vocal when displaying in flight – birds are most active at dusk

SNIPE

Gallinago gallinago | SN | LENGTH 25–28cm

Distinctive wader, recognised by its dumpy, rounded body, rather short legs and very long, straight bill. Sexes are similar.

extremely long bill

Adult and juvenile have mainly buffish-brown upperparts, beautifully patterned with black and white lines and bars. Has distinctive stripes on head, with a streaked and barred breast and flanks, and white underparts.

VOICE Utters 1 or 2 sneeze-like *kreech* calls when flushed. Males perform a 'drumming' display in the breeding season, when a humming sound is produced by vibrating the tail feathers. **HABITS** Feeds by probing its long bill vertically downwards into soft mud, in the manner of a sewing machine. When flushed, rises quickly and flies off fast, sometimes with a zigzag flight pattern. **STATUS AND HABITAT** Invariably associated with waterlogged or boggy ground. In the breeding season, marshes, meadows and moorland bogs are favoured; around 76,000 pairs probably breed here, mainly in Scotland, Ireland and N England. In autumn and winter, it is more widespread and numerous (probably totalling around a million birds), and is found in a wider variety of freshwater habitats.

flight is rapid and direct

pale feather margins align to form stripes on back

JACK SNIPE

Lymnocryptes minimus | JS | LENGTH 18–20cm

Similar to Snipe, but appreciably smaller
and with a relatively shorter bill and
legs; markings on head and back
are striking. Sexes are similar.

forked pale
supercilium

pale feather
margins align to
form stripes on back

moves with a bobbing action

bill is relatively
shorter than
in Snipe

Adult and juvenile have essentially brown upperparts with intricate, cryptic dark markings
on feathers. Back has striking yellow stripes; a greenish sheen can sometimes be discerned.
Head is strikingly marked with dark and pale buff stripes; note the forked, pale supercilium
and lack of a central crown stripe. Neck and breast are streaked, and underparts are white.
VOICE Mostly silent. **HABITS** Moves in a distinctive manner, pumping its body up
and down as it walks. Easily overlooked because it feeds unobtrusively among waterside
vegetation. Very reluctant to fly, preferring to crouch motionless until danger has passed.
STATUS AND HABITAT Scarce winter visitor from N European breeding grounds.
Favours muddy margins of pools and marshes, where tangled and flattened dead stems of
rushes and grasses are a perfect match for its cryptic plumage. Its numbers are hard to assess
accurately, but around 100,000 birds are probably present in most winters in the UK.

BLACK-TAILED GODWIT

Limosa limosa | BW | LENGTH 38–42cm

Large, long-legged wader whose long bill is straight or only very slightly upturned. Compared to Bar-tailed Godwit, note the longer tibia. Sexes are dissimilar in summer.

Summer adult male has a reddish-orange face, neck and breast. Back is greyish but spangled with reddish brown; belly is whitish with barring on flanks. Birds of ssp. *islandica* (breeds in Iceland) have darker red body plumage than males that breed here (ssp. *limosa*). All birds have an orange base to bill. Summer adult female is similar to male but plumage colours are less intense. Winter adult has grey-buff body plumage, palest on belly; undertail is white and base of bill is pink. Juvenile recalls winter adult but is flushed orange on neck and breast; has pale fringes and dark spotting to feathers on back. In flight, all birds reveal a striking contrast between black tail and white rump. Has white wingbars on upperwing; on underwings, whitish coverts contrast with dark flight feathers. **VOICE** Utters a *kwe-we-we* call in flight. **HABITS** Forms flocks outside the breeding season. Feeds by probing mud with its long bill. **STATUS AND HABITAT** Around 100 pairs breed in the UK, favouring wet grassland. In winter, when it favours muddy estuaries for feeding, an influx of Icelandic birds boosts numbers to around 43,000.

JUVENILE   scaly-looking back

legs are proportionately longer than in Bar-tailed Godwit and project further beyond tail in flight

WINTER

SUMMER

white rump contrasts with black tail

WINTER

BAR-TAILED GODWIT

Limosa lapponica | BA | LENGTH 35–40cm

Large wader with a dumpy body and incredibly long, subtly upturned bill. Compared to Black-tailed Godwit, looks shorter-legged (tibia are shorter). Sexes are dissimilar in summer plumage.

Summer adult male has a reddish-orange head, neck and underparts, including the undertail. Back is spangled grey, black and pale buff, and bill is all dark. Summer adult female has a buffish-orange wash to head, neck and breast, and a pale belly and greyish back. Winter adult has a uniform grey-brown head, neck and upperparts; underparts are pale and bill is pink at base. Juvenile recalls a winter adult but has a buffish wash to head, neck and upperparts. In flight, in all birds, note the absence of a wingbar on upperwing; white on rump extends as a wedge to lower back, and tail is barred. **VOICE** Utters a sharp *kve-wee* call in flight. **HABITS** Often feeds along the edge of breaking waves and rising and falling tides, probing sand and mud for invertebrates, notably worms. **STATUS AND HABITAT** Fairly common non-breeding visitor that breeds in the Arctic. Favours estuaries and sandy and muddy beaches. Around 38,000 birds are present in the UK in most years.

WINTER

barred tail grades into white rump and lower back

upperwings are unmarked and lack the white wingbar seen in Black-tailed Godwit

WINTER

long bill is subtly upturned

SUMMER

orange-red colour is usually more extensive on underparts than in Black-tailed Godwit

WHIMBREL

Numenius phaeopus | WM | LENGTH 40–45cm

Smaller than the similar Curlew and with a relatively shorter bill. Head markings are diagnostic, and the distinctive call allows certain identification even when bird cannot be seen. Sexes are similar.

Adult has grey-brown to buffish-brown plumage with fine, dark streaking on neck and breast. Head pattern comprises a pale supercilium and pale median stripe on an otherwise dark crown. Juvenile is similar to adult but plumage is overall warmer buff in appearance. In flight, all

migrating flocks are often vocal, making separation from Curlew easier

birds look similar to slightly paler Curlew, the dark upperwings and barred tail contrasting with white rump and lower back. **VOICE** Distinctive bubbling call typically comprises 7 notes that descend slightly in pitch from start to finish. Song is confusingly similar to that of a Curlew. **HABITS** Migrating birds are often solitary. Feeds both by probing mud and under seaweed for invertebrates. **STATUS AND HABITAT** Around 500 pairs nest in the UK each

year, mostly on Shetland; its favoured habitat is boggy moorland, especially where tussocks provide slightly elevated nesting sites. Also a fairly common passage migrant (around 3,000 birds in most years), seen on coasts. A handful of birds overwinter here.

median crown stripe is not always easy to see

bill is much shorter than in Curlew

bluish legs

CURLEW

Numenius arquata | CU | LENGTH 53–58cm

Distinctive large wader with a long, downcurved bill. Its onomatopoeic call is evocative of windswept uplands in spring, and estuaries in winter. Sexes are similar.

upperwings are uniformly brown

often vocal in flight, which aids identification

Adult has mainly grey-brown plumage that is streaked and spotted on neck and underparts; belly is rather pale. Juvenile is similar to adult but looks overall more buffish brown; has fine streaks on neck and breast, and an appreciably shorter bill. In flight, all birds show rather uniform upperparts, darkest on outer half of wing, a white rump and lower back, and narrow dark barring on the tail. **VOICE** Utters a characteristic *curlew* call and delivers a bubbling song on breeding grounds. **HABITS** Feeds by probing the ground for invertebrates. **STATUS AND HABITAT** Present here year-round. In the breeding season, associated mainly with northern and upland grassland and moorland. Around 66,000 pairs nest in the UK. Outside the breeding season, mainly coastal, favouring estuary mudflats and nearby grassland. Influxes of birds in autumn and winter from mainland Europe boost numbers to around 140,000 birds in the UK.

bill is proportionately much longer than in Whimbrel

GREEN SANDPIPER

Tringa ochropus | GE | LENGTH 21–23cm

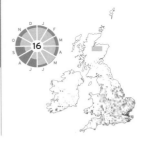

Plump-bodied wader with a bobbing gait. In flight, white rump, dark underwing and yelping alarm call aid identification. Sexes are similar.

upperwing is unmarked brown

tail shows more extensive white than in Wood Sandpiper

JUVENILE

Adult has dark brown upperparts, adorned with small pale spots. Head and neck are streaked, and there is a clear demarcation between dark, streaked breast and clean white underparts. Pale supercilium is bold only in front of eye and legs are greenish yellow. Rump is white and tail has a few broad, dark bands but usually looks all dark. Juvenile is similar to adult but pale spotting on upperparts is more striking. **VOICE** Utters a trisyllabic *chlueet-wit-wit* flight call. **HABITS** Feeds unobtrusively and often first observed when flushed from margins of ponds or ditches. **STATUS AND HABITAT** Widespread and fairly common passage migrant. A few hundred birds also winter in the UK. On migration, favours a range of freshwater habitats, from pond and lake margins to relatively small and overgrown streams and ditches; in winter, Watercress (*Rorippa nasturtium-aquaticum*) beds are also important. A handful of pairs also breed in Scotland.

demarcation between dark breast and white underparts is more striking than in Wood Sandpiper

WOOD SANDPIPER

Tringa glareola | OD | LENGTH 19–21cm

Elegantly proportioned wader with longer legs than its similar-sized cousins. In flight, shows a white rump, pale grey underwings and narrow, dark bars on tail. Sexes are similar.

Adult has brownish upperparts, spangled with pale spots. Head and neck are streaked, and the rather faint streaking and spotting on the breast merges with pale underparts without clear demarcation. Pale supercilium is prominent both in front of, and behind, eye. Legs are yellowish. Juvenile is similar to adult but upperparts are browner

upperwing lacks wingbars but coverts are spangled

barring on tail is more extensive than with Green Sandpiper

and more conspicuously marked with pale buff spots. **VOICE** Utters a distinctive *chiff-iff-iff* flight call. **HABITS** Feeds around freshwater margins, in a deliberate manner. **STATUS AND HABITAT** Widespread and fairly common passage migrant, mainly in early autumn, usually seen on freshwater pools close to the coast; very occasional inland. A handful of pairs attempt to breed each year, favouring boggy ground in the Scottish Highlands.

upperparts are more strikingly pale-spangled than with Green Sandpiper

bill has a yellowish base

yellow legs

COMMON SANDPIPER

Actitis hypoleucos | CS | LENGTH 18–20cm

Active little wader with a characteristic bobbing gait. Overall, looks rather plump-bodied with an elongated tail that extends well beyond the folded wingtips. Sexes are similar.

bobs tail end when walking

pale barring on wing coverts

JUVENILE

flies on bowed wings revealing pale wingbar

Adult has warm brown upperparts with a faint pattern of dark centres and barring to feathers on back and wings. Head and neck are grey-brown, and note the clear demarcation between dark breast and white underparts; white 'tick' extends up sides of breast. Legs are greenish grey. Juvenile is similar to adult but feathers on wing coverts are barred. In all birds in flight, note the obvious pale wingbar and barred white outer-tail, and the absence of a white rump. **VOICE** Utters a whistling *tswee-wee-wee* call in flight. **HABITS** Flies on bowed, fluttering wings, typically just a metre or so above the water. **STATUS AND HABITAT** Locally common migrant breeder. Nests beside upland and northern rivers, streams, lakes and lochs. Around 15,000 pairs breed here. Also a fairly common passage migrant, sometimes seen at inland sites but mainly around the coast. Fewer than 100 winter in the UK, most heading south to Africa.

territorial birds often perch on boulders

GREENSHANK

Tringa nebularia | GK | LENGTH 30–31cm

Elegant, long-legged wader. Can look very white at a distance but a close view reveals finely patterned feathers on its upperparts. Sexes are similar.

1ST-WINTER

Summer adult has mainly grey-brown upperparts but many back feathers have black centres. Head, neck and breast are heavily streaked but underparts are white. Has yellowish-green legs and a long, slightly upturned bill with a 'thick' greyish base. Winter adult is rather uniformly pale grey above and white below. Juvenile recalls a winter adult but upperparts are darker and browner. In flight, all birds show uniform upperwings (wingbars are absent), and a white rump and wedge up back. **VOICE** Utters a distinctive *tchu-tchu-tchu* call. **HABITS** Feeds in a deliberate probing manner, but sometimes actively chases prey. **STATUS AND HABITAT** Scarce breeding species, favouring extensive blanket bogs in Scotland. Around 1,100 pairs nest here and a significant proportion of these birds winter in the UK, mostly on estuaries. Also a passage migrant, occasionally seen inland on fresh waters but mainly on coasts.

SUMMER

1ST-WINTER

WINTER

looks long-legged when feeding in shallows

despite its common name, legs are more yellowish than green

SPOTTED REDSHANK

Tringa erythropus │ DR │ LENGTH 30cm

Elegant cousin of the Redshank, with
proportionately longer legs and a longer bill.
Utters a diagnostic flight call. Sexes are similar.

Summer adult male (sometimes seen in late spring and summer) has almost black body
plumage with a white eye-ring and dotted white fringes to back feathers. However, birds
with mottled, incomplete breeding plumage are more usually encountered. Legs are rich red.
Summer adult female is similar but with more extensive white flecking on flanks. Winter
adult has pale grey upperparts and whitish underparts. Legs are reddish or orange, and note
the pale supercilium. Juvenile recalls winter adult but plumage is much darker overall an
underparts are heavily barred; legs are orange-yellow. In all plumages, bill is dark with an
orange base to lower mandible. In flight, all birds show uniform upperwings that lack a
white trailing edge. **VOICE** Utters a diagnostic *tchewit* call in flight. **HABITS** Feeds in a
deliberate manner, often in water deep enough to require the bird to swim from time to
time. **STATUS AND HABITAT** Regular passage migrant in small numbers; around 400
occur each year in the UK. Nests in the high Arctic and often departs for breeding grounds
surprisingly late in spring, returning as early as Jul. Around 100 birds also
spend the winter in the UK. At all
times they favour estuaries and
coastal pools.

WINTER

bill is
proportionately
longer than
in Redshank

SUMMER

very vocal, and
birds are often
located initially
by call

WINTER

legs darken at the same time birds
acquire full breeding plumage

in flight, lacks white
trailing edge to wing
seen in Redshank

REDSHANK

Tringa totanus │ RK │ LENGTH 28cm

Medium-sized wader with striking orange or red legs.
Generally rather nervous and announces
its presence with shrill alarm call.
Sexes are similar.

WINTER

legs are relatively shorter
than in Spotted Redshank

Summer adult is mainly
grey-brown above and pale
below, but back is heavily marked
with dark spots and neck, breast and
flanks are streaked. Note the faint,
pale supercilium and eye-ring; base
of bill is wholly reddish. Winter adult
has uniform grey-brown upperparts,
including the head, neck and breast,
with paler, mottled underparts. Colours on bill and legs are less intense than in summer.
Juvenile recalls winter adult but plumage is overall browner, feathers on back having pale
notches and margins; legs and base of bill are dull yellow. In flight, all birds show a white
trailing edge to wings, white back and rump, and trailing orange or red legs. **VOICE** Utters a
yelping *tiu-uu* alarm call. Song is musical and yodelling. **HABITS** Feeds by probing soft mud
and actively chasing small prey. **STATUS AND HABITAT** Common resident breeder. In
spring, favours undisturbed damp grassland, moors and marshes; around 24,000 pairs nest in
the UK. Outside the breeding season, an influx from mainland Europe boosts numbers to
around 120,000 birds; estuaries, mudflats and coastal grassland are favoured in winter.

SUMMER

SUMMER

bright orange-red legs

often vocal
in flight

white trailing
edge to wing seen
in flight - absent in
Spotted Redshank

RED-NECKED PHALAROPE

Phalaropus lobatus | NK | LENGTH 18cm

Confiding little wader that spends much of its life swimming. Sexes show role-reversal at the nest and breeding females are brighter than males.

FEMALE, SUMMER

wingbar noticeable in flight

red is restricted to sides of neck and throat

FEMALE, SUMMER

JUVENILE

bill is thin and needle-like by comparison with Grey Phalarope

MALE, SUMMER

male's colours and markings are subdued when compared to female

Summer adult female has brown upperparts, many back feathers having yellow-buff margins. Note the white throat, dark cap and reddish-orange neck; grey breast and mottled flanks grade into white underparts. Bill is dark and feet have lobed toes for swimming. Summer adult male is similar but colours are duller. Winter adult has mainly grey upperparts with distinctive white-fringed feathers, white underparts with a greyish hindcrown and nape, and a black patch through eye. Juvenile recalls winter adult but has brown upperparts and pale buff fringes to back feathers; gradually acquires grey back feathers in autumn. **VOICE** Occasionally utters a sharp *kip* call. **HABITS** Uses its needle-like bill to pick small invertebrates from the water's surface, usually while swimming. Often spins rapidly. **STATUS AND HABITAT** Britain and Ireland are at the southern limit of the species' mainly Arctic breeding range; a small breeding population (around 20 pairs) is confined to the north of the region. Winters at sea and best known here as a scarce passage migrant, mainly in autumn on coastal pools after severe gales.

GREY PHALAROPE

Phalaropus fulicarius | PL | LENGTH 20–21cm

Charming little wader that spends much of its life swimming. Sexes are dissimilar only in breeding plumage (very rarely seen here).

Winter adult has plain grey upperparts, white underparts, a dark cap and nape, and a black 'panda' mark through eye. Bill is shorter and stouter than that of Red-necked Phalarope, with a yellow base. Summer adult female has mainly orange-red plumage with a dark crown and white facial patch, and buff-fringed dark feathers on back. Summer adult male is similar but colours are much duller. Juvenile recalls a winter adult, but breast, neck and back are tinged buff and back feathers are dark with buff fringes. **VOICE** Utters a sharp *pit* flight call. **HABITS** Often spins rapidly on water and feeds by picking invertebrates off the surface. Usually oblivious to human observers. **STATUS AND HABITAT** Nests in the high Arctic and winters at sea in the tropics. Seen here on migration, mostly in autumn and very occasionally in midwinter. Most records (around 160 each year) are coastal, during or just after onshore gales. After particularly bad storms, it sometimes turns up inland, on reservoirs and lakes.

WINTER

bold white wingbar

FEMALE, SUMMER

orange-red element of plumage is much more extensive than in Red-necked Phalarope, and more colourful in female than male

WINTER

yellow-based bill

swims buoyantly

POMARINE SKUA

Stercorarius pomarinus | PK | LENGTH 42–50cm

Large and impressive seabird that shares some plumage features with Arctic Skua but always looks heavier and deeper-chested. Sexes are similar but adults occur in 2 colour morphs.

dark cap

spoon-shaped tail streamers are most obvious in flight

JUVENILE

underparts are barred, especially undertail coverts

Adult pale morph (commonest morph) has a white neck and belly, and otherwise dark grey-brown plumage. Note the yellow flush on cheeks and striking dark breast band. Bill is pinkish with a dark tip; tail streamers are long and spoon-shaped. Adult dark morph is similar structurally, with uniformly dark grey-brown plumage. Juvenile has variably dark grey-brown plumage that is strongly barred on undertail coverts, rump and underwing coverts. Note its dark-tipped pale bill and blunt-ended tail. In flight, all birds show a limited white patch (at base of primaries) in upper outerwing and a double pale crescent at base of primaries on underwing. **VOICE** Silent in the region. **HABITS** Flight is direct, with deep, powerful wingbeats. Harasses other seabirds into giving up food. **STATUS AND HABITAT** Breeds in the high Arctic and its status here is that of a scarce passage migrant. Outside the breeding season and on migration it is a true seabird that seldom comes close to land by choice. Seen at sea on pelagic trips, and near coasts during gales, with occasional inland reports.

ARCTIC SKUA

Stercorarius parasiticus | AC | LENGTH 46cm

Elegant seabird with a buoyant and graceful flight. Sexes are similar but adults occur in 2 colour morphs.

PALE PHASE

PALE PHASE

fast and aerobatic in flight

white breast and belly

JUVENILE

short, pointed tail streamers

uniformly brown underparts

DARK PHASE

All birds have a white patch near underwing wingtip, and a limited but noticeable white patch on upperwing. Only adults have pointed streamers that extend beyond wedge-shaped tail. Adult pale phase has a white neck, breast and belly, a dark cap, and otherwise uniform dark grey-brown plumage. Note the faint yellowish flush on cheeks. Adult dark phase is uniformly dark grey-brown. Juvenile is variably rufous brown but often rather dark. Compared to juvenile Pomarine Skua, note the dainty, dark-tipped pale bill and the wedge-shaped tail that bears tiny central projections. **VOICE** Utters nasal calls near the nest. **HABITS** Feeds by forcing seabirds such as Arctic Terns to relinquish their last meal. Very aerobatic when chasing its quarry. Glides well, and in active flight its powerful wingbeats and narrow, pointed wings can give it an almost falcon-like jizz. **STATUS AND HABITAT** Summer breeding visitor to Scotland; around 2,100 pairs breed here. Regular passage migrant elsewhere, seen at sea from ferries or off coasts during gales.

LONG-TAILED SKUA

Stercorarius longicaudus | OG | LENGTH 36–42cm

Elegant seabird. Recalls an Arctic Skua but smaller and relatively easy to separate: long, pointed wings lack the white patch seen in Arctic's outerwing and adult has long central tail streamers. Sexes are similar.

dark cap

very long tail streamers

pale face and darker breast band are usually good features

limited amount of white in wing

JUVENILE

long, narrow wings

Adult is uniform grey-brown on back and upperside of innerwing; this contrasts with dark outer half of wing and trailing margin of innerwing. Cap is dark and neck and underparts are whitish; note the faint yellow flush on cheeks, visible at close range. Juvenile is variably grey-brown, with some individuals rather dark. Some individuals show a striking pale head. Has a wedge-shaped tail; belly and nape are usually relatively pale, with hint of a darker breast band. Compared to juvenile Arctic Skua, bill is stubbier, outer half being darker than inner half. **VOICE** Silent in the region. **HABITS** Has a light, buoyant Kittiwake-like flight. Does not routinely steal from other birds but will when the opportunity arises, although seemingly half-heartedly – unlike enthusiastic chases undertaken by Arctic Skua. **STATUS AND HABITAT** Scarce passage migrant. Oceanic preferences make it a challenge to see. Opportunities arise on summer pelagic trips from Scilly, and autumn seawatches off SW England and W Wales during westerly gales, and N Norfolk during northeasterlies. Regular spring passage occurs off the Outer Hebrides during strong northwesterlies. Occasionally, storm-driven birds turn up at inland reservoirs; also sometimes feeds in ploughed fields.

GREAT SKUA

Stercorarius skua | NX | LENGTH 48–52cm

**Bulky, 'barrel-chested' seabird with gull-like proportions.
Darker plumage, relatively large
head, dark legs and dark, hook-tipped bill soon
confirm its identity. Sexes are similar.**

striking white
wing 'flashes'

Adult has chocolate-brown plumage, streaked and spotted with
buff. At close range, note the mane of golden-brown feathers
on nape. Juvenile has similar proportions to adult, but back and
head are rather uniformly dark brown, and neck and underparts
are rufous brown and unmarked. In flight, all birds show a striking
white patch on outerwing. **VOICE** Mainly silent. **HABITS** Flight
is powerful and direct. Partly a scavenger, but will also kill
seabirds such as Puffins and force birds as large as Gannets to
regurgitate their last meal. **STATUS
AND HABITAT** Summer
breeding visitor; around 9,600
pairs nest, with Orkney and
Shetland their strongholds.
Nests in loose colonies, normally sited
on moorland close to seabird cliffs.
Also a regular passage migrant, seen
on ferry crossings and from headlands
during onshore gales.

JUVENILE

more uniformly brown
plumage than adult

plumage has a slightly
dishevelled look

powerful
bill

AGEING IN GULLS
HERRING GULL
AS A CASE STUDY

Ageing gulls can be a baffling subject for the novice birdwatcher. But in all species, moulting and plumage follow a standard progression that is easily recognised with a bit of practice. In some smaller gull species it takes just three years to acquire full adult plumage from the point of hatching. With larger gulls the process takes four years. For the ease of the reader, the following images depict the process through four successive winter periods, for Herring Gull.

2nd-winter

1st-winter

2ND-WINTER
A year on from its 1st-winter plumage, this age class has acquired a few plumage features in common with an adult bird, notably the almost uniformly grey back. The bill now has a pale base.

1st-winter

1ST-WINTER
This is a bird in the first winter of its life following hatching the previous summer. It does not share any plumage features with an adult bird. The bill is usually uniformly dark, as is the eye.

2nd-winter

3rd-winter

adult

3RD-WINTER
This age class is very similar to an adult bird but still retains some immature plumage features. Note the brown feathering on the wing, most noticeable in flight. As with all gulls, there is some variation in appearance amongst individuals – some birds moult and mature earlier than others.

3rd-winter

ADULT
This is the typical, familiar Herring Gull, showing uniform grey back and wings (apart from the tips to the flight feathers). Some subtle variation is evident though amongst winter birds: some have more dark streaking on the head than others, and the intensity of the bill colour can vary too.

adult

SABINE'S GULL

Xema sabini | AB | LENGTH 30–35cm

**Distinctive, well-marked gull
that seldom comes close to land
willingly. Sexes are similar.**

JUVENILE

forked tail
with black
terminal band

upperwing pattern
is similar to adult

pattern on
upperwing is
diagnostic

SUMMER

pale feather margins create
scaly appearance
to back

Summer adult has a blue-grey back
and upperwings, a dark hood, dark
wingtips with white spots, and a
yellow-tipped dark bill. In flight,
upperwing pattern is striking and
diagnostic: note the triangular areas
of black, white and grey (cf. juvenile
Kittiwake). Tail is forked. Non-
breeding adult is similar but dark
smudges on nape replace dark hood.
Juvenile has a similar upperwing
pattern to adult, but triangle of grey
on back and upperwing coverts is
replaced by scaly grey-brown. Forked
tail is dark-tipped. **VOICE** Silent in
the region. **HABITS** Flight is buoyant
and powerful. Visits fishing boats and
can be attracted by chumming activity.
STATUS AND HABITAT Breeds
in the high Arctic and winters at sea
in southern oceans. Small numbers
linger in the Western Approaches in
late summer (there are very regular
sightings on pelagic trips from Scilly),
but best known here as an autumn
passage migrant. Mostly seen offshore,
but blown close to land during
onshore gales.

JUVENILE

KITTIWAKE

Rissa tridactyla | KI | LENGTH 38–42cm

Delicate-looking gull, and a true seagull:
its non-breeding period is spent entirely
at sea. Sexes are similar.

unmarked
yellow bill

black 'V' marking
on upperwing

black
wingtips

JUVENILE

black bill, collar and smudge around eye

JUVENILE

Summer adult has a
blue-grey back and
upperwings, and pure
black wingtips (in
flight, these look to have been
dipped in black ink); otherwise
plumage is entirely white. Bill
is yellow, and both eye and legs
are dark. Winter adult is similar
but head is marked with grubby
patches behind eye. Juvenile
has striking black 'V' markings
on each upperwing; back and
upperwing coverts are grey, and
it has a triangle of white on flight
feathers. Note also the dark tip
to tail, black half-collar and dark
markings on head; bill is dark.
In 1st-winter dark half-collar
and black tail tip of juvenile is
gradually lost. **VOICE** Utters a diagnostic *kittee-wake, kittee-wake* call at breeding colonies.
HABITS Flight is buoyant and powerful. **STATUS AND HABITAT** Nests colonially on
coastal cliff ledges, and increasingly on man-made structures such as dockside factories;
around 370,000 pairs breed in the UK. Most spend the non-breeding period far out to sea,
although small numbers occur around harbours in winter.

BLACK-HEADED GULL

Chroicocephalus ridibundus | BH | LENGTH 35–38cm

Our most numerous medium-sized gull. Seasonal
plumage variations exist, although all birds have a
distinctive white leading edge to outerwings that
contrasts with dark wingtips. Sexes are similar.

Adult is pale grey above and
white below, with a red bill
and legs. In summer, has a
chocolate-brown hood and
subtle white 'eyelids'; in
winter, head is white with
dark smudges above and
behind eye. Juvenile is brown
above and paler below, with
an orange flush to upperparts;

SUMMER   WINTER   1ST-WINTER

dark
terminal
band to
tail

unmarked
white tail

leading
white edge
to wing

brown and black
feathering

usually acquires 1st-winter plumage (showing a dark carpal bar, trailing
edge to wings and tail tip) by Oct, and adult plumage a year later.
VOICE Utters raucous calls that include a nasal *kaurrr*. **HABITS**
Usually seen in flocks. Feeds mainly on invertebrates
and small fish, on marshes and around coasts.
Also opportunistic, e.g. taking human
'hand-outs', following the plough
and visiting newly
flooded fields.

**STATUS AND
HABITAT** Resident breeder and migrant
winter visitor. Around 130,000 pairs breed in the
UK, favouring freshwater habitats. Outside the
breeding season, an influx from mainland Europe
swells numbers to more than 2 million individuals;
in winter, found in a wide range of habitats, from
coastal marshes to urban lakes and farmland.

dull red bill

SUMMER

head pattern similar
to that of winter adult

dark smudge
on ear coverts

pale pink legs   1ST-WINTER

WINTER

MEDITERRANEAN GULL

Larus melanocephalus | MU | LENGTH 36–38cm

Attractive gull, superficially similar to Black-headed
but separable in all plumages with experience. Adult's
uniformly pale wings are a reliable feature
year-round. Sexes are similar.

1ST-WINTER   WINTER   SUMMER

pure white wings
in adult birds

hood is black,
not brown as in
Black-headed
Gull, and extends
down nape

bright
red bill

SUMMER

Summer adult has a
pale grey back and wing
coverts, and white flight feathers; in
flight, entire wing can look white. Black
hood contrasts with white 'eyelids'; stout bill
is mainly deep red, its yellow tip defined by
a black sub-terminal band. Legs are deep red.
Winter adult loses dark hood; whitish head has
dark smudges above and behind white 'eyelids'.
Juvenile has grey-brown upperparts with pale
margins to back feathers, and mostly pale underparts with a darkish flush on breast. Bill and
legs are dark, and has a dark terminal band on tail. Plumage of 1st-winter is similar to juvenile
but has a plain grey back and dark smudges above and behind eye. 2nd-year resembles adult
but has black in wingtips. Acquires adult plumage by 3rd-winter. **VOICE** Call is a distinctive
cow-cow. **HABITS** Usually associates with Black-headed Gulls. **STATUS AND HABITAT**
Scarce resident breeder; around 600 pairs nest in the UK. Outside breeding season, mainly
coastal but occasional inland; around 1,800 birds winter here.

dark smudges on head

2ND-WINTER

variable amounts of
black on primaries

bill is more
robust than
in Black-headed
Gull

WINTER

LITTLE GULL

Hydrocoloeus minutus | LU | LENGTH 25–28cm

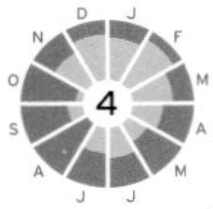

Dainty gull, the smallest of its kind to be seen here.
Seasonal plumage variations exist. Sexes are similar.

dark underwing with white trailing margin

WINTER

1ST-WINTER

black terminal band on tail

dark bar on upperwing

wings pale grey with a white trailing edge, and rounded tips

rosy flush to underparts sometimes visible

Summer adult has pale grey upperwings with white wingtips,
a dark hood, dark bill and short reddish legs. In flight, upperwings
show a white trailing edge and rounded white wingtip;
underwings are dark with a contrasting white trailing
edge. Winter adult is similar but loses dark hood;
the otherwise white head has dark smudges on
crown and ear coverts. Juvenile is overall white
with a striking black bar (forming letter 'W') on upperwings
and back. Has dark markings on mantle, nape and ear coverts,
and a dark tail band. Back in 1st-winter is uniformly pale grey,
hence dark bar is seen only on wings; otherwise resembles
juvenile. Adult plumage is acquired over 2 years. **VOICE**
Utters a sharp *kyeck* call. **HABITS** Buoyant flight gives it a
passing resemblance to a small tern. **STATUS AND HABITAT**
Regular passage migrant and winter visitor. Most records
are coastal, although very occasionally it turns up at inland
freshwater sites. A few dozen birds are seen each winter.

black hood

SUMMER

WINTER

dainty bill

COMMON GULL

Larus canus | CM | LENGTH 40–42cm

Medium-sized gull whose body proportions and
relatively dainty bill allow separation
from the larger Herring Gull. Sexes
are similar.

1ST-SUMMER

dark terminal band to tail

SUMMER

Summer adult has a grey back and
upperwings, the latter with white-spotted
black tips and a broad white trailing
margin. Plumage is otherwise white.
Bill is uniform greenish yellow and
legs are yellowish green. Winter
adult is similar but has dark streaking
on head and neck; bill has duller
colours and a dark sub-terminal
band. Juvenile has pale-edged brown feathers
on back and upperwings, and a pale head
and underparts with dark streaking. Adult
plumage is acquired over next 2 years.
Plumage in 1st-winter is similar to juvenile
but has a grey back; bill is pink with a
dark tip. Plumage in 2nd-winter resembles
adult but black markings on outerwing are
more extensive and band on bill is broader.
VOICE Calls include a mewing *keeow*. **HABITS**
Outside the breeding season often feeds on farmland and
grassy fields. **STATUS AND HABITAT** Resident
breeder. Nests colonially, usually in marshes
or beside lakes; around 48,000 pairs breed
in the UK. Outside the breeding
season, an influx from mainland
Europe boosts numbers to
around 700,000
birds.

dark streaking on head and neck

yellow bill

WINTER

SUMMER

yellow legs

1ST-WINTER

LESSER BLACK-BACKED GULL

Larus fuscus | LB | LENGTH 53–56cm

Similar to Herring and Yellow-legged gulls in size, but adult's combination of a dark grey back and upperwings and yellow legs aids identification. Sexes are similar.

SUMMER

JUVENILE

black wingtips are noticeably darker than otherwise sooty grey upperwings

JUVENILE

WINTER

SUMMER

yellow legs

Summer adult is mostly white with a dark grey back and upperwings (the latter with a white trailing edge). Black wingtips are darker than rest of upperwing (although Baltic birds have almost uniformly dark upperwings). Bill is yellow with an orange spot, and eye's iris is yellow with a red orbital ring. Winter adult is similar but has dark streaks on head and neck, and duller leg and bill colours. Juvenile and 1st-winter have streaked and mottled grey-brown plumage, palest on head. Upperwings appear uniformly dark brown and tail is whitish with a dark terminal band. Eye and bill are dark. Adult plumage is acquired over next 3 years. In 2nd-winter, back is grey, legs are pinkish and pink bill has a dark tip; underparts and tail are paler and have less streaking. 3rd-winter plumage resembles winter adult with more streaking on head and neck, and dark terminal band on tail. **VOICE** Utters a distinctive *kyaoo* and an anxious *ga-ka-ka*. **HABITS** Outside breeding season, often feeds on farmland and roosts on reservoirs. **STATUS AND HABITAT** Locally common breeder. Colonial; around 110,000 pairs nest in the UK on sea cliffs. Many migrate south; around 120,000 birds winter here.

GREAT BLACK-BACKED GULL

Larus marinus | GB | LENGTH 64–79cm

Our largest gull. Recalls Lesser Black-backed but is more bulky; note the adult's darker back and upperwings, massive bill and pink legs. Sexes are similar.

JUVENILE

3RD-WINTER

SUMMER

upperwing is appreciably darker than in Lesser Black-backed Gull

Adult has almost an uniformly dark back and upperwings. Note the white patch at very tip of wings and broad white trailing edge running along almost entire length of wing. Plumage is otherwise white. Bill is yellow with an orange spot. Juvenile and 1st-winter are mottled and streaked grey-brown. In flight, brown upperwings reveal pale panels on upperwing coverts and inner primaries. Bill is dark, legs are dull pink, and whitish tail has a dark terminal band. Adult plumage is acquired over next 3 years. In 3rd-winter, back is dark and bill is pale pink with a dark tip. **VOICE** Utters a deep *kaa-ga-ga* call. **HABITS** Predator of smaller seabirds during the breeding season; diet is more varied and scavenging in winter. **STATUS AND HABITAT** Fairly common resident breeder. Mostly coastal in the breeding season; around 17,000 pairs nest in the UK, usually on the fringes of mixed seabird colonies. Outside the breeding season, more widespread inland and numbers are boosted by influxes from mainland Europe. Around 76,000 birds winter here.

massive bill

SUMMER

pink legs

scavenging as well as predatory diet

3RD-WINTER

HERRING GULL

Larus argentatus | HG | LENGTH 56–62cm

38

variable dark streaking on head

WINTER

Noisy and familiar, and our most numerous large gull. Confusion is possible with Lesser Black-backed Gull. Sexes are similar.

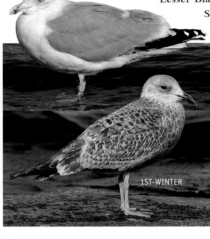

1ST-WINTER

SUMMER

3RD-WINTER

Summer adult has a pale blue-grey back and upperwings, with white-spotted black wingtips; plumage is otherwise white. Legs are pink, bill is yellow with an orange spot near tip, and eye is yellow with an orange-yellow orbital ring. Winter adult is similar but has dark streaks on head and nape. Juvenile and 1st-winter are mottled grey-brown with streaked underparts. Legs are dull pink, bill is dark, and spotted pale tail has a dark tip. Adult plumage is acquired over next 3 years through successive moults. In 2nd-winter back is grey and upperwing has grey areas; tail is dark-tipped but otherwise white. Plumage in 3rd-winter resembles winter adult but with more black on wingtips and hint of a dark tail band. **VOICE** Utters a distinctive *kyaoo* and an anxious *ga-ka-ka*. **HABITS** Often noisy and bold when it is fed regularly. **STATUS AND HABITAT** Locally common resident breeder. Around 130,000 pairs nest in the UK, usually colonially on sea cliffs and islands. Outside the breeding season, more widespread inland as well as on coasts; numbers are boosted to around 730,000 birds by influxes from mainland Europe.

unmarked white head, neck and underparts

SUMMER

pink legs

YELLOW-LEGGED GULL

Larus michahellis | YG | LENGTH 52–60cm

Superficially similar to Herring Gull. Adult's long yellow legs are its best distinguishing feature. Sexes are similar.

SUMMER

1ST-WINTER

subtly less white in wingtips than Herring Gull

Summer adult has a grey back and upperwings (darker than in adult Herring Gull), with more black and less white in wingtips. Winter adult is similar, sometimes with limited dark streaking on head. Juvenile and 1st-winter have a grey-brown back with dark anchor shapes on pale wing coverts, and otherwise dark wings. Head, neck and underparts, although streaked, are markedly paler than in Herring Gull of similar age. Adult plumage is acquired over next 3 years in a similar manner to Herring Gull. Longer legs and wings in all plumages help to separate it from Herring Gull. **VOICE** Similar to that of Herring Gull but perhaps more nasal. **HABITS** Typically consorts with other large gull species. **STATUS AND HABITAT** Present year-round but best known as a non-breeding visitor, seen most frequently in winter.

legs remain pink until fully adult

2ND-WINTER/SUMMER

SUMMER

bill is usually more robust than in Herring Gull

SEABIRDS

GLAUCOUS GULL

Larus hyperboreus | GZ | LENGTH 62–68cm

Similar in size to Great Black-backed but closer to Herring Gull in terms of plumage, apart from the diagnostic white primary feathers. Bill is massive and legs are pinkish at all times. Sexes are similar.

Winter adult has a pale grey back and upperwings, but tips of wings are white and have a broad white trailing margin. Otherwise, plumage is mainly white with a variable extent of dark streaking on head and neck. Eye has a pale iris, and orbital ring is yellow. Summer adult (sometimes seen in late winter) is similar but dark streaking is lost. Juvenile and 1st-winter are mainly pale buffish grey but primary feathers are very pale. Bill is pink with a small black tip. Adult plumage is acquired over next 3 years. Plumage in 2nd-winter is overall very pale with darker streaks on head and neck, and darker marbling elsewhere. In 3rd-winter, plumage is very pale with faint dark streaking on head and neck. **VOICE** Utters a *kyaoo* and an anxious *ga-ka-ka*. **HABITS** Usually mixes with other large gulls. **STATUS AND HABITAT** Non-breeding visitor from Arctic nesting grounds; around 150 birds are seen in most years. Found mainly on the coast, with smaller numbers at inland reservoirs.

1ST-WINTER

1ST-WINTER

similar size to a Great Black-backed Gull

compared to Iceland Gull, head is proportionately larger and bill is massive

WINTER

ICELAND GULL

Larus glaucoides | IG | LENGTH 52–60cm

Recalls a Glaucous Gull in all plumages, but note the smaller size, longer wings, rounded head, relatively small bill and 'gentle' look. Legs are pink at all times. Sexes are similar.

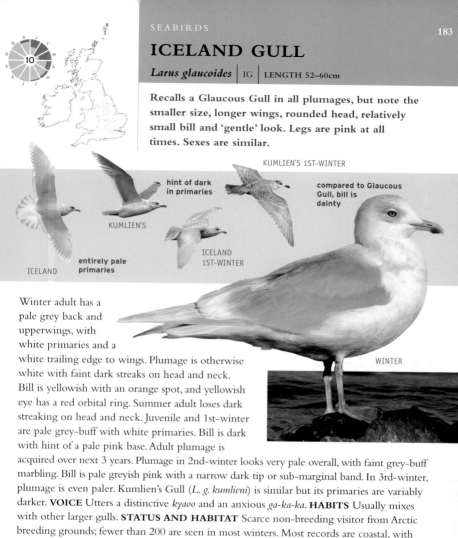

KUMLIEN'S 1ST-WINTER

hint of dark in primaries

compared to Glaucous Gull, bill is dainty

KUMLIEN'S

ICELAND 1ST-WINTER

ICELAND

entirely pale primaries

WINTER

Winter adult has a pale grey back and upperwings, with white primaries and a white trailing edge to wings. Plumage is otherwise white with faint dark streaks on head and neck. Bill is yellowish with an orange spot, and yellowish eye has a red orbital ring. Summer adult loses dark streaking on head and neck. Juvenile and 1st-winter are pale grey-buff with white primaries. Bill is dark with hint of a pale pink base. Adult plumage is acquired over next 3 years. Plumage in 2nd-winter looks very pale overall, with faint grey-buff marbling. Bill is pale greyish pink with a narrow dark tip or sub-marginal band. In 3rd-winter, plumage is even paler. Kumlien's Gull (*L. g. kumlieni*) is similar but its primaries are variably darker. **VOICE** Utters a distinctive *kyaoo* and an anxious *ga-ka-ka*. **HABITS** Usually mixes with other larger gulls. **STATUS AND HABITAT** Scarce non-breeding visitor from Arctic breeding grounds; fewer than 200 are seen in most winters. Most records are coastal, with smaller numbers at inland reservoirs; favours docks and harbours.

primaries are subtly darker than in equivalent age Iceland Gull

1ST-WINTER ICELAND

1ST-WINTER KUMLIEN'S

LITTLE TERN

Sternula albifrons | AF | LENGTH 24cm

12

Our smallest pale tern. Flight is buoyant
and graceful, on slender, swept-back
wings. Sexes are similar.

often
hovers

scaly look
to back

JUVENILE

looks tiny, especially
alongside other 'white' terns

white forehead
and bright yellow
bill

Summer adult has a grey back and upperwings, and a mainly black cap and white forehead;
plumage is otherwise white. Note the black-tipped yellow bill and yellow-orange legs. In
flight, wingtips are noticeably dark. Winter adult (begins to acquire this plumage from late
summer onwards) is similar, but forehead is entirely white and leg and bill colours become
dark. Juvenile is similar to winter adult but back appears scaly and leading edge of wing is
dark. **VOICE** Utters a raucous *cree-ick* call. **HABITS** Often hovers before plunge-diving into
shallow water for small fish and shrimps. **STATUS AND HABITAT** Very locally common
migrant breeder that winters in Africa. Nests in scattered coastal colonies, favouring shingle
and sandy islands and beaches; around 1,900 pairs nest in the UK.

BLACK TERN

Chlidonias niger | BJ | LENGTH 24cm

Elegant wetland bird whose plumage varies considerably according to the time of year and its age. Sexes are similar.

Summer adult has mainly grey upperparts but head, neck, breast and belly are black; note the white undertail and forked, smoky grey tail. Bill and legs are dark. Winter adult (plumage is acquired gradually between Jul and Sep) has darker grey upperparts and entirely white underparts; black on head is restricted to cap, nape and ear coverts, but it also shows a dark 'thumbprint' on breast sides. Moulting birds can look a bit 'moth-eaten'. Bill is dark and legs are dull red. Juvenile is similar to winter adult but back is brownish grey and scaly. **VOICE** Mainly silent. **HABITS** Its buoyant and aerobatic flight is used to good effect when hawking insects or picking food items from the water's surface. **STATUS AND HABITAT** Scarce passage migrant and former rare breeder. Usually favours freshwater wetland habitats, e.g. marshes, lakes and flooded gravel pits. Passage migrants are sometimes seen at sea.

aerobatic in flight and sometimes hovers

incomplete black cap

brownish back

JUVENILE

head and underparts are noticeably darker than rest of sooty grey plumage

SANDWICH TERN

Sterna sandvicensis | TE | LENGTH 41cm

Elegant seabird with powerful, buoyant flight on long, narrow wings. Announces its presence with a loud and distinctive call. Sexes are similar.

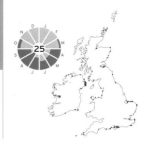

white forecrown

SUMMER

complete black cap

NON-BREEDING

near breeding colonies, often seen carrying fish back to feed young

SUMMER

extremely slender, yellow-tipped black bill

black legs

Summer adult is pale grey on its back and upperwings; has a dark crested cap, but otherwise plumage is white. Legs are black and long, and narrow bill is black with a yellow tip. In flight, wings can look almost pure white, but at close range note that some outer primaries are dark. Winter adult (plumage seen from late summer onwards) is similar but forehead is white. Juvenile is similar to winter adult but back is barred and scaly. **VOICE** Utters a harsh *chee-urrick* call. **HABITS** Dives frequently for fish. **STATUS AND HABITAT** Migrant summer breeder. Often one of the first migrant species to arrive in spring and the last to leave in autumn. Almost exclusively coastal, favouring shallow inshore seas. Around 11,000 pairs nest in the UK, forming colonies on beaches and islands.

ROSEATE TERN

Sterna dougallii | RS | LENGTH 38cm

Our rarest breeding tern and one that is globally threatened. Similar to both its Common and Arctic cousins, but separable with care. Sexes are similar.

SUMMER

long tail streamers

JUVENILE

dark leading edge to innerwing

subtle pink flush to underparts

SUMMER

bill is usually black on at least the outer half (sometimes entirely black)

red legs

Summer adult has pale grey upperparts, a dark cap, and whitish underparts that are subtly flushed pinkish. Note the red-based dark bill (sometimes appears all dark), relatively long red legs and long tail streamers. In flight, looks strikingly pale, particularly on underside; from above, note the dark outer primaries. Winter adult (plumage sometimes seen in late summer) has white on forehead and loses its long tail streamers. Juvenile has white underparts, an incomplete dark cap and scaly upperparts; upperwings are rather uniform except for dark leading edge to innerwing. **VOICE** Utters a disyllabic *chew-vik* call. **HABITS** Plunge-dives for small fish. **STATUS AND HABITAT** Summer migrant breeder. Around 80–90 pairs nest here, mostly in Ireland; all colonies are coastal. Nests are usually sited under vegetation.

COMMON TERN

Sterna hirundo | CN | LENGTH 35cm

25

**Widespread and familiar tern.
Similar to, but separable from,
Arctic Tern. Sexes are similar.**

SUMMER

JUVENILE

innerwing has
dark leading and
trailing edges

SUMMER

dark tips
and shafts
to primaries
often appear
as a dark
'wedge'

Summer adult has grey upperparts, a black cap and whitish underparts. Compared to Arctic, note the black-tipped orange-red bill and relatively longer red legs; underparts are typically paler. In flight from below, only inner primaries look translucent and wings have a rather diffuse dark tip (can be indistinct in spring); from above, outer primaries have dark tips and shafts, forming a dark wedge. Winter adult (plumage sometimes seen in late summer) is similar but acquires white on forehead and dark carpal bar; bill and legs become dark. Juvenile has white underparts, an incomplete dark cap and scaly grey upperparts, the back tinged rufous; both leading and trailing edges of innerwing appear dark when seen from above. **VOICE** Utters various harsh calls, including *kreeear*. **HABITS** Plunge-dives after surface-feeding fish; sizeable numbers gather where feeding is good. **STATUS AND HABITAT** Common migrant breeder. Around 10,000 pairs nest in the UK; most frequent on the coast, but also found inland on flooded gravel pits and reservoirs. Also a common passage migrant, when it is seen mainly on the coast.

back is tinged
rufous

JUVENILE

black-tipped
bill

short tail streamers
compared to Arctic Tern

SUMMER

ARCTIC TERN

Sterna paradisaea | AE | LENGTH 35cm

Elegant and graceful seabird whose flight is
buoyant, on powerful wingbeats. Sexes are similar.

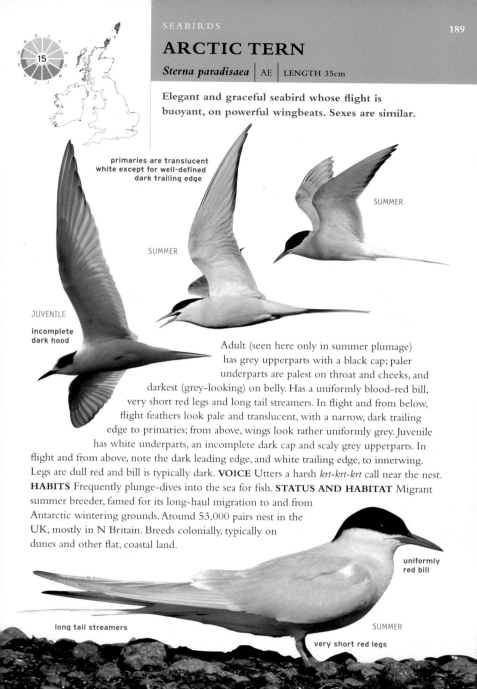

primaries are translucent
white except for well-defined
dark trailing edge

SUMMER

SUMMER

JUVENILE

incomplete
dark hood

Adult (seen here only in summer plumage)
has grey upperparts with a black cap; paler
underparts are palest on throat and cheeks, and
darkest (grey-looking) on belly. Has a uniformly blood-red bill,
very short red legs and long tail streamers. In flight and from below,
flight feathers look pale and translucent, with a narrow, dark trailing
edge to primaries; from above, wings look rather uniformly grey. Juvenile
has white underparts, an incomplete dark cap and scaly grey upperparts. In
flight and from above, note the dark leading edge, and white trailing edge, to innerwing.
Legs are dull red and bill is typically dark. **VOICE** Utters a harsh *krt-krt-krt* call near the nest.
HABITS Frequently plunge-dives into the sea for fish. **STATUS AND HABITAT** Migrant
summer breeder, famed for its long-haul migration to and from
Antarctic wintering grounds. Around 53,000 pairs nest in the
UK, mostly in N Britain. Breeds colonially, typically on
dunes and other flat, coastal land.

uniformly
red bill

long tail streamers

SUMMER

very short red legs

GUILLEMOT

Uria aalge | GU | LENGTH 42cm

Robust and familiar seabird that breeds
in large, densely packed colonies; our
largest auk. Sexes are similar.

SUMMER

chocolate-brown plumage can look dark in poor light

WINTER

white cheeks and
throat, with dark line
running back from eye

Summer adult has a chocolate-brown head and upperparts (darker in northern birds than
southern ones), and white underparts. Bill is dark, dagger-like and straight. So-called 'Bridled
Guillemot' shows white 'spectacles' around eyes. Winter adult has more white on head than
a summer bird; note the white cheeks and throat, and black
line running back from eye. Juvenile recalls a winter adult,
initially with a stubbier bill. **VOICE** Utters nasal, growling
calls at breeding colonies. **HABITS** Swims well and dives
frequently. Flies on whirring wingbeats; the narrow wings
are also used when swimming underwater. **STATUS AND
HABITAT** Locally numerous summer breeder. Nests on
precipitous cliff ledges; in suitable locations sometimes
thousands of birds stand side-by-side. Around 880,000
pairs breed in the UK. Only visits land in the
breeding season; thereafter found exclusively at sea
and seen only occasionally in inshore waters.

dagger-like
bill

SUMMER

upright posture
when standing

BRIDLED FORM

RAZORBILL

Alca torda | RA | LENGTH 41cm

Dumpy seabird with essentially black and white plumage. Easily recognised at close range by its distinctive bill shape. Sexes are similar.

SUMMER

white line from eye to top of bill

WINTER

Summer adult has a black head, neck and upperparts, and white underparts; white trailing edge to innerwing shows as a wingbar in resting bird. Bill is large and laterally flattened; at close range, vertical ridges and white lines can be seen. Winter adult is similar but has a partly white face (throat and cheeks), and bill is smaller. **VOICE** Mostly silent but sometimes utters croaking calls near the nest. **HABITS** Swims well, dives frequently and flies low over the sea on whirring wingbeats.

mainly black upperwings have narrow white trailing edge on inner half, as with Guillemot

SUMMER

clean, white underwing (dusky in Guillemot)

large, 'deep' bill is distinctive

STATUS AND HABITAT Locally common resident breeder. In the breeding season, favours rocky coasts and is present in most rocky-coast seabird colonies in the west and north. Around 110,000 pairs breed in the UK; typical nesting sites include boulder slopes and cliff-side crevices. Outside the breeding season, found at sea and seldom seen close to land.

SUMMER

rather upright posture when standing

BLACK GUILLEMOT

Cepphus grylle | TY | LENGTH 34cm

Distinctive seabird. Often seen close inshore,
off rocky coasts and jetties, usually singly
or in pairs. Sexes are similar.

SUMMER

**white wing patch is obvious
at all times of year**

WINTER

**red gape,
seen when
bird is calling**

Summer adult has mainly dark sooty-brown plumage except
for a striking white patch on wing. At close range, note the
red legs and orange-red gape. Winter adult has scaly grey
upperparts and white underparts; it retains a black tail and
black wings with a contrasting unmarked white wing
patch. Note also the dark bill and eye. In 1st-winter white
wing patch contains dark markings; otherwise similar to
winter adult. **VOICE** Utters high-pitched whistling calls.
HABITS Swims well and dives frequently in search of
bottom-dwelling fish such as Butterfish (*Pholis gunnellus*).
STATUS AND HABITAT Year-round resident of
inshore waters in N Britain; Shetland and Orkney are
its strongholds. The population numbers around
19,000 pairs in the UK. A cavity nester and only
ever locally common near suitable breeding
areas, such as raised boulder beaches.

SUMMER

SUMMER

LITTLE AUK

Alle alle | LK | LENGTH 20cm

Tiny seabird whose dumpy, compact appearance is in part a consequence of its short neck and tiny, stubby bill. Sexes are similar.

WINTER

flight is rapid

only seen near land when forced by severe gales

distinct white markings on otherwise black back

WINTER

short, stubby bill

buoyant when swimming

Winter adult (the plumage typically encountered here) has a black cap, nape and back, and white underparts; at close range, white lines on wings and tiny white crescent above eye can sometimes be discerned. Summer adult (plumage not usually seen here) has a black head, neck and upperparts, and white underparts. **VOICE** Silent in the region. **HABITS** Flies on rapid, whirring wingbeats and can look almost Starling-like on the wing. Swims well and dives frequently. **STATUS AND HABITAT** Scarce non-breeding visitor from Arctic breeding grounds, where its population is numbered in the tens of millions. Probably common offshore in the seas around Britain and Ireland (particularly the N North Sea), but seldom comes close to land except when storm-driven.

PUFFIN

Fratercula arctica | PU | LENGTH 30cm

Endearing and unmistakable seabird. When nesting, often indifferent to people, allowing close views to be obtained at many colonies. Sexes are similar.

SUMMER

pale face and dark crown

SUMMER

flight is fast and agile, on rapid wingbeats

Summer adult has mainly black upperparts. Face is dusky white, and underparts are white with a clear demarcation from the black neck. Legs are orange-red and bill is huge, laterally flattened, and marked with red, blue and yellow. Winter adult is similar but has a dark grey face; bill is much smaller and duller. Juvenile is similar to winter adult but with a relatively small, dark bill. **VOICE** Utters strange groaning calls at the nest. **HABITS** Flies on narrow wings with whirring wingbeats. Swims well and dives frequently in search of fish. **STATUS AND HABITAT** Locally common summer breeder that comes ashore only to nest. Breeds in colonies and nests in burrows on grassy, sloping cliffs and islands; around 580,000 pairs nest in the UK. Outside the breeding season, found far out to sea.

SUMMER

colourful, diagnostic bill

colours are duller and bill size is much smaller than in summer

WINTER

orange-red legs

ROCK DOVE/ FERAL PIGEON

Columba livia │ DV/FP │ LENGTH 33cm

Feral Pigeon is the urban domesticated descendant of Rock Dove, a shy bird of wild and untamed cliffs and coasts. Sexes are similar.

VARIANT

Feral Pigeon plumage is very variable

Feral Pigeon occurs in a wide variety of colour forms, from almost black to pure white; some are similar to the ancestral Rock Dove. Adult and juvenile Rock Doves have blue-grey plumage that is palest on upperwings and back, and flushed pinkish maroon on breast. Note the 2 dark wingbars, seen in standing birds, and dark-tipped tail. In flight, shows a small white rump patch; upperwings have a dark trailing edge and narrow wingbar, while underwings are white. **VOICE** Utters a range of cooing calls. **HABITS** Forms flocks; with Feral Pigeons these can number hundreds of birds. **STATUS AND HABITAT** Rock Dove is a local resident breeder restricted to coasts and cliffs in N and W Britain. Its status can be hard to assess because of feral populations of Feral Pigeons; the combined Rock Dove/Feral Pigeon UK population is estimated at 540,000 pairs. Feral Pigeons are often abundant in most towns and cities in the region, and are occasionally seen on farmland.

sheen on neck feathers is seen in good light

Rock Dove plumage shows little variation

two dark wingbars and a white rump

STOCK DOVE

Columba oenas | SD | LENGTH 33cm

Superficially similar to Woodpigeon
but slimmer, and also separable using
plumage details. Sexes are similar.

lacks white
markings on
neck seen in
Woodpigeon

in flight, upperwings can look rather
uniform except for dark trailing edge
to wings and dark terminal band to tail

dark bars on
wings are not
always well
defined

Adult has rather uniform blue-grey upperparts and paler grey underparts; has a pinkish-maroon flush to breast and an iridescent green patch on side of neck. Shows 2 narrow black bars on upper surface of innerwing and a broad, dark trailing edge. Juvenile is similar but wingbars are faint. In flight, looks short-tailed. **VOICE** During the breeding season, utters a diagnostic and repetitive *oo-u-look* call. **HABITS** Rather solitary in the breeding season but sizeable flocks form in winter. In direct, level flight, wings tend to be flicked more than is the case with Woodpigeon. **STATUS AND HABITAT** Widespread resident breeder that favours areas of wooded farmland and nests in tree-holes; around 260,000 pairs nest in the UK. Outside the breeding season, flocks feed in arable fields.

WOODPIGEON

Columba palumbus | WP | LENGTH 41cm

Plump bird of lightly wooded open country.
Its 'song' is a familiar countryside sound, as is
the loud clatter of wings as it flies off in alarm.
Sexes are similar.

Adult has mainly blue–grey plumage with pinkish maroon on the breast. Note the distinctive
white patch on side of neck and, in flight, prominent transverse white wingbars accentuated
by dark wingtips; also has a dark terminal band on tail. Juvenile is similar to adult but white
mark on neck is missing. **VOICE** Sings a series of *oo-OO-oo, oo-oo* phrases. **HABITS** Aerial
displays are performed in the spring. Forms sizeable flocks outside the breeding season.
STATUS AND HABITAT Resident breeder and the commonest of its kind in Britain.
Has benefited from the popularity of Oilseed Rape (*Brassica napus*) crops; around 5.3
million pairs nest in the UK. Favours arable farmland and grassland fields with a mosaic
of hedgerows and scattered woodlands. Also found increasingly in urban locations.

white 'crescent'
on upperwing
(absent in
Stock Dove)

white marking
on neck

compared
to Stock Dove,
body is much
more plump

COLLARED DOVE

Streptopelia decaocto | CD | LENGTH 32cm

A recent addition to our fauna but now a widespread and familiar sight. Its distinctive call is also well known. Sexes are similar.

pale underwings

Adult has mainly sandy-grey plumage with a pinkish flush to head and underparts. Note the dark half-collar on nape. Black wingtips and white outer-tail feathers are most noticeable in flight. Bill is dark and legs are reddish. Juvenile is similar but has duller colours and pale fringes to back feathers; black half-collar is absent. **VOICE** Utters a repetitive 'song' that comprises a much-repeated _oo-oo-oo_ phrase. **HABITS** Performs a gliding display flight on bowed, outstretched wings. **STATUS AND HABITAT** Spread northwest across Europe in the early 20th century and first recorded here in the 1950s. Today, around 980,000 pairs nest in the UK. Favours gardens and urban areas, as well as farm buildings and grain spills.

narrow
black collar

uniformly
grey-buff
plumage

broad white
trailing edge
to tail

TURTLE DOVE

Streptopelia turtur | TD | LENGTH 27cm

Attractive, well-marked species with the proportions of a Collared Dove but appreciably smaller. Often first detected by its distinctive song. Sexes are similar.

white corners to tail

flight is rapid

scaly appearance to back

rufous feathering on back and innerwing

barring on neck

Adult has a blue-grey head, neck and underparts with a slight pinkish-buff flush on breast. Back and wing coverts are chestnut, the dark feather centres and pale margins creating a scaly appearance. Long, mainly black tail appears wedge-shaped in flight due to white corners. At close range, note the black and white barring on neck. Juvenile is similar but colours are duller and neck markings are absent. **VOICE** Song is a diagnostic purring *coo*. **HABITS** Flight is fast and direct, with jerky, flicking wingbeats. **STATUS AND HABITAT** Migrant summer breeder that winters in Africa. Favours arable farmland with hedgerows and scrub. Has declined due to the widespread use of agricultural herbicides; also shot on migration in the Mediterranean region. Around 14,000 pairs attempt to nest in the UK.

RING-NECKED PARAKEET

Psittacula krameri | RI | LENGTH 40–42cm

Established alien species and colourful
but slightly incongruous addition to the
British list. Has a distinctive long-tailed
outline in flight. Sexes are subtly dissimilar.

Adult male has mainly green
plumage but dark flight feathers
are noticeable on the wing. Has a
red bill and eye-ring, and a pinkish
neck-ring that is dark-bordered
towards its lower margin; this links
to black throat. Adult female and
juvenile are similar but lack any
markings on neck or throat. **VOICE**
Vocal, often announcing
its presence (including
in flight) with loud,
squawking calls.
HABITS Flight is fast,
on rapid wingbeats.
Often seen in small
groups. Roosts in
sizeable flocks outside
the breeding season. **STATUS AND
HABITAT** A feral population (escapees from
captivity and their progeny) is now well
established in parts of the region; around
8,600 pairs breed in the UK, nesting primarily
in tree-holes. The suburban fringes
of London are a stronghold.

nests in
tree holes

FEMALE

narrow
neck ring

green plumage
and parrot-like
appearance are
diagnostic

MALE

MALE

flight is rapid
and direct; long
tail is striking

BARN OWL

Tyto alba | BO | LENGTH 34–38cm

Beautiful owl that can appear ghostly white when caught in car headlights. Its flight is leisurely and slow on rounded wings. Sexes are similar.

facial disc is broadly heart-shaped

flight is buoyant on broad, rounded wings

whitish underparts

subtle, fine grey and black markings on back and innerwing

Adult and juvenile (British race) have orange-buff upperparts speckled with tiny black and white dots. Underparts are white and facial disc is heart-shaped and white. In flight, underwings are pure white. Birds from mainland Europe, distinguishable by their dark orange-buff breast, will sometimes migrate here in winter. **VOICE** Utters a blood-curdling call at night. **HABITS** Usually crepuscular or nocturnal, but in winter, and when chicks need to be fed in summer, sometimes hunts in the late afternoon. Often perches on fenceposts. **STATUS AND HABITAT** Resident breeder; around 4,000 pairs nest in the UK. Small mammals, particularly voles, are important in its diet, and so undisturbed grassland and wetland margins are favoured habitats.

LITTLE OWL

Athene noctua | LO | LENGTH 22cm

Our smallest owl, recognised even in silhouette by its dumpy outline and short tail. Sexes are similar.

Adult has brown upperparts adorned with whitish spots, and pale underparts that have dark streaks. Note its staring yellow eyes. Juvenile is similar but less well marked and lacks spotting on head. **VOICE** Calls include a strange cat-like *kiu*, uttered repeatedly and agitatedly in early evening. Has a distinctive undulating flight. **HABITS** Often active in daylight, making it relatively easy to see. When perched, often bobs its head and body. **STATUS AND HABITAT** Introduced here from mainland Europe in the 19th century and now a fairly widespread resident breeder; around 5,700 pairs nest in the UK. Favours open-country habitats, typically comprising a mosaic of fields and hedgerows. Nests in tree-holes and cavities in stone walls and old buildings.

rounded wings

often active in daytime

staring yellow eyes

compact body shape and proportionately large head

TAWNY OWL

Strix aluco | TO | LENGTH 38–40cm

Our commonest and most familiar owl; nevertheless, you are far more likely to hear one than see one. Sexes are similar.

JUVENILE
very 'fluffy-looking' plumage

underwings can look rather pale when flying bird is caught in car headlights

all dark eyes

beautifully marked brown plumage

Adult and juvenile have variably chestnut-brown or grey-brown plumage. At close range, note the streaked underparts, which can look rather pale, and the dark-streaked, well-marked upperparts. Eyes are dark. In flight, underwings can look rather pale. Young birds typically leave the nest while they are still downy and white. **VOICE** Utters a sharp *kew-wick* and the well-known hooting calls; most vocal in late winter and early spring when territorial boundaries are under dispute. **HABITS** Roosts unobtrusively during the day among branches and foliage of trees; sometimes discovered and mobbed by small songbirds. Flight is leisurely on broad, rounded wings. **STATUS AND HABITAT** Fairly common breeding resident. Favours woodland habitats where its small mammal prey is common; also occurs in gardens and suburban parks with mature trees. Around 50,000 pairs breed in the UK.

LONG-EARED OWL

Asio otus | LE | LENGTH 32–35cm

Well-marked, strictly nocturnal owl. In flight, recalls a Short-eared Owl but note the orange-buff patch that contrasts with the otherwise dark upperwing and lack of ·a white trailing edge to the wings. Sexes are similar.

Adult and juvenile have dark brown upperparts and paler underparts; whole body is heavily streaked. At close range, note the rounded orange-buff facial disc and staring orange eyes. Its 'ear' tufts are appreciably longer than those of Short-eared Owl.

VOICE Mainly silent but a series of deep hoots is sometimes heard in spring. **HABITS** Roosts in deep cover and usually hard to see. When alarmed, sometimes adopts a rather strange, elongated posture with the 'ear' tufts raised. **STATUS AND HABITAT** Resident breeder. Usually nests in conifer plantations and scrub thickets; around 3,500 pairs probably breed in the UK. Disperses outside the breeding season, when roosting sites can include coastal scrub and dense hedgerows. Some birds from mainland Europe winter here.

long ear tufts raised in alarm

barred primaries (cf. Short-eared Owl)

orange eyes

streaking on underparts extends to belly

sometimes discovered roosting in daytime

SHORT-EARED OWL

Asio flammeus | SE | LENGTH 35–40cm

Well-marked owl that often hunts in daylight. Flight is leisurely and slow; glides frequently, and flies holding its rather long, rounded-tipped wings rather stiffly. Sexes are similar.

Adult and juvenile are buffish brown, heavily spotted and streaked on upperparts, including neck; underparts are paler but are also streaked, more heavily on throat and upper breast. Facial disc is rounded; has yellow eyes and short 'ear' tufts. In flight, shows a pale orange-buff patch on upperwings, black-tipped wingtips and a white trailing edge to wings. **VOICE** Displaying birds will sometimes utter deep hoots; otherwise silent. **HABITS** Hunting birds quarter the ground at low level and also frequently perch on fenceposts and grassland tussocks. Displaying birds sometimes rise to considerable heights. **STATUS AND HABITAT** Present year-round but summer and winter distributions differ. Nests on upland and northern moorland; around 1,400 pairs breed in the UK. Outside the breeding season, moves to lowland marshes, coastal grassland and heathland. Some birds from mainland Europe winter here.

dark smudge around yellow eyes is more pronounced than in Long-eared Owl

underparts are rather plain and unmarked, except for dark-streaked throat

white trailing edge to underwing is not always easy to discern

CUCKOO

Cuculus canorus | CK | LENGTH 33–35cm

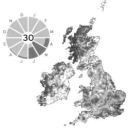

Male's onomatopoeic call is heard far more often than the bird is seen. Occasionally perches on wires overlooking potential egg-laying sites but otherwise secretive. With some individuals, sexes are dissimilar.

looks rather falcon-like in flight

JUVENILE

brown upperparts and strongly barred underparts

Adult male, and most females, have a blue-grey head, neck and upperparts; underparts are white and barred, and eye is yellow. Some adult females are brown and barred on head, neck and upperparts; underparts are white with dark bars. Juvenile is similar to brown adult female but note the white nape patch. **VOICE** Male utters a distinctive *cuck-oo* song during the first 6 weeks or so after its arrival; female has a bubbling call. **HABITS** In low-level flight, recalls a Sparrowhawk. Renowned for its parasitic breeding behaviour: female lays an egg in a songbird's nest and, having evicted its companion eggs or chicks, young Cuckoo is fed by hosts until it fledges. Adult feeds primarily on hairy caterpillars. **STATUS AND HABITAT** Distribution is dictated by ranges of the songbirds used for nest parasitism; classic hosts include Meadow Pipit, Dunnock and Reed Warbler. Around 15,000 birds breed in the UK.

tail is sometimes elevated when bird is excited

mainly blue-grey upperparts are tinged brown on wings

NIGHTJAR

Caprimulgus europaeus | NJ | LENGTH 24–27cm

Intriguing long-winged, long-tailed bird whose nocturnal habits and cryptic plumage make it difficult to see in daytime. Sexes can be separated with care.

MALE and FEMALE

female lacks white patches seen near wingtips of male

male often performs wing-clapping display in flight

Adult male has intricate brown, grey and black markings that, in combination, resemble tree bark. In flight, note the striking white patches near wingtips and corners of tail. Adult female and juvenile are similar but lack the white wing and tail markings. **VOICE** Male utters a distinctive churring song after dark for hours on end. **HABITS** Flight is light and buoyant, with lots of wing-flicking. Takes to the wing at dusk to hawk for insects. Sits motionless on the ground during the day and resembles a fallen branch; will flush only if approached extremely closely. **STATUS AND HABITAT** Summer migrant breeder. Favours lowland heathland and ground where conifer plantations have been felled and cleared; also occurs on heather moors in N Britain. Around 4,600 pairs nest in the UK.

FEMALE incubating female is well camouflaged amongst dead Bracken fronds

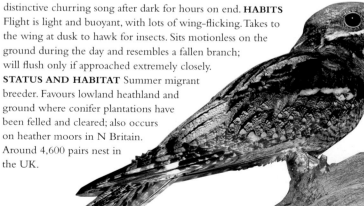

MALE

calling males often perch on bare branches

SWIFT

Apus apus | SI | LENGTH 16–17cm

Familiar summer visitor that is invariably seen
in flight. Recognised by its anchor-shaped
outline and mainly dark plumage. Sexes are
similar.

forked tail and
sickle-shaped
wings

noisy groups of birds are often
encountered near nesting sites

Adult has wholly blackish-brown plumage; in good light, the pale throat can be discerned.
Tail is forked but often held closed in active flight. Juvenile is similar, but plumage is
overall darker while throat is whiter and forehead can look rather pale. **VOICE** Loud, shrill,
screaming calls are uttered by parties of birds as they chase one another overhead at speed.
HABITS Flight is on stiff wings and includes lots of gliding. Apart from when nesting,
spends its life in the air, eating, sleeping and mating on the wing. A large gape allows it to
catch flying insects. **STATUS AND HABITAT** Migrant summer breeder that winters in
Africa. Around 87,000 pairs breed in the UK. Nests are usually associated with man-made
structures: churches and loft spaces in houses are favoured. At other times, birds are seen in
the air, and usually congregate where insects are numerous.

KINGFISHER

Alcedo atthis | KF | LENGTH 16–17cm

Dazzlingly attractive bird with a dagger-like bill. Its diet of fish means it is tied to water. Sexes are separable with care.

plunge-dives into water

dazzling blue back is striking in flight

Adult male has orange-red underparts and mainly blue upperparts; electric-blue back is most striking in flight. Legs and feet are red, and bill is all dark. Adult female is similar but base of lower mandible is flushed red. Juvenile is similar to adult but colours are duller and tip of bill is pale. **VOICE** Utters a distinctive thin, high-pitched *tist-tseee* call in flight. **HABITS** Often perches on overhanging branches; in shade, colours look rather muted. Plunges headlong into water after fish. Sometimes seen in low-level flight speeding along rivers. **STATUS AND HABITAT** Resident of rivers, streams, flooded gravel pits and lakes; nests in holes excavated in steep waterside banks. Around 4,900 pairs breed in the UK. Mainly sedentary but some dispersal occurs in summer (if streams and rivers dry up) or in harsh winters (if water freezes).

combination of bright blue and orange make the species unmistakable

often perches on branches overhanging water

WOODPECKERS

WRYNECK

Jynx torquilla | WY | LENGTH 16–17cm

Unusual member of the woodpecker family whose intricate plumage markings look like tree bark and afford it superb camouflage. Sexes are similar.

Adult has finely marked grey, brown, buff and black upperparts. Underparts are pale and barred, but flushed yellow–buff on throat and flanks. Has dark stripes through eye and down crown, nape and centre of back. Juvenile is similar but crown stripe is less distinct. **VOICE** Mostly silent but territorial birds utter loud, piping, raptor-like *pee-pee-pee* calls. **HABITS** The common name derives from its occasional habit of twisting its neck around. Feeds mainly on the ground, and is particularly fond of ants. In flight, could be mistaken for a large warbler, or even a Dunnock. **STATUS AND HABITAT** Has bred in Scotland (in open, park-like woodland) but its current status is that of scarce passage migrant. Around 250 are reported in most years, mainly from coastal districts and in autumn. Migrants usually favour short turf and scrub patches.

alert birds sometimes adopt an upright posture

slim-bodied appearance

often feeds on the ground, hunting ants and other insects

GREEN WOODPECKER

Picus viridis | G. | LENGTH 32–34cm

Despite its size and colourful plumage, can be tricky to observe because of its shy habits. Sexes are similar but separable with care.

MALE

JUVENILE

often feeds in grassland, searching for ants

undulating flight

red centre to 'moustache' only seen in male

MALE

Adult male has greenish-olive upperparts and whitish underparts. Head has a red crown, black 'mask' and red-centred black 'moustache'. In flight, yellowish rump is striking. Adult female is similar but 'moustache' is all black. Juvenile recalls adult male but is heavily spotted.

FEMALE

VOICE Its laughing call (sometimes referred to as 'yaffling') is distinctive and the 'song' comprises a dozen or so yelping, call-like notes. **HABITS** Climbs trees (using its spiky tail as a support) and excavates timber. Also feeds on the ground, using its long tongue to extract ants from subterranean nests. Flight is undulating. **STATUS AND HABITAT** Widespread resident breeder that favours open woodland, parks and gardens. Around 52,000 pairs breed in the UK; nests in tree-holes.

GREAT SPOTTED WOODPECKER

Dendrocopus major | GS | LENGTH 23–24cm

The larger and commoner of our 2 pied woodpeckers. Often seen climbing tree trunks or in undulating flight. Sexes are separable with care.

MALE

shows extensive white on upperwings in flight

Adult male is mainly black on its back, wings and tail, with obvious white shoulder patches and narrow white barring; underparts are mainly grubby white. Head pattern comprises a white face and throat, and a black cap and nape connected via a black line to a black stripe running from base of bill. Has a red patch on nape and red vent. In flight, white barring and shoulder patches are striking. Adult female is similar but red nape patch is absent. Juvenile recalls adult male but note the red crown and subdued red vent colour. **VOICE** All birds utter a loud *tchick* alarm call. In spring, males 'drum' loudly to proclaim territorial ownership. **HABITS** Excavates timber by drilling with its bill – for food and to create a nest chamber. A frequent garden visitor to peanut feeders. **STATUS AND HABITAT** Widespread resident breeder, with around 140,000 pairs nesting in the UK. Primarily a bird of deciduous woodland but also found in wooded gardens.

MALE

FEMALE

JUVENILE

climbs up vertical trunks and branches

juvenile is often accompanied by adult for a few weeks after fledging

LESSER SPOTTED WOODPECKER

Dendrocopus minor | LS | LENGTH 14–15cm

Our smallest woodpecker. Rather unobtrusive and easily overlooked. Sexes are similar but separable with care.

sometimes feeds on slender branches and twigs

MALE

FEMALE

red cap invites confusion with juvenile Great Spotted (plumage only seen during summer months) but miniature size helps with identification

Adult male has a black back and wings with white barring that creates a ladder-back appearance. Underparts are grubby white with dark streaking. Face is white while nape is black; a black stripe runs from bill, around ear coverts to sides of breast. Note the white-flecked red crown (cf. juvenile Great Spotted Woodpecker). In flight, shows strong white barring on otherwise black back and wings. Adult female and juvenile are similar to adult male but crown is black. In all plumages, vent is white. **VOICE** Male utters a loud, piping, raptor-like *kee-kee-kee* call in spring. Drumming is rapid but rather faint, and is also higher-pitched and longer than that of Great Spotted, averaging 24 strikes per drum (13 for Great Spotted). **HABITS** Usually searches for insects on slender outermost branches of trees. Seldom visits garden feeders. Excavates nest cavities in mature trees. **STATUS AND HABITAT** Thinly scattered resident breeder. Favours deciduous woodland and parkland; often associated with Common Alder (*Alnus glutinosa*). Around 1,500 pairs breed in the UK.

MALE

striking barring on back

INTRODUCING PASSERINES

Sometimes referred to as perching birds, passerines are our most varied group of birds, both in terms of numbers of species and diversity of appearance and habit preferences. Some of our most familiar garden and countryside birds are passerines, and across the group they vary in size from our smallest species to amongst our largest.

As their common name suggests, passerines have feet that allow them to perch. Three toes point forwards and one faces back; this not only provides support and allows the bird in question to stand upright on level surfaces, but it also allows it to grasp twigs and branches with a sure grip.

Passerines are vocal birds and males of some species are among our finest songsters. Many advertise ownership of breeding grounds and attract and retain mates using loud and diagnostic songs. And all species have a repertoire of calls that serve a variety of behavioural functions, including alarm (for example, at the presence of a predator) or contact (with other members of the species in feeding flocks or on migration).

The Nuthatch is a vocal passerine whose distinctive call can be heard throughout much of the year.

The full song of a territorial Robin is a familiar sound in spring.

The Goldcrest is the tiniest passerine and the smallest British bird – its size as depicted here is roughly relative to the size of a Raven.

The Raven is one of our largest birds and the biggest British passerine.

Passerine identification is aided greatly by recognition of their songs. That of the Whitethroat, like many other warblers, is unique and diagnostic, and easily recognised with a bit of practice.

INTRODUCING PASSERINES

The diet of passerines is as varied as the appearance of the birds themselves, but for many species small invertebrates are important for at least part of the year – typically the spring and summer months, when nesting is taking place. Some passerine families, such as warblers, are almost exclusively insectivorous (a misleading description, since spiders and other invertebrates are eaten in addition to insects), while sparrows and buntings rely to great degree on seeds as a source of nutrition. Many crow family members are arch scavengers that, to a certain extent, have predatory habits too. But in shrikes, the predilection for live prey reaches its apogee, the birds behaving like miniature raptors and even having hook-tipped bills to aid the dismemberment of their victims.

There is a clue to the Pied Flycatcher's diet in its name. Insects and other invertebrates are abundant during the breeding season but in short supply here in winter, hence the birds migrate to Africa after nesting has finished.

During the summer months a Waxwing's diet includes plenty of insects, but in winter berries are consumed eagerly.

The Jay has a varied diet that includes everything from seeds to nestlings in the summer months. In autumn, however, it is renowned for collecting and burying acorns as a stash for the winter months. Those acorns that are not rediscovered by the bird and eaten stand a good chance of growing into new oak trees.

Most passerine birds lead rather solitary lives during the breeding season and nest in relative isolation from pairs of the same species. However, outside the breeding season, many form sizeable flocks that migrate, feed and roost together. There is some truth in the saying that there is 'safety in numbers' because there are plenty of eyes on the look-out for danger.

The Starling is one of the most familiar flock-forming passerine birds in the winter months.

PLUMAGE

With many passerine species, visual differences between the sexes are subtle (to our eyes at least) – think of the Wren, Dunnock or Rook, for example. Behavioural differences obviously play an important part for the birds themselves, but for us as observers, it is only when a male is heard singing, or nesting behaviour is observed, that we can be sure of gender in certain species. However, among a select group of passerines (certain finches, buntings and chats, for example) there are striking differences in plumage too, although as a generalisation these differences are much more apparent in breeding plumage than during the winter months.

Although differences between the sexes in some passerine species is hard to discern, those between the male and female Chaffinch are striking.

RED-BACKED SHRIKE

Lanius collurio | ED | LENGTH 16–18cm

Distinctive predatory passerine. Dispatches insects and other prey using its powerful hook-tipped bill. Sexes are dissimilar.

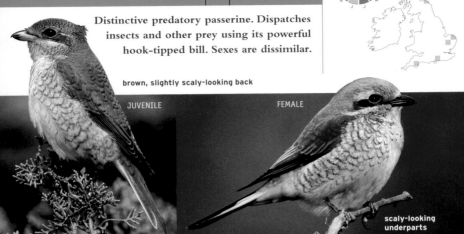

brown, slightly scaly-looking back

JUVENILE

FEMALE

scaly-looking underparts

Adult male has a reddish-brown back, blue-grey cap and nape, and whitish underparts, flushed pink on breast and flanks. Has a broad black band through eye; grey rump and white sides to base of tail are striking in flight. Adult female is similar but colours are muted, dark eye patch is fainter and underparts have dark vermiculations. Juvenile has barred brown upperparts and pale underparts strongly marked with dark vermiculations; dark eye patch is most prominent behind eye. **VOICE** Utters a harsh *tchek* call when agitated. **HABITS** Often perches on dead branches or wire fences for long periods. **STATUS AND HABITAT** Formerly extinct as a breeding species (having once been a widespread summer visitor), but one or two pairs have bred again recently. Best known as a scarce passage migrant; around 200 are recorded in a good year. Nesting birds favour commons and heaths; migrants are usually found in coastal scrub.

black 'mask' and reddish-brown back are diagnostic

stout, hook-tipped bill

MALE

scans for potential prey from an elevated perch

GREAT GREY SHRIKE

Lanius excubitor | SR | LENGTH 22–26cm

Bulky, predatory passerine with a powerful hook-tipped bill. Spends long periods perched on the tops of bushes or wires. Sexes are similar.

Adult has a grey cap and back, white underparts and a broad black mask through eye; note the white patch on wings at base of primaries, and white sides to long black tail. Juvenile (unlikely to be encountered here) is similar but has faint barring on underparts and black elements of plumage are washed out. **VOICE** Utters a harsh, trilling call. **HABITS** Can be remarkably elusive for such a large and well-marked bird: hides in deep cover. Prey includes small mammals and birds; food is sometimes impaled on a spike to facilitate butchering. **STATUS AND HABITAT** Scarce winter visitor from breeding grounds in N mainland Europe. A hundred or so are recorded in a good year; most records are from heaths and open country with scattered bushes and wires.

striking white wing markings seen in flight

upperparts are grey, but birds can look very black and white in strong light, and at a distance

often perches in a prominent position

CHOUGH

Pyrrhocorax pyrrhocorax | CF | LENGTH 38–40cm

All-dark Jackdaw-sized corvid,
recognised by its long, downcurved
red bill. Sexes are similar.

Adult has glossy black plumage. Legs are reddish pink and downcurved bill is bright red.
Juvenile is similar but leg colour is duller and bill is dull yellow. In flight, note the broad
'fingered' wingtips seen in all birds. **VOICE** Utters a distinctive *chyah* call; with standing
birds, this is typically accompanied by the caller flexing and flicking its wings in a seemingly
agitated manner. **HABITS** Bill is used to probe the ground for invertebrates. Forms flocks
outside the breeding season. Has superb aerobatic skills. **STATUS AND HABITAT** Scarce
resident breeder with extremely restricted habitat
preferences. Associated almost exclusively with
coasts, favouring sea cliffs with short turf for
feeding, and caves and cavities for nesting. Very
small numbers are found inland. Around 300
pairs probably breed in the UK.

very vocal,
even in flight

red, downcurved
bill and red legs
are diagnostic

plumage has a glossy
sheen in good light

JACKDAW

Corvus monedula | JD | LENGTH 31–34cm

Our most widespread and familiar small
corvid, and an opportunistic feeder, quick to
exploit any new food source.
Sexes are similar.

silvery-grey nape

Adult has mainly smoky-grey plumage, darkest on wings and crown; at close range, note
the pale blue-grey eye and silvery-grey nape. Juvenile is similar although plumage often
has a brownish tinge and eye is darker and duller. **VOICE** Utters a characteristic *chack* call.
HABITS Walks with a distinct swagger and is aerobatic in flight. Forms flocks outside the
breeding season. **STATUS AND HABITAT** Widespread and common resident
breeder. Equally at home on farmland or sea cliffs, and in towns and
villages. Requires a combination of areas of short vegetation for
feeding, and holes and cavities for nesting: caves, rock crevices,
old buildings and even chimneys are used. Around 1.3
million pairs nest in the UK. Outside the breeding
season, influxes from mainland Europe join
our resident birds.

beady pale
eye

MAGPIE

Pica pica | MG | LENGTH 45–50cm

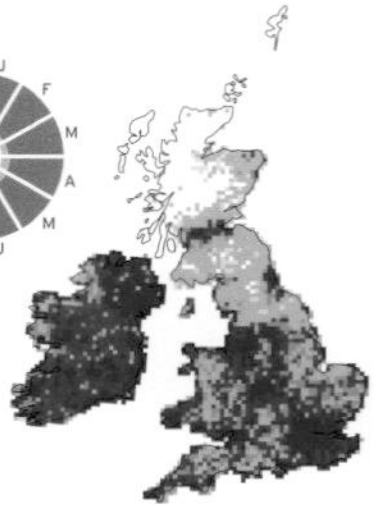

Familiar and unmistakable long-tailed black and white
bird with a distinctive call. Often seen on roadside
verges. Sexes are similar.

rounded,
black-and-white
wings

iridescent sheen is
only seen in good light

very long tail

Adult and juvenile have mainly black plumage with a contrasting white belly and white
patch on closed wing. At close range and in good light, a bluish-green sheen can be seen
on wings and tail. In flight, outer half of short, rounded wings appears strikingly white.
VOICE Utters a loud, rattling alarm call. **HABITS** An opportunistic omnivore: diet includes
fruit, insects, animal road-kills, and the eggs and young of birds; it will also happily scavenge
discarded leftover food scraps in towns. Nest is a long-lasting large twiggy structure, usually
built among dense tree branches. Outside the breeding season it is often seen in small groups.
STATUS AND HABITAT Widespread resident breeder. Favours a range of lightly wooded
habitats, including towns and villages. Around 550,000 pairs nest in the UK.

JAY

Garrulus glandarius | J. | LENGTH 33–35cm

Colourful and wary bird whose raucous calls
are heard more often than the bird itself is seen.
Its most striking feature is the white rump,
seen as it flies away. Sexes are similar.

white rump is diagnostic
in a bird of this size

loud screeching
calls often
uttered in
flight

broad, rounded
wings

white
undertail

colourful chequerboard
pattern is unique and
diagnostic

Adult and juvenile have mainly pinkish-buff body plumage except for white rump, undertail
and lower belly. Tail is black and wings are marked with a black and white pattern and
chequerboard patch of blue, black and white. Note also the black 'moustache', streaked pale
forecrown and pale eye. **VOICE** Utters a loud, harsh scream. **HABITS** Each bird buries
thousands of acorns in autumn as a food supply for winter. **STATUS AND HABITAT**
Widespread resident breeder and primarily a woodland bird; its precise distribution is linked
to the presence of mature oak trees. Acorns form an important part of its diet for much of
the year, but in summer it becomes an opportunistic omnivore, taking invertebrates as well as
eggs and young of other birds. Around 170,000 pairs nest in the UK. If the acorn crop fails
in mainland Europe, influxes from there may occur.

PASSERINES

ROOK

Corvus frugilegus | RO | LENGTH 43–48cm

Familiar open-country bird, often seen in large flocks feeding in fields or at colonial tree-nest sites, which are noisy and active from Mar to May. Sexes are similar.

Adult has all-black plumage that reveals a reddish-purple iridescence at certain angles. Bill is long, narrow and rather pointed, with a bare patch of whitish skin at base. Juvenile is similar but patch of bare white skin at bill base is absent. In all ages has a distinctive peaked crown. In flight, shows a long, rounded tail. **VOICE** Utters a grating *caw-caw-caw…* call. **HABITS** Diet is omnivorous: uses its long bill to probe the ground for invertebrates, notably earthworms and leatherjackets, and seeds and roots. Nests colonially, building large twig nests in clumps of tall trees. Roosts communally in winter. **STATUS AND HABITAT** Widespread resident breeder, associated mainly with farmland. Flocks forage in grassland and ploughed fields. Around a million pairs probably nest in the UK. In winter, population is joined by birds from mainland Europe.

fully-feathered face

JUVENILE

pale, bare skin on face

long bill

in good light, feathers have an iridescent sheen

RAVEN

Corvus corax | RN | LENGTH 55–65cm

Our biggest passerine and appreciably larger than Carrion Crow or Rook. Recognised on the ground by its size and massive bill. Sexes are similar.

Adult and juvenile have mainly black plumage, but in good light an oily or metallic sheen can be seen. In flight, note the long, thick neck, heavy bill and wedge-shaped tail. Rather shaggy throat appears ruffled when bird is calling. Incredibly aerobatic, tumbling and rolling in mid-air. **VOICE** Utters a loud, deep *cronk* call. This often alerts observers to the presence of distant flying birds. **HABITS** Generally wary and alert. Often seen in pairs or small family groups. Carrion forms the basis of this scavenging species' diet. **STATUS AND HABITAT** Local resident breeder. Formerly the westerly bias to its distribution in part reflected a history of persecution, as well as the relatively sanitised nature of farmland in E Britain. Today, it has spread back into many former haunts and is now found in areas of rolling wooded countryside, desolate upland areas, and rugged and windswept coasts. Around 7,000 pairs nest in the UK.

very vocal

massive bill

oily sheen to feathers seen in good light

wedge-shaped tail

CARRION CROW

Corvus corone | C. | LENGTH 43–50cm

Archetypal member of the crow family, and
the species most likely to be seen singly or
in pairs, rather than in flocks.
Sexes are similar.

**broad wings
and direct
flight**

**uniformly black plumage that
looks glossy in bright light**

Adult and juvenile have all-black plumage that appears glossy in good light. Legs and stout
bill are dark; base of bill is entirely feathered (cf. Rook). In flight, note the broad wings and
long, rather square-ended tail. **VOICE** Utters a harsh, trumpeting, slightly slurred *creeaa-
creeaa-creeaa* call. **HABITS** Generally extremely wary, and justifiably so because it is widely
persecuted. An opportunistic feeder, taking both carrion and live prey. Far less gregarious
than either Rook or Jackdaw. **STATUS AND HABITAT** Widespread resident throughout
England and Wales; in Scotland, largely confined to the south and east of a line between the
Firth of Clyde and Dornoch Firth. The zone of hybridisation with Hooded Crow (which
lives north and west of the line) is along the Scottish section of this line. Favours a wide
variety of habitats, from farmland and seashores to moorland and relatively urban locations.
Around a million pairs breed in the UK; the nest is usually constructed in a tree.

HOODED CROW

Corvus cornix | HC | LENGTH 43–50cm

Closely related to Carrion Crow and very similar structurally. Formerly treated as geographically separate subspecies, but now elevated to full species status. Sexes are similar.

Adult and juvenile have mainly grubby grey body plumage with black wings and tail; head is black, and black throat and centre of upper breast form a straggly black bib. In flight, grey body underparts and back contrast sharply with black tail, wings and head. **VOICE** Utters a harsh, trumpeting, slightly slurred *creeaa-creeaa-creeaa* call. **HABITS** Generally wary. An opportunistic feeder, taking both carrion and live prey. Not usually gregarious but small groups may gather at sites of good feeding, notably on coasts in winter. **STATUS AND HABITAT** Widespread resident in Scotland, north and west of a line between the Firth of Clyde and Dornoch Firth. The predominant resident 'crow' in Ireland and on the Isle of Man. Favours a wide variety of habitats, from farmland and moorland to seashores; the latter are particularly favoured in winter. Around 260,000 pairs breed in the UK; the nest is usually constructed in a tree.

pale grey belly and underwing coverts are obvious in flight

grey elements of plumage can assume a subtle lilac hue in some lights

GOLDEN ORIOLE

Oriolus oriolus | OL | LENGTH 22–24cm

Stunningly colourful bird. Has an unmistakable
song and is far more frequently heard than
it is seen. Sexes are dissimilar.

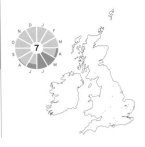

Adult male has mainly bright yellow plumage with black on wings, tail and lores. Bill is red.
Adult female has a similar plumage pattern but yellow colour is less intense and underparts
are pale and faintly streaked. Juvenile is similar to adult female but upperparts are green
and underparts are more heavily streaked. **VOICE** Song is a rich, fluty, tropical-sounding
wee-lo-weeow, with variations on the theme. Also utters various harsh
disyllabic calls; some are Jay-like or cat-like. **HABITS** Generally
rather shy and easily overlooked in dappled foliage. Sightings
are invariably brief and often involve birds in flight. **STATUS
AND HABITAT** Scarce summer breeder that winters in
Africa. A few pairs breed in most years, mainly in mature
poplar plantations in East Anglia. Also a scarce passage
migrant, with perhaps 100 or more recorded
in most years, mainly on coasts.

red bill
and dark
'mask'

bright yellow plumage
is diagnostic in a
bird of this size

streaked
underparts

MALE

FEMALE

BLUE TIT

Cyanistes caeruleus | BT | LENGTH 11–12cm

Colourful little bird and a familiar garden favourite. Sexes are similar but, on average, males have slightly brighter colours than females.

white face with dark line through eye

manoeuvrable in flight, on rounded wings

yellow underparts

Adult has a greenish back, blue wings and yellow underparts. The mainly white head is demarcated by a dark blue collar that connects to a dark eye-stripe and dark bib; cap is blue. Has a pale wingbar, bill is short and stubby, and legs are bluish. Juvenile is similar to adult but colours are subdued, particularly the blue elements of plumage. **VOICE** Call is a familiar, chattering *tser err-err-err*. Song contains whistling and trilling elements. **HABITS** Frequent visitor to bird-feeders in winter. Nests in tree-holes in natural settings, and readily uses nest boxes. **STATUS AND HABITAT** Common resident breeder, widespread everywhere except on northern and smaller offshore islands; around 3.4 million pairs breed in the UK. Favoured habitat is deciduous woodland but also frequently found in parks and gardens.

compact body shape

stubby bill

GREAT TIT

Parus major | GT | LENGTH 14–15cm

Familiar bold woodland bird, and also a frequent garden visitor. Well marked and colourful, with a song as distinctive as its appearance. Sexes are separable with care.

60

width of dark central line on belly allows separation of the sexes

MALE

white cheek is framed with black

pale wingbar

Adult male has striking white cheeks that contrast markedly with otherwise black head; black throat continues as a thick black line down centre of breast to legs on otherwise yellow underparts. Upperparts are greenish and blue with a white wingbar. Adult female is similar to adult male but with a narrower black line on breast that breaks up at legs. Juvenile plumage pattern hints at that seen in adult, with much duller and paler colours overall. **VOICE** Utters a harsh *tche-tche-tche* alarm call. Song is a striking variation on a *teecha-teecha-teecha* theme. **HABITS** Visits peanut feeders and bird tables in winter. Uses nest boxes with a suitable size entrance hole; in natural settings, nests in tree-holes. **STATUS AND HABITAT** Common resident breeder; widespread, but absent from most N Scottish islands. Favours a range of wooded habitats and is a common garden resident. Around 2.5 million pairs breed in the UK.

CRESTED TIT

Lophophanes cristatus | CI | LENGTH 11–12cm

Distinctive little bird, easily recognised by its conspicuous crest. Has very precise habitat requirements and a restricted British range. Sexes are similar.

Adult has a striking black and white barred crest. Has a black line through the eye and bordering ear coverts, on a head that is otherwise mainly whitish; in addition, note that the black throat and black collar demarcate the head. Upperparts are otherwise brown and underparts are buffish white. Bill is narrow and warbler-like. Juvenile is similar to adult but plumage colours and markings are less striking. **VOICE** Utters a high, trilling call. Song is a rapid, almost warbler-like series of call-like notes and whistles. **HABITS** Feeds mainly on insects and other invertebrates in summer, but supplements its diet with seeds at other times of the year. **STATUS AND HABITAT** Very local resident breeder, found only in ancient Caledonian pine forests and mature and open Scots Pine (*Pinus sylvestris*) plantations in the Scottish Highlands. Requires standing dead tree stumps: nests in holes excavated in decaying wood. Around 1,500 pairs breed here.

beady red eye

black throat and collar

crest is diagnostic in a bird of this size

narrow, pointed bill

WILLOW TIT

Poecile montana | WT | LENGTH 12–13cm

Superficially very similar to Marsh Tit but separable with care. Voice is the most useful identification feature, along with subtle plumage differences and distinct habitat preferences. Sexes are similar.

excavates nest hole

Adult and juvenile have a black cap and bib, whitish cheeks, a grey-brown back and pale grey-buff underparts. Bill is short and legs are bluish. Compared to Marsh Tit, cap is dull, not shiny, and extends onto upper mantle, and bib is relatively large. In addition, neck appears thicker (species is often described as 'bull-necked') and a pale panel can usually be seen on otherwise grey-brown wings. **VOICE** Utters a distinctive and nasal *si-si tchay-thcay-tchay* call. Song is rather musical and warbling. **HABITS** Excavates its own nest holes; decaying stumps of birch trees are ideal. **STATUS AND HABITAT** Declining resident breeder, commonest in the southern half of Britain. Seldom found in the same habitat as Marsh Tit. Willow Tit favours damp wooded areas: Common Alder (*Alnus glutinosa*) carr and waterside willow scrub are ideal. Also sometimes found in conifer plantations. Around 3,400 pairs breed in the UK.

neck is thicker when compared to Marsh Tit

dull, matt black cap

pale wing panel, not seen on Marsh Tit

MARSH TIT

Poecile palustris | MT | LENGTH 12–13cm

Pugnacious little woodland bird. Superficially similar to Willow Tit and the more frequently encountered of the two. Subtle differences in plumage, structure and calls can be used to separate them. Sexes are similar.

Adult and juvenile have a black cap and bib. Cheeks are whitish, upperparts are uniform grey-brown and underparts are pale grey-buff. Compared to Willow Tit, cap is glossy, not dull, and bib is relatively small (features are not always easy to discern in the field). Pale wing panel is largely absent. Bill is short and often shows an obvious pale spot at base. Legs are bluish. **VOICE** Utters a loud, sneezing *pitchoo* call. Song is a loud and repeated *chip-chip-chip…* **HABITS** Nests in existing holes in trees and will occasionally use nest boxes in shady places. Visits feeders, and forages on the ground, more frequently than Willow Tit. **STATUS AND HABITAT** Widespread resident breeder, associated with deciduous woodland, and wooded parks and gardens. Around 41,000 pairs nest in the UK.

black bib is small, relative to that of Willow Tit

glossy cap only obvious in bright light

uniform grey-buff underparts

BEARDED TIT

Panurus biarmicus | BR | LENGTH 16–17cm

Charming reedbed specialist with a compact, rounded body and very long tail. Its distinctive call has earned it the affectionate nickname of 'Pinger'. Sexes are dissimilar.

MALE

long tail

striking black 'moustache'

plain, unmarked face

FEMALE

JUVENILE

invariably seen climbing reeds

Adult male is mainly sandy brown on body and tail, with black and white markings on wings and a distinctive black undertail. Head is blue-grey, with conspicuous black 'moustaches' that flank throat. At close range, note the beady yellow eye and yellow bill. Adult female is similar but head is sandy brown, palest on throat, and undertail is pale. Juvenile is similar to adult female but back is blackish, throat is whiter, and eye colour is darker and duller; also has dark lores. Juvenile male has a yellow bill while that of female is dark. **VOICE** Utters a diagnostic high-pitched *ping* call. Soft, rasping song is seldom heard. **HABITS** Adept at climbing reed stems; feeding birds move tail constantly. Flight is undulating on whirring wingbeats. Outside the breeding season, usually encountered in small flocks. **STATUS AND HABITAT** Resident breeder, associated exclusively with extensive reedbeds. Around 630 pairs nest in the UK. Mostly sedentary but some dispersal occurs in early autumn.

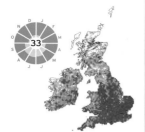

LONG-TAILED TIT

Aegithalos caudatus | LT | LENGTH 14cm

Delightful little bird with a proportionately
very long tail (9cm tail accounts for most
of its length) and almost spherical body.
Sexes are similar.

Adult can look rather black and white at a
distance. At close range, note the pinkish-
chestnut patch on scapulars and whitish
wing-feather fringes on the otherwise black
back and wings. Head is mainly whitish
with a broad black band running above eye;
underparts are whitish but suffused with pink
on flanks and belly. Bill is dark, short and
stubby. Juvenile is similar but pinkish elements
of plumage are absent and face is more
uniformly dark. Note: Scandinavian birds are
seen occasionally in winter; they are similar
but have white heads. **VOICE** Utters a rattling
tsrrr contact call and a thin *tsee-tsee-tsee*. Soft,
twittering song is easily overlooked. **HABITS**
Moves in a rather jerky fashion and has an
undulating flight. Has acrobatic feeding habits
and is often seen in animated small flocks.
Nest is ball-shaped, made from feathers and
spiders' silk, and camouflaged with lichens.
STATUS AND HABITAT Resident breeder,
associated mainly with deciduous woodland,
areas of scrub and mature hedgerows.
Around 330,000 pairs
nest in the UK.

short,
rounded
wings

pure white
head

NORTHERN
RACE

very short
stubby bill

very long tail

pinkish flush
to underparts

COAL TIT

Periparus ater | CT | LENGTH 10–11cm

Tiny, well-marked bird with rather
warbler-like proportions.
Sexes are similar.

white line down nape

two whitish
wingbars

pinkish yellow, or
buff wash to flanks

Adult ssp. *britannicus* (seen here) has white cheeks and a white nape patch on an otherwise black head. Back and wings are bluish grey and underparts are pale pinkish buff. Has 2 white wingbars and a dark, needle-like bill. Juvenile is similar to adult but plumage colours and pattern are less striking. Note that Irish birds (ssp. *hibernicus*) have a subtle yellow flush on cheeks and underparts. **VOICE** Utters a thin call. Song is a repeated *teechu-teechu-teechu…*, higher-pitched, more rapid and weaker than that of Great Tit. **HABITS** Often feeds in an energetic and acrobatic manner, frequently on outermost twigs and branches on trees. Visits garden feeders in rural locations. Nests in tree-holes and will occasionally use a nest box. Often joins mixed-species feeding flocks in winter. **STATUS AND HABITAT** Widespread resident breeder, with around 680,000 pairs nesting in the UK. Most numerous in conifer forests and plantations, but also common in mixed and deciduous woodland.

SHORE LARK

Eremophila alpestris | SX | LENGTH 16–17cm

Distinctive, well-marked lark. Sexes are similar, although females usually have duller head markings than males.

WINTER

black breast band

striking black markings on face

sandy buff upperparts

SPRING

Breeding plumage adult (seen in autumn and late spring) has sandy-brown upperparts, streaked on back but unstreaked on nape. Underparts are mainly white but with a striking black breast band and faint buff streaks on flanks. Head is yellow with a black band through eye and ear coverts, and a black forecrown that extends backwards to form 2 'horns'. Winter adult is similar, but colours and markings on head are less distinct and 'horns' are absent. Juvenile's markings are reminiscent of an adult, but upperparts have pale spots. In flight, shows a black and white outer-tail. **VOICE** Flight call is a thin *see-seer*. **HABITS** Feeds unobtrusively and can be difficult to locate when foraging among saltmarsh plants. **STATUS AND HABITAT** Has bred in Scotland, but its status is essentially that of a scarce winter visitor, with around 70–100 in the UK in most years. Restricted to coastal habitats, typically favouring saltmarshes. Usually discovered in small feeding flocks comprising 3–10 birds.

PASSERINES

WOODLARK

Lullula arborea | WL | LENGTH 15cm

Small, rather short-tailed lark. Unobtrusive and easy to overlook were it not for its beautiful yodelling song. Sexes are similar.

Adult has streaked sandy-brown upperparts and mainly pale underparts, although breast is streaked and flushed with buff. Note the chestnut ear coverts, pale supercilium that meets on the nape, and black and white marking at the angle of the leading edge to the wing. Juvenile is similar but pale margins to feathers on back give it a scaly appearance. In flight, short tail obvious. **VOICE** Song is a series of fluty, yodelling notes, often delivered in flight but sometimes while bird is perched in a tree. Call is a yodelling *deet-luee*, reminiscent of a snatched phrase from the song. **HABITS** Outside the breeding season, wandering birds sometimes associate loosely with flock-forming songbirds such as Skylarks. **STATUS AND HABITAT** Scarce resident breeder. Associated with heathland sites where a mosaic of short turf (for feeding) and longer grassland (for nesting) occurs. Also found where conifer plantations have been felled and heathland regrowth has begun. Around 3,100 pairs breed in the UK. Rather nomadic outside the breeding season.

dark-edged chestnut ear coverts

distinctive, fluty song

tail is short, relative to that of Skylark

long hind claw

SKYLARK

Alauda arvensis | S. | LENGTH 18cm

Rather nondescript, streaked brown bird. Best known
for its incessant trilling and fluty song, usually delivered
in flight. Sexes are similar.

Adult has streaked sandy-brown upperparts and paler underparts; breast is marked with
streaks and flushed with buff. Has a short crest that is raised occasionally. In flight, note
the whitish trailing edge to wings and white outer-tail feathers. Juvenile is similar but pale
feather margins on back give it a scaly appearance, and brown feathers on face and crown
have pale tips. **VOICE** Song, most often delivered in flight, is a rapid and varied mixture of
trilling and whistling notes; it sometimes includes elements of mimicry. Call is a rolling *chrrrp*.
HABITS Singing birds are often airborne for long periods, sometimes rising to great heights.
STATUS AND HABITAT Widespread resident breeder associated with grassy habitats, from
meadows and coastal grassland to moors and heaths. Wildlife-unfriendly agricultural methods
exclude it from most areas of intensive farming. Around 1.4 million pairs nest in the UK.
Outside the breeding season, numbers may be boosted by birds on migration from mainland
Europe. In winter, absent from most upland breeding sites, and flocks tend to concentrate in
lowland districts.

song is often delivered in flight

rather nondescript
buffish-brown upperparts

pale trailing
edge to wings

streaked
breast

SAND MARTIN

Riparia riparia | SM | LENGTH 12cm

Our smallest hirundine, typically seen hawking for insects over water, sometimes even picking them off the surface. Sexes are similar.

excavates nest burrow in sand bank

dark breast band

Adult has sandy-brown upperparts and mainly white underparts with a striking brown breast band. In flight, wings are rather triangular in outline and tail is short and forked. Juvenile is similar but pale margins to feathers on the back create a scaly appearance. **VOICE** Utters a range of rasping *jsee-jsee-jsee* calls. **HABITS** Agile in flight, which includes periods of gliding and rapid, fluttering wingbeats. Catches insects on the wing and typically feeds over water in the vicinity of its breeding colony. Sometimes perches on overhead wires, alongside Swallows. **STATUS AND HABITAT** Widespread summer breeder that winters in Africa. Nests colonially, excavating burrows in sandy banks beside rivers and in sand and gravel quarries. Around 100,000 pairs probably breed in the UK, although in the recent past the population has been much higher.

uniform sandy brown upperparts

HOUSE MARTIN

Delichon urbicum | HM | LENGTH 12–13cm

Familiar summer visitor that is easily recognised
in flight by its rather black and white appearance
and conspicuous white rump. Sexes are similar.

Adult has mainly blue-black upperparts with a striking and contrasting white rump;
underparts are wholly white. In flight, wings look triangular in outline and tail is forked.
Juvenile is similar but underparts are rather grubby white and upperparts are duller. **VOICE**
Utters a distinctive *prrrt* call in flight. Twittering song is often delivered from overhead wires
in the vicinity of its nest. **HABITS** Breeding birds gather mud from margins of drying
pools. On migration, often congregates over fresh water, catching insects in low-level
flight. **STATUS AND HABITAT** Migrant summer breeder that winters in Africa. Typically
associated with urban areas; its rounded mud nest is commonly constructed under eaves and
overhangs of houses, in loose colonies. Very occasionally breeds on cliffs
and near cave entrances. Around 510,000 pairs nest in the UK.

white rump

blue sheen to
upperparts seen
in good light

white
underparts
contrast with
dark tail

forked tail

SWALLOW

Hirundo rustica | SL | LENGTH 19cm

Familiar migrant visitor, recognised in flight by
its pointed wings and long tail streamers. Sexes
are similar although, on average, males have
longer tail streamers than females.

tail streamers create impression
of deeply forked tail

JUVENILES

brick-red
face

Adult has blue-black upperparts and white underparts except for a
dark chest band and brick-red throat and forecrown. Juvenile is
similar but has shorter tail streamers and a pale buffish-red throat.
In all ages throat appears dark in flight. **VOICE** Utters a sharp *vit*
call in flight. Male sings a twittering 'sparrow-like' song, often
while sitting on overhead wires near the nest site. **HABITS**
Gathers mud for nest-building from margins of drying
pools. On migration and after breeding, birds often
congregate in large numbers over freshwater
lakes, perching on overhead wires and roosting
in reedbeds. **STATUS AND HABITAT**
Widespread summer breeder that winters
in Africa. Around 760,000 pairs nest in the
UK. During the breeding season, usually
associated with margins of rural
villages and farmyards. Typically
nests under eaves or in barns or
sheds, attaching a half-
cup-shaped nest of mud
to a wall or rafter.

MALE

blue sheen seen
on upperparts
in good light

tail streamers
are particularly
long in male

WREN

Troglodytes troglodytes | WR | LENGTH 9–10cm

Tiny bird with dumpy proportions, mainly dark brown plumage and a habit of cocking its tail upright. The presence of unseen birds is often detected by hearing the distinctive call. Sexes are similar.

SHETLAND RACE

northern, island races are typically darker and more rufous than their southern counterparts

Adult and juvenile have dark reddish-brown upperparts with barring on wings and tail. Underparts are greyish white with a buff wash to flanks. Has a striking pale supercilium, bill is needle-like and legs are reddish. **VOICE** Very vocal. Utters a loud, rattling alarm call and its song is loud and warbling, ending in a trill. **HABITS** Rather unobtrusive as it creeps through low vegetation in search of insects; can look rather mouse-like. **STATUS AND HABITAT** Widespread resident breeder. Found in a variety of habitats, from woodlands and hedgerows to scrub patches, gardens and coastal cliffs; the common factor is dense undergrowth. Population fluctuates from year to year – it suffers badly in severe winters, but in good seasons around 7.7 million pairs nest in the UK.

very vocal

short, rounded wings

GOLDCREST

Regulus regulus | GC | LENGTH 9cm

Our smallest breeding bird. Has a passing resemblance to a *Phylloscopus* warbler but the large, white-ringed dark eye, thick neck and colourful crown stripe allow separation. Sexes are dissimilar.

FEMALE

FEMALE

needle-like bill

acrobatic as it searches for food

MALE

face is plain and unmarked except for pale ring around eye

small, rounded body

Adult male has greenish upperparts with 2 pale wingbars, and yellow-buff underparts. Note the black-bordered orange crown and needle-like bill. Adult female is similar but crown colour is yellow. Juvenile is similar to adult but crown markings and colours are absent. **VOICE** Utters a thin, high-pitched *tsee-tsee-tsee*. Song comprises a series of high-pitched phrases and ends in a flourish. **HABITS** Typically forages high in the tree canopy for invertebrates, sometimes hanging from twigs or hovering. **STATUS AND HABITAT** Widespread and common woodland resident. Favours conifers but also found in deciduous woodland and scrub, especially in winter. Around 520,000 pairs nest in the UK, and influxes from N mainland Europe may almost double the population in winter.

FIRECREST

Regulus ignicapilla | FC | LENGTH 9–10cm

Tiny bird, and only marginally larger than a Goldcrest. Has distinct and diagnostic markings and colours. Sexes are dissimilar.

MALE

1ST-WINTER

extremely active in search of invertebrates such as aphids and spiders

MALE

golden flush

striking markings on face allow separation from Goldcrest

rounded body shape is similar to that of Goldcrest

Adult male has yellow-green upperparts with 2 pale wingbars. Underparts are buffish white but flushed golden yellow on sides of neck. Has a dark eye-stripe, broad white supercilium and orange-centred black crown stripe. Adult female is similar but crown centre is yellow. Juvenile is similar to adult but lacks markings and colour on crown. **VOICE** Utters a thin *tsuu-tsee-tsee* call. Song comprises a series of thin, high-pitched notes and ends abruptly. **HABITS** Constantly active in its search for small invertebrates. **STATUS AND HABITAT** Rare breeding bird, passage migrant and winter visitor. Around 550 pairs nest in the UK, mainly in S England, favouring mature woodland; territories are often centred on large and mature conifer trees with a Holly (*Ilex aquifolium*) understorey. Passage migrants and wintering birds are typically associated with coastal woodland and scrub.

RECOGNISING WARBLER GENERA

Warbler identification can be a real challenge, not only for the novice but on occasions also for more experienced birdwatchers. The songs and calls of common species are a great help, but of course most birds are silent for long periods too. Fortunately, there are a few useful plumage pointers that separate the various genera of warblers. Assigning a mystery bird to a genus is a useful first step in the identification process.

Cetti's Warbler

GENUS *CETTIA*

Represented in Britain by just one species: Cetti's Warbler is a skulking bird with a distinctive voice. Like other members of the genus it is a relatively large-bodied warbler with a long, rounded tail, relatively short wings and medium-length undertail coverts. The sexes are similar in plumage terms.

Willow Warbler

GENUS *PHYLLOSCOPUS*

Sometimes referred to as 'leaf warblers', these birds are small and relatively compact, and are generally very active. The bill is rather small and thin, the primary projection of the wings varies according to species, the tail is subtly forked and the undertail coverts are relatively short. The sexes are usually similar in plumage terms.

Whitethroat

GENUS *SYLVIA*

Characterised by a rounded head and short wings, *Sylvia* warblers have a short but stout bill. The tail is relatively long and square-ended in most species, and some have white outer-tail feathers. In most species, the sexes are dissimilar in plumage terms.

GENUS *LOCUSTELLA*

This warbler genus includes one common species (Grasshopper Warbler) and several rarer ones (covered in this book's companion volume). In general, they are skulking birds with a rather rounded head, relatively long wings, a long, broad and rounded tail, and very long undertail coverts. The sexes are similar in plumage terms.

GENUS *ACROCEPHALUS*

Acrocephalus warblers have a distinctive elongated head shape, created by the sloping forehead and rather long bill. The wings are relatively short (compared to *Locustella* warblers, for example), the tail is rather long and the undertail coverts are long (but not as long as in *Locustella* warblers). The sexes are similar in plumage terms.

GENUS *REGULUS*

Firecrest and Goldcrest are not closely related to true warblers, but because of their appearance and habits they are treated here as honorary members of the group. They are tiny, extremely active birds with a rounded body, relatively short wings and tail, and a thin bill. Both species have striking head patterns and wing markings. The sexes are subtly dissimilar.

Grasshopper Warbler

Reed Warbler

Firecrest

CETTI'S WARBLER

Cettia cetti | CW | LENGTH 14cm

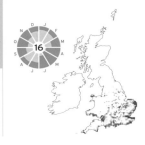

Rather bulky but unobtrusive wetland warbler whose loud, explosive song is often the first indication of its presence. Sexes are similar.

Adult and juvenile have dark reddish-brown upperparts, including the tail. Underparts are contrastingly pale, with a whitish throat, grey on face and breast, and grey-buff on belly. Legs are reddish and bill is dark-tipped. Undertail coverts are short, brown and tipped darker in all ages. **VOICE** Usual call is a loud *pluut* but often also a rattling *plurrrr*. Song is an explosive *chee, chippi-chippi-chippi*. Most vocal in spring, but snatches of song are sometimes heard at other times of year. **HABITS** Vaguely reminiscent of an outsized Wren and sometimes cocks its rounded tail up in a similar manner to that species. Spends much of its time in dense cover. **STATUS AND HABITAT** Colonised Britain in the latter half of the 20th century and now a very local resident breeder. Around 2,000 pairs nest in the UK, favouring scrubby margins of marshes and isolated clumps of bushes in extensive reedbeds.

upperparts appear warm rufous brown

a vocal bird, and arguably our loudest songster

short undertail coverts

favours wetland scrub on fringes of reedbeds

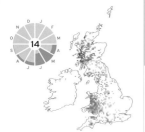

WOOD WARBLER

Phylloscopus sibilatrix | WO | LENGTH 11–12cm

A rather large *Phylloscopus* warbler with bright plumage colours, a distinctive song and precise habitat requirements. Sexes are similar.

Adult and juvenile have olive-green upperparts, a bright yellow throat and supercilium, and clean white underparts. Note the rather dark eye-stripe and pale pink legs. **VOICE** Utters a sharp *tsip* call. Its song, which has been likened to a coin spinning on a plate, starts with ringing notes and accelerates into a silvery trill. **HABITS** Nests on the ground but spends much of its time foraging for insects in the tree canopy. Can be surprisingly hard to spot amongst dappled foliage. **STATUS AND HABITAT** Local migrant summer breeder that winters in Africa. Favours mature woodlands with tall trees, limited ground cover and generally a closed canopy; Sessile Oak (*Quercus petraeus*) woodlands are used in W and N Britain, Beech (*Fagus sylvatica*) woods elsewhere. Around 6,500 pairs nest in the UK.

a colourful songster with a distinctive song

yellow flush to head and upperparts

associated with mature native woodland

clean white underparts

WILLOW WARBLER

Phylloscopus trochilus | WW | LENGTH 11cm

46

Superficially very similar to Chiffchaff but separable
with care on plumage details and song. Also has
subtly different habitat preferences to
its cousin. Sexes are similar.

JUVENILE

strikingly
yellow

upperwings
are unmarked

Adult has olive-green upperparts, a yellow throat and grubby white underparts. Note
the pale supercilium and pinkish-yellow legs. Overall, plumage is brighter compared to
Chiffchaff and primary feathers project further, relative to exposed length of tertials (primary
projection is equal to exposed tertials). Juvenile is similar but plumage is paler and more
yellow overall, particularly on underparts. **VOICE** Utters a disyllabic *hueet* call, similar to that
of Chiffchaff. Song comprises a tinkling, descending phrase that ends in a slight flourish; it is
endlessly repeated by newly arrived birds in spring. **HABITS** Nests on the ground but
forages for insects among foliage. **STATUS AND HABITAT** Widespread
migrant summer breeder that winters in Africa. Around 2.2 million
pairs nest in the UK. Favours wooded or partly wooded habitats;
birch woodland and areas of willow scrub are
particularly favoured.

compared to most Chiffchaffs,
Willow Warbler's plumage
is brighter

relative long primary projection

pinkish legs

CHIFFCHAFF

Phylloscopus collybita | CC | LENGTH 11cm

Tiny warbler, probably best known for its onomatopoeic song. One of the earliest migrants to arrive in spring. Sexes are similar.

Adult and juvenile have grey-brown upperparts and pale greyish underparts suffused with yellow-buff, particularly on the throat and breast. Bill is thin and needle-like, while legs are black (cf. leg colour in Willow Warbler). Has a shorter primary projection than Willow Warbler (equal to two-thirds of exposed tertials). **VOICE** Call is a soft *huitt*, shorter and harsher than Willow Warbler's *hueet*. Song is a continually repeated *chiff-chaff* or *tsip-tsap*, heard most frequently in early spring but sometimes uttered in snatches by migrants in late summer. **HABITS** A restless feeder, constantly on the move in foliage in search of invertebrates. **STATUS AND HABITAT** Mainly a migrant summer breeder; around 1.1 million pairs nest in the UK. During the breeding season it is associated with mature deciduous woodland with a dense understorey of shrubs. In autumn, most British breeders migrate south and winter around the Mediterranean. Also a common passage migrant. Several hundred birds are present in winter; some of these will be from mainland Europe.

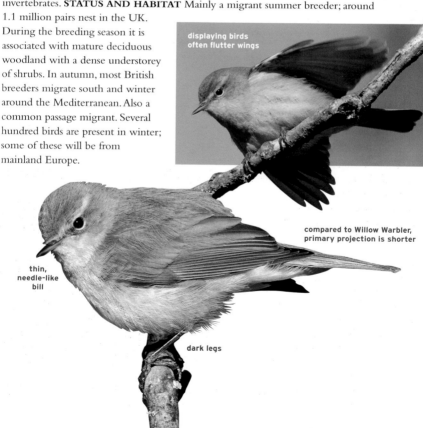

displaying birds often flutter wings

compared to Willow Warbler, primary projection is shorter

thin, needle-like bill

dark legs

GARDEN WARBLER

Sylvia borin | GW | LENGTH 14–15cm

A bulky warbler that has rather nondescript plumage but one of the most attractive songs of all British birds. Sexes are similar.

subtle grey patch on side of neck

upperparts are rather uniform grey-brown

a beautiful songster

buffish wash to breast and flanks

Adult and juvenile have rather uniform grey-brown upperparts and pale underparts with a buffish wash, particularly on breast and flanks. Legs are grey, grey bill is relatively short and stubby, and note the subtle grey patch on side of neck; the latter is a useful identification feature although not always easy to discern. **VOICE** Call is a sharp *chek-chek*. Song is rich and warbling; could be confused with that of Blackcap but is even more musical, some phrases having a thrush-like quality, often bubbling on uninterrupted for long periods. **HABITS** Typically unobtrusive and borderline shy. Usually feeds in, and sings from, deep cover. **STATUS AND HABITAT** Widespread and fairly common migrant summer breeder that winters in Africa. Around 170,000 pairs nest in the UK, favouring areas of deciduous woodland and mature scrub.

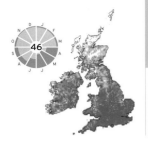

BLACKCAP

Sylvia atricapilla | BC | LENGTH 14–15cm

Well-marked and distinctive warbler with an engaging, musical song. Distinctive coloration makes it easy to identify in all plumages. Sexes are dissimilar.

distinct black cap

buffish brown back and wings

grey face

MALE

reddish-chestnut cap

FEMALE

Adult male has grey-brown upperparts and paler dusky-grey underparts, palest on throat and undertail. Has a pale eye-ring and diagnostic black cap. Adult female and juvenile have grey-brown upperparts, pale buffish-grey underparts (palest on throat and undertail) and a reddish-chestnut cap; note also the pale eye-ring. **VOICE** Utters a sharp *tchek* alarm call. Song is a rich and musical warble; it is similar to that of Garden Warbler but lacks the thrush-like tones, usually contains jaunty 'dancing' phrases, has discernible finish and doesn't bubble along. **HABITS** Usually feeds in cover but often sings from an exposed perch. **STATUS AND HABITAT** Mainly a migrant summer breeder. Around 1.1 million pairs nest in the UK, favouring a range of habitats, from deciduous woodland with dense undergrowth to areas of scrub and mature gardens and parks. Also a passage migrant; the departure in autumn of breeding birds often overlaps with the arrival of migrants from mainland Europe, around 1,000 of which winter here.

LESSER WHITETHROAT

Sylvia curruca | LW | LENGTH 12–13cm

**Small and relatively short-tailed *Sylvia* warbler.
Its habits are rather secretive, but fortunately
the distinctive song makes it easy to pinpoint
and identify. Sexes are similar.**

Adult and juvenile have a blue-grey crown, dark mask, and grey-brown on back and wings.
Underparts are pale, whitish on throat but washed with pale buff on flanks. Legs are dark
and grey bill is dark-tipped, and pale iris can sometimes be discerned. **VOICE** Utters a harsh
chek alarm call. Song comprises a distinctive tuneless rattle, sung on one note, and usually
preceded by a short warbling phrase. **HABITS** Usually keeps to dense cover and often scolds
intruders with its harsh call. **STATUS AND HABITAT** Migrant summer breeder that winters
in Africa and S Asia. Around 74,000 pairs nest in the UK, favouring areas of mature scrub
and hedgerows with dense ground cover. Seldom found in mature woodland. Also a passage
migrant in small numbers.

distinctive songster

pale iris is not always obvious

grey cap contrasts with white
throat and buffish-brown back

pale buff
wash to
flanks

WHITETHROAT

Sylvia communis | WH | LENGTH 13–15cm

Familiar warbler of open country. Males
in particular often perch conspicuously,
allowing good views to be obtained.
Sexes are separable with care.

Adult male has a blue-grey cap and face,
grey-brown back and obvious rufous-
brown edges to feathers on wings. Throat
is strikingly white, while remaining
underparts are pale but suffused with
pinkish buff, especially on breast. Legs
are yellowish brown and bill is yellowish
with a dark tip. Dark tail has white outer
feathers. Adult female and juvenile are
similar to adult male, but cap and face
are brownish and pale underparts (apart
from white throat) are suffused with pale
buff. **VOICE** Utters a harsh *check* alarm
call. Song, sung from an exposed perch
or in flight, is a rapid and scratchy warble
delivered in a distinct phrase. **HABITS**
Adopts a rather horizontal posture
when perched, sometimes with its tail elevated. **STATUS AND
HABITAT** Migrant summer breeder that winters in Africa.
A characteristic bird of overgrown hedgerows, heaths and
scrub-covered slopes by the sea. Around 1.1 million
pairs breed in the UK.

song is often
delivered in
flight

1ST-WINTER

brown iris is
emphasised
by white
eye-ring

rufous-brown feather edges

white
throat

pinkish-brown legs

DARTFORD WARBLER

Sylvia undata | DW | LENGTH 12–13cm

Perky little warbler that frequently cocks its long tail up at an angle. Sexes are dissimilar.

Adult male has blue–grey upperparts and reddish underparts with a white belly. Note the small white spots on throat, beady red eye and reddish eye-ring, and pinkish-yellow legs. Adult female is similar but colours are duller and throat in particular is rather uniformly pale. Juvenile is similar to adult female but colours are even more subdued, with back and wings appearing brownish. Long tail is obvious in flight. **VOICE** Distinctive *tchrr-tche* call is often the first clue to the species' presence in an area. Song is a rapid, scratchy warble. **HABITS** Occasionally perches conspicuously on prominent gorse stems, but is usually skulking and rather secretive. **STATUS AND HABITAT** Local resident breeder, associated with heathland, particularly where mature gorse bushes are at least 1m tall. Resident year-round in some areas but in winter many birds move to the coast. Numbers vary from year to year (mortality is high in cold winters), with around 3,200 pairs nesting in the UK in a good year.

WINTER

long tail is often cocked up

WINTER

short, rounded wings

MALE, SUMMER

needle-like bill

singing birds sometimes perch in the open

GRASSHOPPER WARBLER

Locustella naevia | GH | LENGTH 13cm

Skulking and unobtrusive warbler that is heard far more frequently than it is seen. Sexes are similar.

well-marked brown
upperparts

most vocal at dusk
or after dark

adept at creeping
through wetland
vegetation

very long undertail
coverts that are streaked

Adult has streaked olive-brown upperparts; underparts are paler but flushed buffish brown on breast. Has long undertail coverts (extending well beyond primary tips on folded wing), characteristic of members of the genus *Locustella*; these are adorned with dark streaks. Juvenile is similar but underparts are usually tinged with a more intense yellow-buff suffusion. **VOICE** Utters a sharp *tssvet* call. Song is reeling and sung continuously for minutes on end; some liken it to the 'song' of a bush-cricket, while to others it is mechanical-sounding. Sings mainly at night. **HABITS** Can look rather mouse-like as it creeps its way through vegetation. **STATUS AND HABITAT** Summer migrant breeder that winters in Africa and S Asia; usually associated with damp, rank grassland with Bramble (*Rubus fruticosus*) patches and clumps of rushes. Around 13,000 pairs breed in the UK.

SEDGE WARBLER

Acrocephalus schoenobaenus | SW | LENGTH 12–13cm

Well-marked wetland warbler whose lively and distinctive
song is a useful aid to identification. Sexes are similar.

striking head pattern contrasts
with that of Reed Warbler which
is rather plain and unmarked

song is sometimes
delivered in flight

warm brown rump

Adult has dark-streaked sandy-brown upperparts and pale underparts that are flushed
orange-buff on breast and flanks. Head is marked with a dark-streaked crown, striking
pale supercilium and dark eye-stripe. Juvenile is similar but faint streaking can usually be
discerned on breast. **VOICE** Utters a sharp *chek* alarm call. Song comprises a series of rasping
and grating phrases interspersed with trills and whistles. **HABITS** Often sings from an
exposed perch or bush, sometimes in flight. **STATUS AND HABITAT** Widespread migrant
summer breeder that winters in Africa; around 260,000 pairs nest in the UK. Favoured habitats
include rank marshy vegetation, patches of scrub on fringes of reedbeds, and overgrown
ditches choked with vegetation. Also seen as a passage migrant in spring and autumn.

REED WARBLER

Acrocephalus scirpaceus | RW | LENGTH 13–14cm

Familiar wetland warbler. Has rather nondescript brown plumage but its song is distinctive enough to allow identification even when the bird itself cannot be seen. Sexes are similar.

Adult has sandy-brown upperparts with a noticeable reddish-brown flush to rump. Underparts are pale with a buffish flush to flanks. Legs are dark and bill is thin and needle-like. Has a hint of a pale supercilium and eye-ring. Juvenile is similar but upperparts are warmer brown and underparts are more intensely flushed buff. **VOICE** Utters a sharp *tche* call. Rhythmic song contains grating and chattering phrases, some of which are repeated 2 or 3 times, plus some elements of mimicry. Very much the rhythm and blues player to Sedge Warbler's jazz musician! **HABITS** Often works its clambering way up reed stems to view human intruders on its territory. Its woven cup-shaped nest is attached to upright reed stems; the species is a favourite host for the Cuckoo. **STATUS AND HABITAT** Locally common migrant summer breeder that winters in Africa; around 130,000 pairs nest in the UK. The species is restricted to reedbeds.

very subtle eye-ring and supercilium

overall, plumage is rather plain sandy-brown

slender, needle-like bill

subtle buffish-brown flush to flanks

long undertail coverts

PASSERINES

NUTHATCH

Sitta europaea | NH | LENGTH 14cm

Dumpy, short-tailed woodland bird. Often descends tree trunks head downwards in a jerky manner (the only species able to do this). Sexes are rather similar.

black stripe through eye

broad, rounded wings

very vocal, especially in spring

Adult has blue-grey upperparts, a black eye-stripe, white cheeks and orange-buff underparts; on average, males have a more intense reddish-buff flush to rear of flanks than females. Juvenile is similar to adult female but colours and eye-stripe are less intense. **VOICE** Utters an insistent and loud *zwiit*, repeated regularly if bird is agitated. Song typically comprises a series of loud *pee-pee-pee* notes. **HABITS** Chisel-like bill is used to prise insects from tree bark and to hammer open acorns wedged into bark crevices. Nests are made in tree-holes and typically mud is plastered around the entrance to reduce the size of the hole. **STATUS AND HABITAT** Resident breeder associated with deciduous and mixed woodland; also occurs in gardens and parks with mature trees. Around 220,000 pairs nest in the UK.

chisel-like bill

able to climb vertically down tree trunks

TREECREEPER

Certhia familiaris | TC | LENGTH 12–13cm

Unobtrusive little woodland bird. Easily overlooked as it creeps up tree trunks, probing bark for insects and spiders with its needle-like bill; overall, it can look almost mouse-like. Sexes are similar.

Adult and juvenile have streaked brown upperparts and silvery-white underparts subtly suffused with buff towards rear of flanks. Has a downcurved needle-like bill, grubby whitish supercilium and broad zigzag buffish barring on wings. **VOICE** Utters a thin, high-pitched *tseert* call. Short song comprises a series of high-pitched notes and ends in a trill. **HABITS** Spiky tail is used as a support when climbing. Typically feeds by spiralling around and up a tree trunk, then dropping down to the base of an adjacent tree to repeat the process. Nests are usually constructed in crevices in and behind tree bark. **STATUS AND HABITAT** Resident breeder favouring deciduous and mixed woodlands. Around 180,000 pairs nest in the UK.

downcurved, needle-like bill

creeps up tree trunks

streaked brown upperparts are a match for tree bark

tail feathers are used as props when climbing

WAXWING

Bombycilla garrulus | WX | LENGTH 18cm

**Distinctive and much-admired winter visitor.
In flight, its silhouette is rather Starling-like.
Sexes are subtly dissimilar.**

crest can be
raised or
lowered

1ST-WINTER

outline in flight
recalls that of
Starling

Adult male has mainly pinkish-buff plumage that is palest on belly. Has a crest, black throat and black mask through eye. Rump is grey, undertail is chestnut and dark tail has a broad yellow tip. Wings have white and yellow margins, and red, wax-like projections. In the adult female, the yellow tip to tail is narrower. In 1st-winter birds, white margins to flight feathers are absent, as are the red, wax-like projections. **VOICE** Utters a trilling call. **HABITS** Migrants to Britain are often remarkably indifferent to human observers, allowing superb views to be obtained. Usually seen in small flocks. **STATUS AND HABITAT** Migrant winter visitor from breeding grounds in N mainland Europe. Numbers vary from year to year. In most seasons, several hundred spend the winter here, but if the berry crop fails in NE Europe then the influx may involve thousands of birds. By late winter, most end up visiting berry-bearing trees in suburban areas.

pinkish-buff
plumage

colourful and
diagnostic wing
markings

yellow tip
to tail

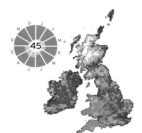

STARLING

Sturnus vulgaris | SG | LENGTH 20–22cm

Familiar bird of urban and rural areas. Extremely vocal and mimics both animate and inanimate sounds. Sexes are separable with care in summer.

rather plain and unmarked brown plumage

JUVENILE

Summer adult (both sexes) has dark plumage with an oily sheen, reddish legs and a yellow bill; base of lower mandible is blue in male; female has a few pale spots on underparts. Winter adult (both sexes) has numerous white spots adorning the dark plumage; bill is dark. Juvenile is grey-brown; bill is dark. 1st-winter bird retains grey-brown head and neck but acquires white-spotted dark plumage elsewhere. In flight, wings look triangular. **VOICE** Utters various clicks and whistles. Song includes mimicry of other birds and man-made sounds. **HABITS** Walks with a swagger. Feeds in grassland. Forms large flocks outside breeding season. **STATUS AND HABITAT** Abundant resident breeder (suburban areas) and winter visitor (mainly farmland). Around 1.8 million pairs nest in the UK. Influxes from Europe can boost winter numbers to the tens of millions.

oily-looking sheen to plumage is seen in good light

SUMMER

usually seen in sizeable flocks outside the breeding season

white spots most obvious outside the breeding season

WINTER

RING OUZEL

Turdus torquatus | RZ | LENGTH 25–26cm

Distinctive upland counterpart of the Blackbird that is typically associated with wild and remote locations. Sexes are dissimilar.

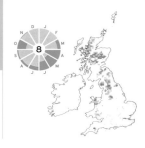

Adult male has mainly black plumage but with a striking white crescent on breast and pale fringes to wing feathers. Legs are dark, bill is yellowish and, at close range, pale fringes to feathers on dark underparts can be discerned. Adult female is similar but overall the dark elements of plumage are browner and pale crescent on breast is grubby white. In 1st-winter birds, plumage looks rather uniformly dark with pale feather fringes all over, and hint of adult's pale crescent on breast. In all birds in flight, pale fringes to wing feathers give the wings a silvery look. **VOICE** Utters a harsh *tchuck* alarm call. Song comprises short bursts of fluty phrases. **HABITS** Usually alert and wary on its breeding grounds, less so on migration. **STATUS AND HABITAT** Migrant summer breeder that favours rugged moorland habitats and lower mountain slopes; territories usually include rocky outcrops, used as lookouts for intruders. Around 6,900 pairs nest in the UK. Sometimes observed on migration, when most records are from coastal districts.

female's plumage is a browner version of the male

FEMALE

bold white crescent

pale feather edges create a scaly appearance

MALE

BLACKBIRD

Turdus merula | B. | LENGTH 25–28cm

Familiar and distinctive ground-dwelling thrush with a predilection for gardens and suburban locations. Sexes are dissimilar.

yellow bill

MALE

MALE

glossy black plumage

FEMALE

rather uniform brown plumage, subtly spotted on underparts

Adult male has uniformly blackish plumage. Legs are dark but bill and eye-ring are yellow. In the otherwise similar 1st-winter male, bill is dark and eye-ring is dull. Adult and 1st-winter females have brown plumage, darkest on wings and tail, and palest on throat and breast; breast is streaked. Juvenile is similar to adult female but back and underparts are marked with pale spots. **VOICE** Utters a harsh and repeated *tchak* alarm call, often at dusk or if it is disturbed by a prowling cat. Male is an excellent songster with a rich and varied repertoire. **HABITS** In urban settings, often indifferent to people and easy to observe. **STATUS AND HABITAT** Common resident breeder and migrant winter visitor. Favours a wide range of habitats, including gardens and parks, woodland and scrub, farmland, moors and coasts. Around 4.9 million pairs nest in the UK. Outside the breeding season, influxes from N mainland Europe can treble the population.

SONG THRUSH

Turdus philomelos | ST | LENGTH 23cm

Dainty, well-marked thrush whose beautiful and distinctive song contributes to its appeal. Sexes are similar.

orange-buff underwing coverts

Adult has warm brown upperparts with hint of an orange-buff wingbar. Underparts are pale but well marked with dark 'arrowhead' spots; note the yellowish-buff wash to breast. In flight, orange-buff underwing coverts are a clue to its identity. Juvenile is similar but markings and colours are less intense. **VOICE** Utters a thin *tik* call in flight. Song is loud and musical, and comprises phrases that are repeated 2 or 3 times. **HABITS** Feeds mainly on soil invertebrates. Also well known for smashing snails on regularly used 'anvils'. **STATUS AND HABITAT** Resident breeder and migrant visitor. Favours habitats with a mosaic of open ground and dense vegetation, plus trees and shrubs: woodland, parks and mature gardens are ideal. Around 1.1 million pairs nest in the UK. Outside the breeding season, many birds from N Britain move south and some migrate to the Continent. Overall, however, the winter population is boosted by influxes from N mainland Europe.

arrowhead-shaped dark spots on underparts

yellowish-buff wash to breast

as well as being smaller, body is much slimmer than rather pot-bellied Mistle Thrush

MISTLE THRUSH

Turdus viscivorus | M. | LENGTH 27cm

Appreciably larger than Song Thrush. Has a loud and distinctive call and song. Sexes are similar.

white underwing coverts

Adult has grey-brown upperparts with hint of a white wingbar. Underparts are pale but marked with large round dark spots, and flanks are washed orange-buff. In flight, note the white underwings and white tips to outer-tail feathers. Juvenile recalls an adult but back has teardrop-shaped white spots. **VOICE** Utters a loud and distinctive rattling alarm call. Its loud song is Blackbird-like but contains brief phrases and long pauses. **HABITS** Often sings in dull weather, even when it is raining. **STATUS AND HABITAT** Resident breeder and migrant visitor that favours areas of open woodland, parks and mature gardens. Around 160,000 pairs nest in the UK. Outside the breeding season, many northern and upland districts are vacated and some birds migrate to the Continent. However, the overall winter population is boosted by influxes from N mainland Europe.

subtle white wingbar

compared to a Song Thrush, dark spots on underparts are rounded, not arrowhead-shaped

FIELDFARE

Turdus pilaris | FF | LENGTH 24–26cm

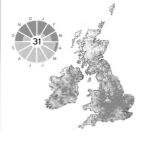

Large, plump thrush. Typically encountered in sizeable winter flocks, often with Redwings. Sexes are similar.

white underwing coverts

Adult has a blue-grey head with a pale supercilium, and a chestnut back. Breast and flanks are washed with orange-yellow and heavily spotted, while rest of underparts are whitish. In flight, note the pale grey rump and white underwings. Juvenile is similar but has pale spots on wing coverts. **VOICE** Utters a harsh *chack-chack-chack* call; night-migrating flocks can be detected by these calls. Song (seldom heard here) comprises short bursts of subdued fluty phrases. **HABITS** Recent arrivals often congregate where berries and fallen fruit are in good supply. Thereafter, flocks are usually nomadic. **STATUS AND HABITAT** Common non-breeding visitor. Numbers vary from year to year, but around 700,000 are usually present in the UK from Oct to Mar. Small numbers (a dozen or so pairs) usually nest here each year.

breast in particular is flushed orange-yellow, more so in some birds than others

grey rump

beautifully patterned underparts

REDWING

Turdus iliacus | RE | LENGTH 20–22cm

Well-marked and attractive thrush that forms winter flocks and often associates with Fieldfares. Sexes are similar.

Adult has grey-brown upperparts and pale underparts that are neatly dark-spotted and flushed with orange-red on flanks and underwings. Has prominent white stripes above eye and below cheeks. Juvenile is similar but with pale spots on upperparts and subdued colours on flanks. **VOICE** Utters a thin, high-pitched *tseerp* in flight; often heard on autumn nights as migrating flocks pass overhead. Song (seldom heard here) comprises short bursts of whistling and fluty phrases. **HABITS** Flocks are usually nomadic and seldom stay put for more than a few days. **STATUS AND HABITAT** Common winter visitor in variable numbers; in most years a million or so birds are present in the UK. Favours open countryside, but also suburban gardens and parks in harsh weather. Feeds on berries and fallen fruit while supplies last; also forages for soil and leaf-litter invertebrates. Several dozen pairs usually nest here, mainly in open woodland in NW Scotland.

bold facial markings

orange-red underwing coverts

orange-red flanks

SPOTTED FLYCATCHER

Muscicapa striata | SF | LENGTH 14cm

**Perky little bird with rather
undistinguished plumage.
Perched birds adopt an upright
posture. Sexes are similar.**

subtle
streaking
on breast

Adult has grey-brown upperparts that are streaked
on the crown, and pale greyish-white underparts
that are heavily streaked on the breast. Juvenile is
similar but has pale spots on back and dark spots on
throat and breast. **VOICE** Utters a thin, buzzy *tsee*
call. Song is simple and includes thin, call-like notes.
HABITS Uses regular perches from which to make
insect-catching aerial sorties, during which it looks
long-winged. Becomes remarkably unobtrusive when
nesting and easily overlooked at this time. **STATUS
AND HABITAT** Migrant summer breeder that
winters in Africa. Numbers have declined in recent
years but around 30,000 pairs still nest in the UK,
favouring open woodland with sunny clearings, and
parks and gardens; often nests around
habitation. Also seen
at coastal migration
hotspots in
spring and
autumn.

JUVENILE

subtle streaking
on crown

rather nondescript
grey-brown upperparts

perches for
extended periods
before making aerial
sorties after insects

PIED FLYCATCHER

Ficedula hypoleuca | PF | LENGTH 12–13cm

Well-marked and distinctive insect-catching bird with very precise habitat requirements. Sexes are dissimilar.

Summer adult male has black upperparts, white underparts and a bold white band on the black wings; note the small white patch at base of bill. Autumn adult male, adult female (at all times) and 1st-winter birds have a similar pattern to summer adult male but the black elements of the plumage are replaced by brown. **VOICE** Utters a sharp *plit* call repeatedly when alarmed. Song is sweet and ringing. **HABITS** Forages and performs fly-catching aerial sorties in the tree canopy. Readily takes to the provision of nest boxes. **STATUS AND HABITAT** Local migrant summer breeder that winters in Africa. Around 19,000 pairs nest in the UK each year. Hillsides cloaked in Sessile Oak (*Quercus petraeus*) woodland are favoured; this preference is reflected in the species' westerly breeding range.

JUVENILE

striking white markings on wings

unobtrusive when perched in tree foliage

FEMALE

1ST-WINTER

MALE

bold black and white plumage

DIPPER

Cinclus cinclus | DI | LENGTH 18cm

13

Dumpy bird that is invariably associated with water. At a distance, and in harsh light, it can look black and white. Sexes are similar.

DARK-BELLIED RACE

always found near water

uniformly dark belly

Adult ssp. *gularis* (seen here) is dark grey-brown on wings, back and tail. Head is reddish brown, and throat and breast are white, appearing like a bib. Belly grades from reddish chestnut at front to blackish brown at rear. Legs and feet are stout and powerful. Juvenile has the proportions of an adult, but upperparts are greyish while underparts are pale but heavily barred everywhere except on throat. **VOICE** Utters a shrill *striitz* call. **HABITS** Usually seen perched on boulders in fast-flowing streams and rivers, or flying on whirring wingbeats low over water. Submerges readily, swimming underwater and walking on the bottom while searching for invertebrates. **STATUS AND HABITAT** Resident breeder, associated with fast-flowing streams and rivers (also favoured by Grey Wagtail) where caddisfly larvae and mayfly nymphs are common. Around 11,000 pairs nest in the UK. Very occasionally, a mainland European Dipper turns up in winter; this subspecies is recognised by its uniformly dark brown belly.

white throat and belly are often obvious at a distance, even in dull light

compact body shape

scaly appearance to feathers on back

JUVENILE

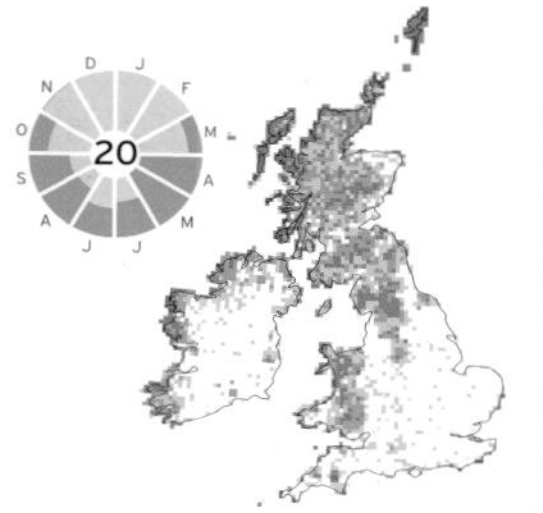

WHEATEAR

Oenanthe oenanthe | W. | LENGTH 14–16cm

A bird of open country. In flight, all birds show a
white rump and inverted black 'T' marking
on the otherwise white tail. In other
plumage respects, sexes are dissimilar.

white rump
and sides
to tail

plumage is usually
uniform buffish
brown

JUVENILE

Adult male has a blue-grey crown and back, black mask and wings, and pale underparts with
an orange-buff wash on breast. Has a white supercilium; legs and bill are dark. Adult female
is mainly grey-brown above, darkest on wings. Face, throat and breast are
pale orange-buff and underparts are otherwise whitish. Note the pale
supercilium. In 1st-winter, upperparts are grey-brown to buffish brown,
underparts are pale, and face, throat and flanks have a buffish–orange
wash. In the Greenland race (ssp. *leucorhoa*, seen here on migration),
orange-buff suffusion is more extensive and intense. **VOICE** Utters
a sharp and distinctive *chak* alarm call, like 2 pebbles being knocked
together. Song is fast and warbling. **HABITS** Perches prominently
on boulders or fenceposts, often adopting an upright posture and
bobbing up and down when agitated. **STATUS AND HABITAT**
Migrant summer breeder, typically
associated with short, grazed
turf and open moors. Around
230,000 pairs nest in the
UK. Also seen on
migration in
spring and
autumn.

black 'mask' and
white supercilium
are striking

MALE

often adopts
an upright
stance when
perched

FEMALE

dark legs

ROBIN

Erithacus rubecula | R. | LENGTH 13–14cm

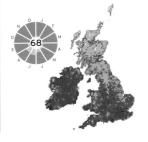

One of the nation's favourite birds. Often
bold in garden settings but usually more
shy in the countryside. Sexes are similar.

numerous pale spots

Adult is almost unmistakable, with its striking orange-red face, throat and
breast, bordered by blue-grey to the sides and with a sharp demarcation
from white belly. Upperparts are buffish brown with a faint buff wingbar.
Juvenile has brown upperparts, marked with pale buff
spots and teardrop-shaped streaks; pale buff underparts
have darker spots and crescent-shaped markings. **VOICE**
Most vocal in spring but its rather plaintive, melancholy
song can be heard in almost any month. Alarm call
is a sharp *tic*. **HABITS** Strongly and conspicuously
territorial and notoriously aggressive towards rival
intruders. **STATUS AND HABITAT** Widespread
resident breeder, with around
6 million pairs nesting in
the UK. Migrants from
mainland Europe pass
through in the autumn
and some remain here
in winter.

JUVENILE

**orange-red face,
throat and breast
are diagnostic**

**bold and perky bird that
often becomes tame
in garden settings**

NIGHTINGALE

Luscinia megarhynchos | N. | LENGTH 16–17cm

Rather secretive bird. Best known for its powerful, musical song, delivered both by day and at night. Sexes are similar.

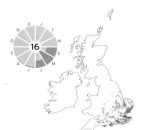

Adult and juvenile have rich-brown upperparts overall; tail and rump are warmer reddish chestnut than back, and note the hint of grey on face and sides of neck. Underparts are a rather uniform greyish white, suffused with pale buffish brown on breast. **VOICE** Song is rich and varied, and includes fluty whistles and clicking sounds; typically starts with a rich, whistling *tu-tu-tu-tu*, before embarking on its more complex repertoire. Call is a frog-like croak. **HABITS** Usually unobtrusive and keeps to deep cover; silent birds are easily overlooked. **STATUS AND HABITAT** Migrant summer breeder that winters in Africa; around 6,700 pairs nest in the UK. Favours scrub, overgrown hedgerows and coppiced woodland with dense undergrowth.

usually sings from cover, and often at night

plumage is rather nondescript but song is rich and easily recognised

reddish-brown rump and tail

PASSERINES

BLACK REDSTART

Phoenicurus ochruros | BX | LENGTH 14cm

Bold, perky bird that often perches conspicuously, quivering its striking red tail. Sexes are dissimilar.

1ST-WINTER

uniform grey-brown plumage

striking red tail is a feature shared with Redstart

Adult male has mainly slate-grey body plumage that is darkest (almost black in spring) on face and breast. Also has a white wing patch and whitish lower belly; legs and bill are dark. Adult female and immature birds have rather uniform grey-brown body plumage, darkest on wings and palest on lower belly. Pale eye-ring emphasises the dark eye. **VOICE** Utters a whistling *svit*, or *svit-it-it* call. Song comprises various whistles and curious crackling, static-like phrases. **HABITS** Some individuals can be remarkably confiding. **STATUS AND HABITAT** Scarce breeder; around 30 pairs nest in the UK, favouring industrial and urban locations. More numerous as a passage migrant. Some autumn migrants remain, boosting the winter population to around 400 individuals between Oct and Mar; most favour coastal sites.

white wing patch

MALE

the only red-tailed songbird likely to be seen here in winter

REDSTART

Phoenicurus phoenicurus | RT | LENGTH 14cm

Robin-sized bird, the males of which are particularly striking. In all plumages, note the distinctive dark-centred red tail. Sexes are dissimilar.

FEMALE

always shows an orange flush to underparts

MALE, 1ST-WINTER

Adult male has a grey back, nape and crown, black face and throat, and orange-red underparts that are most colourful on breast. Has a white forehead and supercilium; legs and bill are dark. Adult female has grey-brown upperparts and head, and an orange wash to rather pale underparts. Plumage of 1st-winter birds recalls their respective adults, but pale feather fringes make markings less distinct and colours duller; underparts appear barred or scaly. **VOICE** Utters a soft *huiit-tut-tut* call and a sharp ticking when alarmed. Song is tuneful but melancholy. **HABITS** Perched birds continually pump their tail up and down. Nests in holes in gnarled trees, in stone walls and in nest boxes. **STATUS AND HABITAT** Summer migrant breeder; around 100,000 pairs nest in the UK. Favours open woodland (particularly Sessile Oak, *Quercus petraeus*) with scattered mature trees and short ground vegetation.

black face and white supercilium

colourful red tail shows up well in flight

MALE

MALE

rich orange-red underparts

WHINCHAT

Saxicola rubetra | WC | LENGTH 12–14cm

Superficially similar to Stonechat but separable on plumage details. Male in particular is strikingly marked and colourful. Sexes are dissimilar.

MALE

MALE

orange flush to breast

often perches prominently on vegetation

Adult male has streaked brown upperparts with a striking white supercilium. Margins of throat and dark ear coverts are defined by a pale stripe but throat itself, along with breast, are orange; underparts are otherwise whitish. Bill and legs are dark. Adult female's plumage pattern is similar but colours and contrast are less intense; supercilium is grubby white and breast is only subtly flushed with orange. Plumage of 1st-winter is similar to adult female but upperparts appear more spotted. In all birds, short tail is mainly dark but sides to tail base are whitish. **VOICE** Utters a whistling *whi-tuc* alarm call. Song is rapid and warbling. **HABITS** Often perches on fencelines. **STATUS AND HABITAT** Migrant summer breeder that favours rough grassy slopes with scattered scrub. Around 47,000 pairs nest in the UK. Also seen on migration, especially on coasts.

bold pale supercilium

FEMALE

1ST-WINTER

STONECHAT

Saxicola rubicola | SC | LENGTH 12–13cm

Small, compact bird with a relatively short, dark tail. When perched, frequently flicks its tail while uttering a harsh alarm call. Sexes are dissimilar.

Adult male has a blackish head, white on side of neck, and a dark back. Breast is orange-red, grading into pale underparts. Bill and legs are dark and brown rump appears spotted or streaked. In autumn, pale feather fringes make head appear paler; these wear away during the winter months. Adult female recalls adult male but colours are muted; in particular, head and back are uniformly streaked brown and pale patch on side of neck appears grubby. In 1st-winter, upperparts and head are streaked sandy brown, and underparts are buffish orange. **VOICE** Utters a harsh *tchak* call, like 2 pebbles being knocked together. Rapid, warbling song is rather Whitethroat-like. **HABITS** Often perches on sprays of gorse or fencelines. **STATUS AND HABITAT** Locally common resident breeder, favouring heaths and commons, and scrub-covered coastal slopes. Around 56,000 pairs nest in the UK. Many adults are year-round residents of suitable territories (except in severe winters); 1st-winter birds often disperse in autumn and concentrate around coasts.

MALE, WINTER

compared to female
Whinchat, face is plain

MALE

MALE

FEMALE

territorial
males perch
on prominent
pieces of
vegetation

HOUSE SPARROW

Passer domesticus | HS | LENGTH 14–15cm

Widespread species with an affinity for human habitation. When fed in urban parks, it becomes tame, sometimes taking food from the hand. Sexes are dissimilar.

**grey cap
(chestnut in Tree Sparrow)**

MALE, WINTER

grey-brown rump

bold wingbars

greyish-white flanks

MALE, SUMMER

FEMALE

**rather nondescript head markings
except for pale buff supercilium**

Adult male has a grey crown, cheeks and rump. Nape, sides of crown, back and wings are chestnut brown, underparts are pale grey, and throat and breast are black. Bill is dark and legs are reddish. In winter, pale feather tips make colours appear less intense; bill is paler. Adult female has mainly brown upperparts, including crown; back is streaked with buff. Underparts are pale grey and has a pale buff supercilium behind eye. Juvenile is similar to adult female but plumage pattern is less distinct. **VOICE** Utters a range of chirping calls. **HABITS** Frequently dust-bathes. Small groups are often seen sitting on roofs, uttering familiar sparrow chirps. **STATUS AND HABITAT** Widespread resident breeder that favours villages, towns and farms. Around 5.1 million pairs nest in the UK, using roof spaces, holes in walls and other cavities.

TREE SPARROW

Passer montanus | TS | LENGTH 13–14cm

Well-marked bird and a more rural counterpart
of House Sparrow; sometimes occurs alongside
that species. Sexes
are similar.

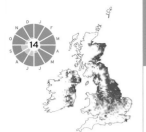

Adult has a chestnut cap, striking black
patch on otherwise whitish cheeks, and
a black bib. Underparts are greyish white,
and back and wings are streaked brown;
has striking white wingbars. Juvenile
is similar but facial markings are duller,
darker and less distinct. **VOICE** Utters House
Sparrow-like chirps, but also a sharp *tik-tik* in flight.
HABITS Outside the breeding season, forms flocks
and sometimes feeds alongside buntings and finches
in fields. Nests in tree-holes and readily uses nest
boxes. **STATUS AND HABITAT** Local resident
breeder; numbers have declined catastrophically
in recent years. Around 180,000 pairs nest in the
UK now. Occasionally found on outskirts of villages
but more usually associated with untidy arable farms,
feeding on grain spills.

white wingbars

chestnut crown
and black patch on
cheeks allow easy
separation from
House Sparrow

unlike House Sparrow,
sexes are similar

buffish wash on flanks

PASSERINES

DUNNOCK

Prunella modularis | D. | LENGTH 13–14cm

Sparrow-like bird but with a thin, warbler-like bill. Generally rather skulking but males are comparatively bold in spring. Sexes are similar.

narrow, pointed bill

streaked flanks

warbler-like song is a harbinger of spring

chestnut-brown back

Adult shows heavy streaking on its chestnut-brown back. Underparts are mostly bluish grey but flanks are boldly streaked with brown and chestnut. Face is bluish grey with brown streaking on ear coverts and crown. Also has a faint, pale wingbar. Bill is needle-thin and dark, and legs are reddish pink. Juvenile is similar but with bolder streaking. **VOICE** Song is energetic and warbler-like; alarm call is a thin, piping *tseer*. **HABITS** The species' territorial and reproductive behaviour is complex. Usually sings from a prominent perch or highest tangle in a Bramble (*Rubus fruticosus*) patch, from early Mar onwards. Often flicks its wings. **STATUS AND HABITAT** Widespread resident breeder of woodlands, hedgerows, and gardens with dense cover. Around 2.3 million pairs nest in the UK.

PIED WAGTAIL

Motacilla alba yarrellii and **White Wagtail**
M. a. alba | PW | LENGTH 18cm

Pied Wagtail is a black, grey and white bird that
pumps its tail up and down. White Wagtail is seen
here on migration. Sexes are dissimilar.

Pied Wagtail summer adult male has mainly white underparts and black upperparts with
a white face and striking white wingbars. Legs and bill are dark and outer-tail feathers
are white. Winter adult male has a white throat and less extensive black on breast. Adult
female recalls adult male in appropriate season but back is dark grey, not black. Juvenile and
1st-winter birds have greyish upperparts with a black rump, whitish underparts, and a faint
yellowish wash on face. All ages show smoky grey flanks. White Wagtail is similar to Pied
in its various plumages except that back and rump are always grey, not black, and flanks are
cleaner white with only a small amount of grey. **VOICE** Utters a loud *chissick* call. **HABITS**
Flight is bounding. **STATUS AND HABITAT** Pied Wagtail is a resident breeder, with around
460,000 pairs nesting in the UK. It favours areas of short turf such as farmland, coastal
grassland, playing fields and car parks. In winter, birds from upland regions move south.
A few White Wagtails nest here in the north,
but it is better known as a widespread
passage migrant, mainly to western
coastal districts.

MALE, PIED

JUVENILE, PIED

white wingbars

MALE, WHITE

long tail

MALE, PIED

FEMALE

back is much
blacker than in
White wagtail

YELLOW WAGTAIL

Motacilla flava flavissima | YW | LENGTH 16–17cm

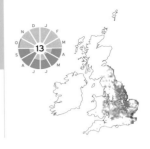

Delightful long-tailed bird. Searches
for insects on the ground, sometimes
feeding at the feet of grazing animals.
Sexes are dissimilar.

FEMALE   MALE

yellow elements of
plumage are much less
intense than in male

white outer-tail
feathers

Adult male has greenish-yellow upperparts and striking yellow underparts that extend to face; note the yellow supercilium, white outer-tail feathers and whitish wingbars. Adult female is similar but plumage is duller and yellow coloration less intense. Juvenile has olive-buff upperparts and pale underparts; note the whitish throat, yellow flush to undertail, white outer-tail feathers and pale wingbars. Legs are black in all ages. Blue-headed Wagtail *M. f. flava* (mainland Europe race) sometimes turns up here. Only the male is distinctive: similar to male Yellow Wagtail but with a bluish cap and ear coverts, and a white supercilium. **VOICE** Utters a distinctive *tsree-ee* call. **HABITS** Sometimes perches on barbed-wire fences in its favoured wetland habitats **STATUS AND HABITAT** Migrant summer breeder that favours water meadows and damp, grazed grassland; around 15,000 pairs nest in the UK. Also seen on migration, particularly in areas of short coastal grassland.

pale
wingbars

bright yellow plumage

MALE, SUMMER

GREY WAGTAIL

Motacilla cinerea | GL | LENGTH 18cm

Elegant bird with a strikingly long tail. Invariably
associated with flowing fresh water
and often perches on mid-stream
boulders. Sexes are dissimilar.

MALE, SUMMER

coloration is more lemon yellow than
Yellow Wagtail's egg-yolk yellow

striking black and
white facial markings

FEMALE

MALE

yellow rump
and white
outer-tail
feathers

Summer adult male has blue-grey upperparts and lemon-yellow
underparts. Black bib contrasts with white sub-moustachial
stripe and white supercilium. Bill is dark, legs are reddish and
outer-tail feathers are white. Summer adult female is similar but
bib is typically whitish and variably marked with grey, while underparts are paler with the
yellow coloration striking only on vent. Winter adults are similar to their respective summer
plumages but with white throats. Juvenile and 1st-winter birds resemble winter adult female.
VOICE Utters a sharp *tip-tip* call in flight. **HABITS** Tail is continually pumped up and down.
STATUS AND HABITAT Resident breeder that favours fast-flowing stony watercourses;
around 35,000 pairs nest in the UK. Outside the breeding season, some northern and upland
birds move south to lowland freshwater sites.

TREE PIPIT

Anthus trivialis | TP | LENGTH 15cm

Superficially similar to Meadow Pipit but separable with care using plumage details, voice and habitat preferences. Sexes are similar.

Adult has sandy-brown upperparts adorned with dark streaks. Underparts are pale, whitish and unmarked on throat and belly, but boldly streaked and flushed with yellow-buff on breast and flanks. Has a striking pale supercilium, pale spot on rear edge of ear coverts and dark sub-moustachial stripe. Legs are pinkish and outer-tail feathers are white. Juvenile is similar. In all ages has a short hind claw. **VOICE** Flight call is a buzzing *spzzzt*. Song (delivered in flight but starting from a tree perch) comprises an accelerating trill that ends with thin, drawn-out notes as the bird parachutes down, usually to a different tree-top perch. **HABITS** Spends more time perched in trees than other pipits. **STATUS AND HABITAT** Migrant summer breeder. Around 88,000 pairs nest in the UK, favouring open woodland with grassy clearings and heaths with scattered trees. Also seen on coasts on migration.

pale supercilium

song is typically given in flight, starting from, and ending on, a tree perch

pale wingbars

streaking and yellow-buff wash on breast and flanks

MEADOW PIPIT

Anthus pratensis | MP | LENGTH 14–15cm

Rather nondescript, streaked brown bird that is ground-dwelling and feeds on invertebrates. Sexes are similar.

coloration is usually warmer buff in autumn compared to spring

1ST-AUTUMN

subtle pale wingbars

Adult has streaked brown upperparts and pale underparts adorned with dark streaks; buffish-yellow flush to flanks and breast is particularly noticeable in autumn. Throat is pale and unmarked, and bird has a pale eye-ring, pale lores, hint of a short, pale supercilium and a buff sub-moustachial stripe. Legs are pinkish and outer-tail feathers are white. Juvenile is similar but streaking on underparts is less extensive. In all ages has a very long hind claw. **VOICE** Utters a *pseet-pseet-pseet* call and has a descending song delivered in flight, but that typically starts and ends on the ground. **HABITS** Often found in loose flocks both on migration and in winter. **STATUS AND HABITAT** Present year-round. During the breeding season, favours rough grassy habitats, from coastal meadows, heaths and downs to grassy moorland; around 1.9 million pairs nest in the UK. Outside the breeding season, most numerous in lowland areas and near coasts; passage migrants from N Europe boost numbers in autumn.

subtle pale wingbars

streaking on breast and flanks

SPRING

ROCK PIPIT

Anthus petrosus | RC | LENGTH 16–17cm

Bulky and rather dark pipit, invariably
found within sight of the sea.
Sexes are similar.

overall looks rather uniformly dark in flight

AUTUMN

Adult and juvenile have streaked, dark grey-brown upperparts and
rather grubby whitish underparts that are heavily streaked on
breast and flanks. Throat is pale and there is an indistinct pale
supercilium and eye-ring; note the indistinct sub-moustachial
stripe and dark malar. Legs and bill are dark, and outer-tail
feathers are greyish white. **VOICE** Utters a single *pseet*
call, and has a Meadow Pipit-like song that is delivered
in flight but starts and ends on a cliff-side rocky
outcrop. **HABITS** Outside the breeding season,
small groups often gather where feeding is
good. **STATUS AND HABITAT** Resident
breeder whose distribution is almost
exclusively coastal. During the breeding
season favours rocky coasts and cliffs;
around 34,000 pairs nest in the UK.
Outside the breeding season,
more widespread around
coasts and often found
feeding on beach
strandlines.

SPRING

rather
indistinct
pale wingbars

plumage colours and streaking
are more intense in breeding
season than at other times

greyish-white
outer-tail feathers

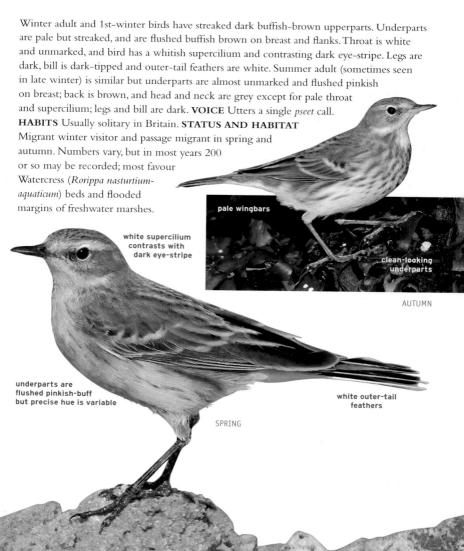

WATER PIPIT

Anthus spinoletta | WI | LENGTH 16–17cm

Bulky pipit that was formerly treated as a
race of Rock Pipit. Almost always associated
with freshwater habitats. Sexes are similar.

Winter adult and 1st-winter birds have streaked dark buffish-brown upperparts. Underparts
are pale but streaked, and are flushed buffish brown on breast and flanks. Throat is white
and unmarked, and bird has a whitish supercilium and contrasting dark eye-stripe. Legs are
dark, bill is dark-tipped and outer-tail feathers are white. Summer adult (sometimes seen
in late winter) is similar but underparts are almost unmarked and flushed pinkish
on breast; back is brown, and head and neck are grey except for pale throat
and supercilium; legs and bill are dark. **VOICE** Utters a single *pseet* call.
HABITS Usually solitary in Britain. **STATUS AND HABITAT**
Migrant winter visitor and passage migrant in spring and
autumn. Numbers vary, but in most years 200
or so may be recorded; most favour
Watercress (*Rorippa nasturtium-
aquaticum*) beds and flooded
margins of freshwater marshes.

pale wingbars

clean-looking
underparts

AUTUMN

white supercilium
contrasts with
dark eye-stripe

underparts are
flushed pinkish-buff
but precise hue is variable

white outer-tail
feathers

SPRING

CHAFFINCH

Fringilla coelebs | CH | LENGTH 15cm

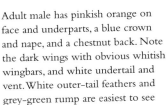

Common and widespread bird whose
song is a familiar sound in spring.
Sexes are dissimilar.

FEMALE

bold white wingbars

Adult male has pinkish orange on
face and underparts, a blue crown
and nape, and a chestnut back. Note
the dark wings with obvious whitish
wingbars, and white undertail and
vent. White outer-tail feathers and
grey-green rump are easiest to see
in flight. Colours are brightest in spring and early summer. Adult female and juvenile are
mainly buffish brown, palest on face and underparts; note the pale wingbars on otherwise
rather dark wings. **VOICE** Utters a distinct *pink pink* call. Song comprises a descending
trill with a characteristic final flourish. **HABITS** Outside the breeding season, forms flocks
and feeds mainly on seeds; while nesting, insects form a significant proportion of its diet.
STATUS AND HABITAT Present year-round in gardens, parks and woodlands; 5.8 million
pairs nest in the UK. Outside the breeding season, influxes from N mainland Europe boost
numbers, and winter flocks feed in open woodland and fields.

**extensive white on wings and tail
is revealed in flight**

**bill is blue in breeding
season, grey-brown
at other times**

MALE

MALE

**pinkish face,
throat and
breast**

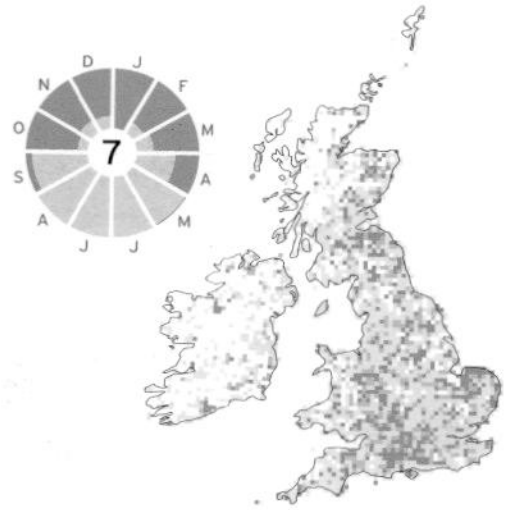

BRAMBLING

Fringilla montifringilla | BL | LENGTH 14–15cm

Distinctive finch, recognised in flight
by its white rump and absence of white
outer-tail feathers. Sexes are dissimilar.

pale face is framed
by dark lines

FEMALE, WINTER

Winter adult male has an orange
throat, breast and lesser wing coverts;
underparts are otherwise white with
dark spots on flanks. Head and back
are blackish; feathers have grey-
buff fringes that gradually wear off.
Wings are dark with pale feather
margins and striking whitish-orange
wingbars. Bill is yellow with a dark
tip. Summer adult male (occasionally
seen here) is similar but hood, back
and bill are blackish. Adult female is
similar to winter male but colours
are less intense, pale fringes obscure
dark feathers on back, and head is
pale grey-brown with dark lines on
sides of crown and nape. Juveniles are
similar to respective sex winter adults
but duller. **VOICE** Calls include a
harsh, nasal *jseeerrp*. Song (seldom heard here) comprises
a series of buzzing notes. **HABITS** Forages for
seeds on woodland floor; seeds of Beech (*Fagus
sylvatica*) are favoured. Winter flocks often
mix with Chaffinches. **STATUS AND
HABITAT** Occasionally nests here
but best known as a migrant
winter visitor in variable
numbers; typically around
285,000 birds are
present in winter
in the UK.

pale rump shows up well in flight,
even in distant flocks

head becomes blacker
through the winter as pale
feather tips wear away

yellowish
bill

orange tone
to coloration
is subtly different
from pinkish hue
of Chaffinch

bold wingbars, lower one
flushed with orange

MALE, WINTER

GREENFINCH

Chloris chloris | GR | LENGTH 14–15cm

Distinctive finch with a relatively large, conical pinkish bill. All birds show a yellowish patch on wings. Sexes are dissimilar.

overall yellowish green
with grey on cheeks
and wings

MALE

MALE

yellow sides
to base of tail

Adult male is yellowish green, darkest on back, and with grey areas on face, sides of neck and wings. Intensity of body colour increases throughout winter as pale feather fringes wear. Adult female is similar but colours are duller, and has faint streaking on back. Juvenile recalls adult female but back and pale underparts are obviously streaked. In all plumages, note the yellow bar on closed wing (wingbar in flight) and yellow sides to base of tail (brightest on adult male). **VOICE** Utters a sharp *jrrrup* call in flight. Song either comprises well-spaced wheezy *weeeish* phrases or a series of rapid, trilling whistles, sometimes delivered in flight. **HABITS** Wingbeats are exaggeratedly slow when bird is performing a song flight. **STATUS AND HABITAT** Resident breeder associated with parks, gardens and hedgerows; around 1.7 million pairs nest in the UK. Influxes from mainland Europe boost winter numbers, when flocks are also found in open country.

streaked
underparts

JUVENILE

compared to male, plumage is
less colourful and more streaked

FEMALE

GOLDFINCH

Carduelis carduelis | GO | LENGTH 12cm

Colourful bird whose combination of yellow wingbars and white rump (seen in all birds) is diagnostic. Sexes are similar.

Adult has a striking black and white pattern on head with a colourful red face. Back is buffish brown, and underparts are mainly whitish but suffused with pale buff on flanks and sides of breast. Wings are black with a yellow wingbar and white tips to flight feathers; also has white tips to black tail feathers. Conical bill is relatively long and pale pinkish buff. Juvenile is mainly buffish white, streaked brown on flanks, back and head. **VOICE** Utters a tinkling, trisyllabic call. Song is twittering and rapid, containing call-like elements. **HABITS** Forms flocks outside the breeding season. Often feeds on seeds of Wild Teasel (*Dipsacus fullonum*) and thistles. **STATUS AND HABITAT** Resident breeder; around 1.2 million pairs nest in the UK, favouring scrub, deciduous woodland margins and mature gardens. Outside the breeding season, flocks favour wayside ground and field margins. Most of our Goldfinches move south in autumn; many winter in mainland Europe, returning in Feb and Mar.

narrowly pointed conical bill, ideally suited to extracting seeds from Teasel heads

colourful facial markings are diagnostic

unmarked face

JUVENILE

yellow wingbar

white feather tips

LINNET

Linaria cannabina | LI | LENGTH 13–14cm

Delightful little finch of wayside habitats. Summer male
is colourful but in other plumages the bird is rather
nondescript. All birds have a grey bill
but otherwise sexes are dissimilar.

JUVENILE

streaked throat and breast

**white patch on
wings is seen in flight**

Summer adult male has a grey head with a rosy-pink forecrown, and a chestnut back. Pale
underparts are flushed rosy pink on breast. Has a whitish patch on wings, pale sides to forked
tail, and a streaked throat. Winter adult male is similar but rosy-pink elements of plumage are
dull and brownish or obscured by pale feather tips. Adult female has a brown back, grey-brown
head and pale underparts that are streaked and spotted, a grey-buff flush on breast, and a
whitish patch on wings. Juvenile is similar to adult female but duller and more
streaked. **VOICE** Utters a distinctive *tetter-tett* call. Male's twittering, warbling
song is usually delivered from a prominent perch. **HABITS** Outside the
breeding season, forms flocks that mix with other finch species and
buntings. **STATUS AND HABITAT** Resident breeder;
around 410,000 pairs nest in the UK, favouring scrub
and hedgerows, and mature gorse patches on heaths and
near coasts. At other times, forms loose flocks that
feed on weedy wayside ground and in
ploughed and stubble fields.

**pink
forecrown**

**chestnut
back**

**greyish bill seen
at all times**

FEMALE

**male is particularly colourful
in breeding season**

MALE

TWITE

Linaria flavirostris | TW | LENGTH 13–14cm

Dumpy-bodied little finch. In many ways the northern and upland counterpart of Linnet; useful features for separation include bill colour (grey in summer, yellow in winter) and unstreaked throat. Sexes are subtly dissimilar.

subtly pink rump is only seen in males, and best appreciated in flight

Summer adult male has dark-streaked brown upperparts, a pinkish rump (not always easy to see), and white margins to flight and tail feathers. Pale underparts are heavily streaked, especially on breast and flanks; face and throat are buffish brown.

Winter adult male is similar but has subdued markings, and head and breast are warm buffish brown. Adult female and juvenile are similar to winter male, although rump is brown, not pink. All ages are told from Linnet by lack of spotting and streaking on unmarked buff throat. **VOICE** Utters a characteristic, sharp, nasal, twanging *tveeht* call. Song comprises a series of trilling and rattling notes. **HABITS** Forms flocks outside the breeding season. **STATUS AND HABITAT** Upland and northern breeder, favouring heather moorland and coastal and island grassland; around 10,000 pairs nest in the UK. Outside the breeding season, found on saltmarshes and coastal fields. Its range extends south in winter, when influxes from N mainland Europe boost numbers.

yellow bill

FEMALE

MALE

pinkish rump

SISKIN

Spinus spinus | SK | LENGTH 11–12cm

Charming little finch, recognised in all plumages by its broad yellowish wingbar, yellow rump and yellow sides to tail, these features most obvious in flight. Sexes are separable with care.

bright yellow wingbars

JUVENILE   MALE, AUTUMN

MALE

streaked flanks

Adult male has striking yellowish-green upperparts, with streaking on back, and a black cap and bib. Breast is flushed yellow-green but underparts are otherwise whitish with bold streaking on flanks. Note the dark wings, yellow wingbars, yellow rump and yellow triangles at base of tail. Adult female is similar but with duller colours; head is rather uniform, and it lacks male's black cap and bib. Juvenile is mainly streaked grey-brown, palest on head and underparts; wing and tail patterns are similar to those of adults. **VOICE** Utters disyllabic whistling or twittering *speeoo* calls. Song comprises a series of twittering, almost warbling, phrases. **HABITS** Outside the breeding season, forms flocks that feed acrobatically on tree seeds. **STATUS AND HABITAT** Resident breeder; around 410,000 pairs nest in the UK, mainly in conifer woodlands and mature gardens. More widespread in winter, favouring Alder (*Alnus glutinosa*) and birch woodlands; numbers are boosted by influxes from mainland Europe.

rather narrow, conical bill

black cap, and other dark elements of plumage, are most intense in breeding season

bright yellow plumage overall

MALE, SPRING

BULLFINCH

Pyrrhula pyrrhula | BF | LENGTH 16–17cm

Attractive but unobtrusive finch. Its soft but distinctive call is heard more frequently than the bird itself is seen. All birds reveal a white rump as they fly away. Sexes are separable.

Adult male has a deep rosy-pink face, breast and belly. Back and nape are blue-grey, and cap and tail are black. Has a white wingbar on otherwise black wings. Bill is stubby and dark. Adult female is similar, but rosy-pink elements of plumage are dull buffish pink. Juvenile is similar to adult female but head is uniformly buffish brown. **VOICE** Utters a distinctive monosyllabic soft, piping *pew* call, sometimes delivered in a duet by a pair. The quiet song, which is seldom heard, comprises slow, fluty notes. **HABITS** Rather secretive. Often encountered in pairs. **STATUS AND HABITAT** Resident breeder, found in woodlands, hedgerows and mature gardens. Around 190,000 pairs nest in the UK.

FEMALE

muted colours compared to male

stubby bill

black cap

MALE

white rump

MALE

rosy-pink is distinctive, the colour subtly different from that seen in any other British bird

PASSERINES

LESSER REDPOLL

Acanthis cabaret | LR | LENGTH 12–14cm

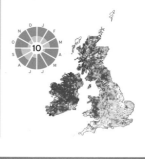

conical yellow bill

Well-marked little finch whose bill is yellow and conical. Sexes are subtly dissimilar.

MALE

streaked underparts

red forecrown

pale wingbars

FEMALE

forked tail

Adult male has heavily streaked grey-brown upperparts that are darkest on back. Underparts are pale but also heavily streaked. Has a red forecrown, black bib and lores, white wingbar, and pale, streaked rump; usually shows a pinkish-red flush to breast. Adult female and immatures are similar to adult male but lack the pinkish flush to breast. In all ages has well-marked, dark-streaked undertail coverts. **VOICE** Utters a rattling *chek-chek-chek* call in flight. Song comprises a series of wheezing and rattling notes. **HABITS** Outside the breeding season, forms restless flocks that feed acrobatically in tree tops, sometimes with Siskins. **STATUS AND HABITAT** Present year-round. Around 190,000 pairs nest in the UK, favouring birch woodland. Outside the breeding season, occurs in both birch and Common Alder (*Alnus glutinosa*) woodlands, feeding on seeds of these trees. Many British breeders move south in autumn, but influxes from mainland Europe ensure the species is still widespread in winter.

COMMON REDPOLL

Acanthis flammea | FR | LENGTH 12–14cm

Noticeably larger than the similar Lesser Redpoll, but appreciably paler and colder-looking in all plumages and separable from that species with care. Sexes are subtly dissimilar.

red forecrown

pale, subtly streaked rump

overall much paler than Lesser Redpoll

pale wingbars

Adult male has streaked pale grey-buff upperparts that are darkest on back. Underparts are pale and streaked. Has a red forecrown, black bib and lores, white wingbar, and pale, streaked rump; sometimes has a red flush to breast. Adult female and immatures are similar to adult male but lack the pinkish flush to breast. In all ages shows streaking on undertail, most obvious and broad on central undertail covert. **VOICE** Utters a rattling *chek-chek-chek* call in flight. Song comprises a series of wheezing and rattling notes. **HABITS** Mixes with flocks of Lesser Redpolls. **STATUS AND HABITAT** Winter visitor from N mainland Europe that is usually found in birch or Common Alder (*Alnus glutinosa*) woodlands, feeding on seeds of these trees. Around 300 individuals occur each year, most records coming from east coasts of England and Scotland.

COMMON CROSSBILL

Loxia curvirostra | CR | LENGTH 15–17cm

Common and Scottish crossbills combined

Distinctive finch that has evolved cross-tipped mandibles for extracting seeds from conifer cones. Sexes are dissimilar.

FEMALE

invariably seen feeding on cones of coniferous trees

mostly uniform yellowish-green plumage, darkest on wings

MALES

very vocal, especially in flight

overlapping bill tips is a feature unique to this genus among British birds

Adult male has mainly red plumage but with brownish wings. Adult female has mainly yellowish-green plumage but with brownish wings. Immature birds are similar to adults of their respective sexes but plumage colours are duller. Juvenile is grey-brown and heavily streaked. **VOICE** Utters a sharp *kip-kip-kip* flight call. **HABITS** Feeds primarily on the seeds of larch and spruce species. Forms single-species flocks outside the breeding season. Nesting takes place early in the year, often in Feb or Mar. **STATUS AND HABITAT** Resident breeder, seldom found outside mature conifer woodland with trees of cone-bearing age; around 39,000 pairs nest in the UK. Being entirely dependent on conifer seeds, birds have to wander extensively and nomadically if food in a given area is depleted. Hence, numbers in any given area vary throughout the seasons and from year to year. Occasional irruptions occur from mainland Europe if the cone crop there fails.

mostly uniform red plumage

MALE

SCOTTISH CROSSBILL

Loxia scotica | CY | LENGTH 15–17cm

Very similar to Common Crossbill but has a more robust bill, adapted to extract seeds from cones of mature Scots Pines (*Pinus sylvestris*). Sexes are dissimilar.

circle shows general centre of distribution

Adult male has mainly red plumage but with brownish wings. Adult female has mainly yellowish–green plumage but with brownish wings. Immature birds are similar to adults of their respective sexes but plumage colours are duller. Juvenile is grey-brown and heavily streaked. **VOICE** Utters a sharp *kip-kip-kip* flight call, similar to, but slightly deeper than, that of Common Crossbill. **HABITS** Nests early in the year (Feb or Mar sometimes). Outside the breeding season, small groups feed in mature Scots Pine (*Pinus sylvestris*) trees. The sound of falling cones hitting the ground can indicate the presence of feeding birds. **STATUS AND HABITAT** Resident breeder and Britain's only endemic bird species; restricted to relict areas of native Scots Pine in the Highlands. Around 6,800 pairs nest here and birds tend not to stray since the cone crop appears consistently reliable.

FEMALE

bill is much larger and much more robust than in Common Crossbill

mostly uniform yellowish-green plumage, darkest on wings

reddish plumage

MALE

drinks at woodland pools

HAWFINCH

Coccothraustes coccothraustes | HF | LENGTH 17–18cm

A giant among finches, recognised by its massive
conical bill; the large head and thick neck match
the bill proportions. Sexes are separable.

MALE

MALE

**extensive white on wings
and tail is revealed in flight**

**proportionately
massive bill**

**relatively large head
and thickset body**

**plumage pattern is
similar to male but
colours are
subdued**

FEMALE

Adult male has mainly
pinkish-buff plumage
with grey on neck,
black lores and bib, and a
brown back. Has a broad
whitish wingbar, blue-
black flight feathers
and a broad white tip
to short tail. Bill is dark
metallic grey in summer but buffish
brown in winter. Adult female is
similar but colours are muted; an
additional pale panel on wings
is seen in some birds. Juvenile is
similar to adult female but plumage
colours are even duller and patterns
less distinct. **VOICE** Utters a sharp,
almost Robin-like *tsic* call. Song is
quiet and subdued, and is seldom
heard. **HABITS** Bill is used to crack
hard-cased seeds of trees such as Hornbeam (*Carpinus betulus*) and cherries, notably Wild
Cherry (*Prunus avium*). In flight, the short tail contributes to the species' characteristic front-
heavy silhouette. Generally shy and easily overlooked. Outside the breeding season, forms
small flocks. **STATUS AND HABITAT** Resident breeder, associated mainly with mature
deciduous woodland; orchards, parks and large gardens are visited if suitable seed-bearing
trees are present. Around 800 pairs nest in the UK.

REED BUNTING

Emberiza schoeniclus | RB | LENGTH 14–15cm

Well-marked bunting and a familiar bird of wetland margins during the summer months. Sexes are dissimilar.

MALE

white outer-tail feathers

Summer adult male has a black head, throat and bib, and a white collar and sub-moustachial stripe. Underparts are otherwise whitish with faint streaking, back is dark, and wings have reddish-brown feather margins. Males and females in all other plumages have heads marked with dark brown and buffish-brown stripes, a pale sub-moustachial stripe, dark brown and buff stripes on back, and reddish-brown margins to wing feathers; pale underparts are streaked on flanks and breast. Males also show a suggestion of summer head pattern, notably dark spotting on throat and bib. All ages have obvious white outer-tail feathers, most noticeable in flight. **VOICE** Utters a thin *seeu* call. Song is simple, chinking and repetitive. **HABITS** Singing males often perch prominently. Outside the breeding season, associates with other ground-feeding buntings and finches. **STATUS AND HABITAT** Resident breeder that favours scrubby margins to wetlands and reedbed fringes; occasionally found on farmland, particularly in Oilseed Rape (*Brassica napus*) fields. Around 230,000 pairs nest in the UK. During autumn, passage migrants from Scandinavia move down the east coast of Britain to winter in France.

black hood

striking facial markings

streaked back

reddish-brown back and wings

FEMALE

MALE

SNOW BUNTING

Plectrophenax nivalis | SB | LENGTH 16–17cm

Plump-bodied bunting. Sexes are dissimilar and
plumage varies throughout the year, but all birds
show a lot of white on innerwing, rump and
tail – features that are striking in flight.

Summer adult male has mainly white plumage with a blackish back and black, and white
on wings; in some birds, white elements of plumage are suffused with orange-buff. Legs
and bill are black. Summer adult female is similar, but back is brownish and it has variable
amounts of streaked brown and buff on head, neck and sides of breast. Winter adults and
1st-winter birds have mainly white underparts
and buffish-orange upperparts. Winter adult
males have the whitest wings, face and
underparts. Bill is yellowish and legs are black
in all birds. **VOICE** Utters a rolling *prrrt* call
in flight. Song is twittering but tone is clearly
bunting-like. **HABITS** Forms flocks outside
the breeding season. **STATUS AND HABITAT**
Resident breeder, winter visitor and
passage migrant. Around 60 pairs
nest here, favouring outcrops
on desolate mountains in the
Scottish Highlands. Best known
as a winter visitor to coastal
grassland and sandy beaches;
more than 10,000 are
present in most years.

1ST-WINTER

yellow
bill

white
elements of
plumage are
variably flushed
with buffish-brown

1ST-WINTER

shows a
considerable
amount of white
on wings

bill is black only in
breeding season

MALE, SUMMER

LAPLAND BUNTING

Calcarius lapponicus | LA | LENGTH 14–16cm

Well-marked bunting, seen here mainly in non-breeding plumage. Sexes are hard to tell apart at that time.

Summer adult male (seldom seen here) has a black face and throat defined by a striking white line; crown is black and nape is chestnut. Underparts are otherwise white, back is streaked brown and black, and bill is yellow. Summer adult female (seldom seen here) has a pale suggestion of male's striking head pattern; pale underparts are streaked on flanks, and back is streaked brown. Winter adults and juvenile have a reddish-brown face with a dark line defining ear coverts and pale, unmarked lores, contributing to open-faced look; crown is dark with a subtle, pale median stripe. Back is streaked brown; reddish-brown wing panel is defined by 2 whitish wingbars. Whitish underparts are streaked on flanks; juveniles are also streaked on breast, while adults show hint of a black bib. **VOICE** Utters a distinctive rattling *tiddlip-tew* call in flight. **HABITS** Seen in small flocks in winter, often with other ground-feeding songbirds. Solitary, newly arrived migrants can be tame but otherwise species is rather wary. **STATUS AND HABITAT** Mainly a winter visitor, favouring coastal fields and saltmarshes; around 700 are usually present. Also an autumn passage migrant, seen on coasts.

reddish-brown wing panel

pinkish bill

1ST-AUTUMN

chestnut nape is most intense in late spring and summer

bill is yellow only in breeding season

MALE, SUMMER

YELLOWHAMMER

Emberiza citrinella | Y. | LENGTH 15–17cm

A colourful bunting with an easily recognised song and an attractive appearance. Sexes are dissimilar.

FEMALE
has more extensive dark markings than in male

WINTER FEMALE/1ST-WINTER

colours are much less intense than in adult birds in summer, but overall still looks distinctly yellow

MALES

Summer adult male has a mainly yellow head marked with faint dark lines, yellow underparts, and a reddish-brown back and wings. Has a chestnut flush to breast and streaking on flanks; rump is reddish brown and bill is greyish. In winter, yellow elements of adult male's plumage are subdued or absent, and dark streaking on head and underparts is more extensive. Adult female has a streaked greenish-grey head and breast, streaked pale yellow underparts and a brown back with a reddish-brown rump. Juvenile is similar to adult female but with more distinct streaking. **VOICE** Utters a rasping *zit* call. Song is often rendered as 'a little bit of bread and no cheese'. **HABITS** Outside the breeding season, forms flocks and sometimes mixes with finches and other buntings. **STATUS AND HABITAT** Resident breeder; around 700,000 pairs nest in the UK, favouring open grassland or farmland fields with scattered scrub and mature hedgerows. In winter, flocks feed in stubble fields, at grain spills or on short grassland.

head is overall yellow with only subtle dark markings

reddish-brown rump

chestnut markings on breast and flanks

MALE

CIRL BUNTING

Emberiza cirlus | CL | LENGTH 16–17cm

Similar to Yellowhammer but separable at all times.
Male is distinctive and all birds have an olive-grey rump
(reddish-brown in Yellowhammer). Sexes are dissimilar.

Adult male's distinctive head pattern comprises a black throat and eye-stripe, separated
and defined by yellow. Breast, nape and crown are greenish grey and underparts are yellow,
flushed and streaked chestnut on flanks; back is reddish brown. Colours are less distinct
in winter than in summer. Adult female has dark and yellowish stripes on head, a streaked
greenish-grey crown, nape and breast, and streaked yellowish underparts; back is reddish
brown. Juvenile is similar to adult female but yellow elements of plumage are pale. **VOICE**
Utters a sharp *tziip* call. Song is a rather tuneless rattle, reminiscent of that of Lesser
Whitethroat. **HABITS** Outside the breeding season, usually forms small single-species flocks.
STATUS AND HABITAT Resident breeder, restricted to coastal districts of SW
England. Around 860 pairs nest here, favouring low-intensity farmland with
a mosaic of mature hedgerows and scrub patches.

compared to a female or winter
Yellowhammer, overall looks more
streaked with much less intense
yellow flush to plumage

1ST-WINTER

FEMALE

diagnostic
facial
pattern

streaked, reddish-brown
back

compared to Yellowhammer, note
the olive (not reddish-brown) rump

MALE

MALE

CORN BUNTING

Emberiza calandra | CB | LENGTH 16–18cm

Rather nondescript bunting. Easiest to detect in spring by listening for its distinctive song. Sexes are similar.

stubby, yellowish bill

streaked brown plumage

presence is often first indicated by hearing its jingling song

dangles legs in short-distance flights

Adult and juvenile appear rather plump-bodied. Upperparts are brown and streaked, while underparts are whitish, streaked on breast and flanks and flushed with buff, especially on breast. Stout bill is yellowish. **VOICE** Utters a *tsit* call. Jingling song has been likened to jangling keys, and is usually sung from a fencepost or overhead wire. **HABITS** Often perches on fencelines. Dangles its legs when flying short distances. Outside the breeding season, forms flocks and associates with other ground-feeding passerines. **STATUS AND HABITAT** Resident breeder that has seriously declined in recent years due to changes in agricultural practices. Nowadays, favours traditionally managed meadows and crop fields (especially Barley, *Hordeum vulgare*); around 11,000 pairs nest in the UK. Feeds in stubble fields in winter and sometimes wanders from breeding habitats at this time.

Axillaries The group of feathers that form the 'armpit' of the bird.

Bill Beak.

Carpal The 'wrist' of a bird, forming the bend of the wing.

Coverts Small contour feathers found on the upperwing, underwing, uppertail and undertail.

Culmen The upper ridge of the bill.

Drumming The sound made by a woodpecker on wood, or the sound made by the vibrating outer-tail feathers of the Snipe.

Exposed tertials The visible extent of the three feathers found between the primaries and coverts on the folded wing.

Eye-ring Coloured ring of feathers that surrounds the eye (cf. orbital ring).

First-winter A description of the plumage acquired by a bird during its first winter after hatching.

Forewing The leading half of the upperwing, best seen in flight.

Fourth-winter A description of the plumage acquired by a bird during its fourth calendar winter after hatching, the next plumage being adult.

Gape The soft mouth of a bird, between the upper and lower mandibles.

Genus (pl. genera) In taxonomy, the rank of genus sits between family and species, e.g. Reed Warbler is in the family Acrocephalidae and genus *Acrocephalus*, and its species name is *scirpaceus*.

Immature A young bird in its first plumage.

Irruptive A species that irregularly moves to an area in which it is not usually found.

Jizz The feel of a species gained from the general impression, size and shape.

Lekking A communal display.

Lores The area between the bill and the eye.

Malar The area in front of and below the sub-moustachial stripe.

Mandible The bill is made of two mandibles, the upper and the lower.

Mantle The back.

Moustachial stripe A stripe that runs from the bill to below the eye, forming a 'moustache'.

Nape The hind neck.

Orbital ring Ring of bare skin around the eye, often brightly coloured (cf. eye-ring).

Passage migrant A species that occurs only as it passes through Britain and Ireland.

Primaries The main flight feathers found on the outer half of the wing and forming the 'hand'.

Primary projection The visible extent of the primary feathers beyond the tertials on the folded wing.

Redhead The females of the sawbills (mergansers and Goosander).

Ringing The act of fitting a uniquely numbered metal ring on a bird's leg for scientific research.

Scapulars A group of feathers that form the shoulder of the bird between the back and folded wing.

Seabird A species that spends the largest part of its life cycle at sea.

Second–winter A description of the plumage acquired by a bird during its second calendar winter after hatching.

Secondaries A group of relatively large flight feathers that form the inner part of the wing.

Spatulate Spoon-like.

Speculum The coloured 'square' found on the innerwing of a duck.

Sub–adult Adult-like plumage, but retaining some immature features.

Sub–moustachial strip The contrasting line of feathers below the moustachial stripe.

Supercilium The stripe that runs above but not through the eye.

Taxonomy The scientific classification of living organisms based on shared characters. Animals, including birds, are arranged in a taxonomic hierarchy from subspecies and species rank, up through genus, family, order, class, division and kingdom.

Tertials The three feathers that can be seen on the folded wing between the small coverts and the primaries.

Third–winter A description of the plumage acquired by a bird during its third calendar winter after hatching.

Tibia The area of the leg above the 'knee'.

Topography Description of the external features of a bird.

Vent The area underneath the tail, formed by the undertail coverts.

Visible migration The observation of birds that can be seen migrating during daylight hours.

Wattle A brightly coloured fleshy structure on the heads of certain species.

SURVEYS CITED

BirdTrack is organised by the BTO in a partnership with the Royal Society for the Protection of Birds (RSPB), BirdWatch Ireland, the Scottish Ornithologists' Club (SOC) and Welsh Ornithological Society (WOS).

Bird Atlas 2007–11 was a partnership project run by BTO, BirdWatch Ireland and SOC, aiming to map the distribution and abundance of all bird species in Britain and Ireland.

The Breeding Bird Survey is run by the BTO and is a partnership between BTO, the Joint Nature Conservation Committee (JNCC) and the RSPB.

Wetlands Bird Survey (WeBS) is a partnership between BTO, RSPB and JNCC, in association with the Wildfowl and Wetlands Trust (WWT).

Balmer, D., Gillings, S., Caffrey, B., Swann, B., Downie, I. and Fuller, R. (2013). *Bird Atlas 2007–11. The Breeding and Wintering Birds of Britain and Ireland*. British Trust for Ornithology.

Harrap, S. and Redman, N. (2010). *Where to Watch Birds in Britain and Ireland*. Christopher Helm.

Mullarney, K., Svensson, L. and Zetterstrom, D. (2009). *Collins Bird Guide*. HarperCollins.

Sample, G. (2010). *Collins Bird Songs and Calls*. HarperCollins.

Vinicombe, K.E., Harris, A. and Tucker, L. (2014). *The Helm Guide to Bird Identification*. Christopher Helm.

USEFUL WEBSITES

BirdTrack (website dedicated to tracking migration and the distribution of birds)
www.birdtrack.net

BirdWatch Ireland
www.birdwatchireland.ie

British Ornithologists' Union (BOU)
www.bou.org.uk

British Trust for Ornithology (BTO)
www.bto.org (more detailed maps can be found at www.bto.org/mapstore)

Royal Society for the Protection of Birds (RSPB)
www.rspb.org.uk

Scottish Ornithologists' Club (SOC)
www.the-soc.org.uk

Wildfowl and Wetlands Trust
www.wwt.org.uk

The Wildlife Trusts
www.wildlifetrusts.org

Xeno Canto (website dedicated to bird sounds)
www.xeno-canto.org